I0006380

Mechanical Graphics

Finsbury Technical Manuals.

EDITOR OF THE SERIES,

PROFESSOR SILVANUS P. THOMPSON,

D.Sc., B.A., M.I.E.E., &c.

Finsbury Technical Manuals.

MECHANICAL GRAPHICS:

A SECOND COURSE IN MECHANICAL DRAWING.

WITH PREFACE BY PROFESSOR PERRY, B.Sc., F.R.S.

ARRANGED FOR USE IN TECHNICAL AND SCIENCE AND ART INSTITUTES, SCHOOLS, AND COLLEGES.

BY

GEO. HALLIDAY,

WHITWORTH SCHOLAR;

INSTRUCTOR IN MECHANICAL DRAWING AND LECTURER ON MECHANISM AT THE CITY AND GUILDS OF LONDON INSTITUTE TECHNICAL COLLEGE, FINSBURY.

E. & F. N. SPON, 125, STRAND, LONDON.

NEW YORK: 12, CORTLANDT STREET.

1889.

ASTOR LIBRARY
JUN
2
1893
NEW YORK

PREFACE.

THE course of instruction given in the Mechanical Department of the Finsbury College to all first-year students of the Mechanical, Electrical, and Chemical Departments, requires students who hear lectures on Practical Mechanics to practise also Mechanical Drawing, to work numerical and graphical exercises, and to work in the Mechanical Laboratory. Mr. Halliday in this book illustrates part of the course of instruction for those first-year students of whom he has charge. I have never interfered with Mr. Halliday in his method of teaching these subjects, which he groups under the general term 'Mechanical Graphics,' and I am sure that his method is greatly deserving of praise.

It is, I think, the first time that such subjects as Practical Plane Geometry, Practical Descriptive Geometry, Graphical Statics, the loads in the parts of Hinged Structures, and Calculations on Link Motions, and other forms of Valve Motion, have been treated together.

Even in the Practical Plane and Descriptive Geometry portion it will be seen that a certain amount of originality of treatment has been introduced, notably in the part on Curves; and the pictures of inclined planes. There is, of course, more chance of originality in the treatment of Graphical Statics and Valve Motions, and of this chance Mr. Halliday has availed himself.

I am glad to say that beginners are able in one year to do all the work given in this book, and, when one questions them, their answers show that they understand what they have been doing. If Mr. Halliday proves as useful an author as he has proved to be a lecturer and instructor, he will have conferred great benefits on students by writing this book.

JOHN PERRY.

INTRODUCTION.

THE subject which is generally named Practical Geometry, in syllabuses like those of the Science and Art Department, is being developed in many directions, and now includes Graphical Statics, Perspective, Valve Motions—whereas at one time it merely meant problems on the straight line, triangles, and circles. It has become a question whether the name Practical Geometry is a suitable name under which might be included the subjects above indicated. It appears that the subject really includes all constructions which can be made by means of the ordinary apparatus used by the draughtsman for the purpose of finding the positions of required points or lines, or numerical answers to mechanical problems ; and this being so, perhaps it would be better to call the subject by a new name which will comprehend all. The methods for finding answers to the problems, are all mechanical—that is, obtained by the use of straight edges and instruments. The answers are presented in the form of a picture, and the best name, the most general name, appears to be Mechanical Graphics.

Mechanical Graphics may be made the subject of long study in any one of its subdivisions ; but there are general and useful principles underlying each. By a knowledge of these the student and draughtsman is enabled to solve a great many of the problems which come before him every hour, and it is for the purpose of laying these principles before him that this book has been prepared.

The general syllabus of the book is intended as a first year's course in Mechanical Graphics for persons beginning a technical training, and is a second course of Mechanical Drawing

Tracing being the first. The syllabus is Professor Perry's, and he directs that drawing of models of machine details be taken along with it. This sketching and drawing of machine details will form the third course in the instruction of mechanical drawing—a course which will appear at an early date.

The step-by-step style in which more difficult problems are approached is due to the instruction the author received in the classes of Professor Rowden, Glasgow.

The drawings have mostly been taken from the sheets executed by the first-year students at the Finsbury Technical College, though most of the descriptive sketches illustrating problems on inclined planes were done by Mr. Hamilton, while the drawings in the chapter on Graphical Statics were done by Mr. Jameson, both second-year students at the above College in 1889.

As the drawings have been published just the same size as they were executed in the class, it is hoped they will be found of more use to the student in helping to find, by the application of his dividers, where he may have gone wrong as he proceeds to work each problem which has been worked; and, as the work is very fully illustrated, the more advanced student will be able better to study the methods of construction from the drawings alone, without reference to the text.

Messrs. Reeves and Sons, Cheapside, have kindly arranged a full set of Drawing apparatus for working the exercises in this and the First Course of Mechanical Drawing. They call it the Finsbury Drawing Apparatus.

CONTENTS.

MECHANICAL GRAPHICS.

SECTION I.

PLANE GEOMETRY.

CHAPTER I.

INSTRUMENTS.

1. MECHANICAL GRAPHICS is the science which treats of the methods for representing lines and solids on paper, and for obtaining solutions of mathematical and physical problems by drawing construction.

2. By the knowledge of the principles of Mechanical Graphics the engineer who wishes to build a structure or a machine is enabled to draw it out in full and in detail, and therefore to determine the exact size and shape of each part before ever he proceeds to construct it. He also, in the case of a machine, can draw the movable parts in any number of different positions, and thus determine whether any one movable part in its cycle of operations will obstruct the motion of another. He thus by his knowledge obviates the necessity of incurring the expense of making first a model of the machine, or the risk and almost certainty of having parts to throw away when neither model nor drawing is made.

The labour, time, and money of the practical engineer are also often saved by a knowledge of mechanical graphics, when he has to solve a problem in applied physics. For the solution of such problems as finding the centre of gravity of bodies, or of the resultant of forces which act on the members of a braced structure due to the action of external forces, practical mathematics offers only long and wearisome methods, while by drawing only a few simple lines with the pencil the answer is readily obtained.

3. Before going on to study Mechanical Graphics proper, it will be well for the student to become thoroughly acquainted with the drawing instruments he will have to use, and for that purpose to take a course of Tracing. If he has a friend who is employed as a civil engineering draughtsman, he cannot do better than borrow from him some of his machine drawings and trace them; but if he has not, his best course will then be to supply himself with a tracing copybook, published by E. & F. N. Spon, and go through it very earnestly and carefully; and he should not leave this kind of work until he has been told by some draughtsman that his tracings would satisfy the requirements of the drawing office.

4. The instruments the student will find necessary for the study of Mechanical Graphics are a T square, pen and pencil compasses, having legs 5 inches or 6 inches long, pen and pencil bow compasses, and two set squares with angles 30°, 45°, and 60°. The 60° set square may be 10 inches long on one side containing the right angle, and the sides of the 45° set square may be 5 inches long. A very convenient drawing-board for a beginner measures 19 inches by 13 inches, and the blade of the T square ought not to be longer than the board, because in class his neighbour may come against it accidentally and so cause mistakes. A 12-inch scale and a protractor will complete his kit.

The pencil and pen points of the compasses should be a little shorter than the needle-point, as this allows one to hold the compasses vertically when the needle-point has entered slightly into the centre of the curve being made. Pencils should be sharpened like a flat chisel, as this enables one to make finer and better lines, and the lead keeps its point for a greater length of time.

The rules and instructions given in the tracing copybook should be carefully observed by the student when he inks in his work.

CHAPTER II

DIVISION OF LINES.

5. ONE of the most common problems which will come in the ordinary course of the student's work is the division of lines into two or into any number of equal parts, or into parts bearing certain proportions to each other. Very often when the experienced draughtsman has to divide a line into two equal parts he does so by trial. Two of the methods for solving this problem are the following:—

6. Suppose A B, Fig. 1, is given, and the middle point is to be found. Open the pencil until the distance is about three-quarters of the length of the line. Then, with B as centre,

Fig. 1.

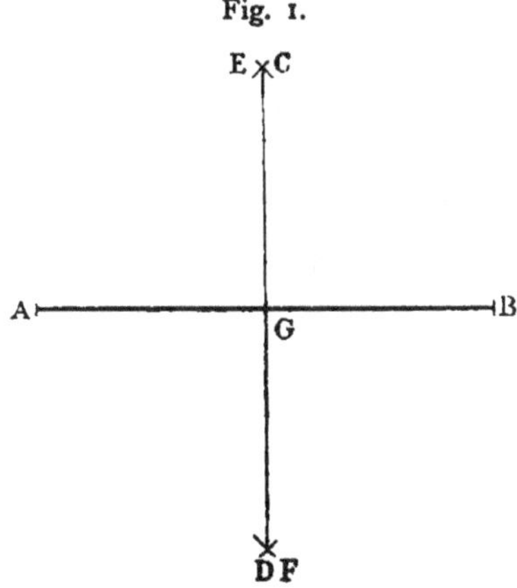

describe the arcs C and D, and with A as centre the arcs E and F. By means of the set square draw a thin line through the points where the arcs cut each other. The point G will be the middle of the line.

7. Another method very often adopted by practical men is to open the compasses until the distance between the points, as nearly as one can judge, is equal to half the line, and

draw from each end as centre two arcs cutting the line. Then make a mark, as nearly as one can judge, between the two arcs. A, Fig. 2, shows a case where the distance guessed

Fig. 2.

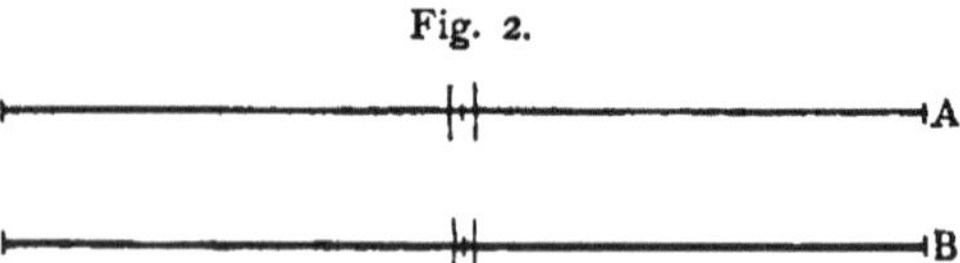

was greater than half the line, and B a case where the distance was less.

Exercise 1. Draw a line $2\frac{5}{8}$ inches long and divide it into two equal parts by both methods.

8. To divide a line into any number of equal parts we employ a theorem demonstrated in the 6th book of Euclid. It is the following. If we have two lines as A C and A E, Fig. 3, inclined to each other and meeting at a point, and if we draw two other lines as B C and C E parallel to each other and cutting the lines, then whatever number of times the length of A C contains the length of A B, the length of A E will contain the length of A D exactly the same number of times.

Fig. 3.

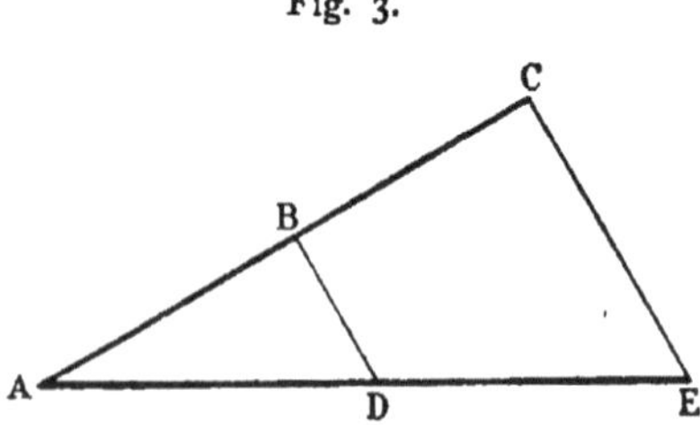

9. For example, if A C is twice the length of A B, then A E will just be twice the length of A D. Sometimes the relationship which exists between the lines is put in the form of a fraction in the following way:

$$\frac{\text{Length A C}}{\text{Length A B}} = \frac{\text{Length A E}}{\text{Length A D}};$$

or again

$$\frac{\text{Length A B}}{\text{Length B C}} = \frac{\text{Length A D}}{\text{Length D E}};$$

or,

$$\frac{\text{A B}}{\text{A D}} = \frac{\text{A C}}{\text{A E}}.$$

10. The lines may be divided into a greater number of parts than two. In Fig. 4, where the lines B H, C I, D J, &c., are all parallel to each other,

$$\frac{\text{A B}}{\text{A H}} = \frac{\text{B C}}{\text{H I}} = \frac{\text{C D}}{\text{I J}} \text{ etc.}$$

Fig. 4.

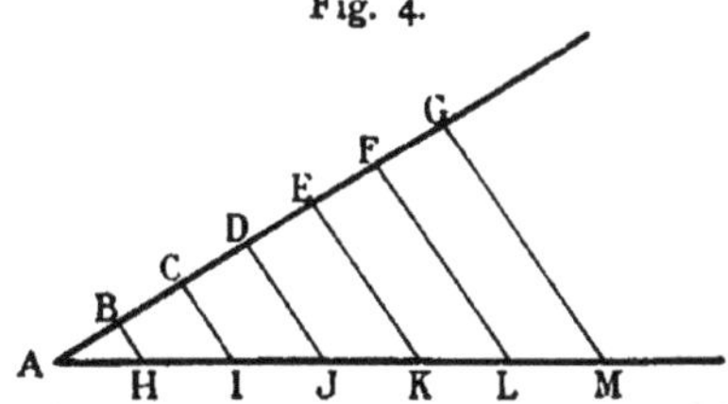

11. If one of the lines be divided into equal parts then the lengths of the sections of the other line will also be all equal to one another. This enables one to divide any given line into any number of parts, whether it be of an even number of inches in length or otherwise.

Suppose, for example, that a line A B is to be divided into three equal parts. Draw from A any line A C inclined to A B at much the same angle as that shown in Fig. 5. The angle should not be much greater or less than that shown, for if it is one finds by experience that the divisions required are not so exactly correct. Then measure off from A three equal lengths, either by means of the scale directly or by stepping the compasses three times along A C; but in either case the total length of the three divisions should be about equal to the length of A B. Join D the last point and B, and draw from E and F the other divisions, the lines E G and F H parallel to D B. The sections A H, H G, and G B will be equal to one another, and the line **A B** will be divided into three equal sections.

Fig. 5.

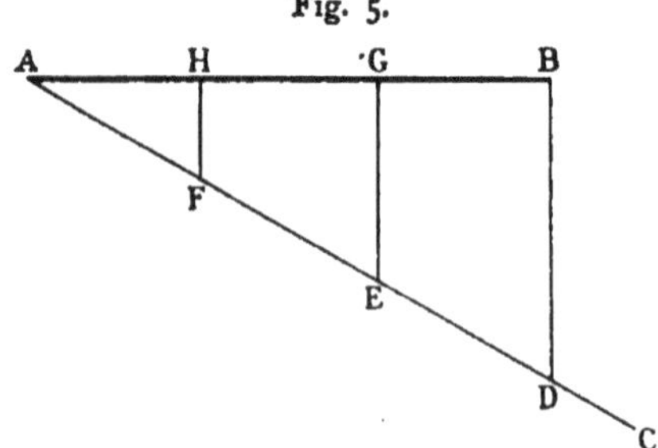

Ex. 2. Divide a line $2\frac{7}{8}$ inches long into three equal parts.

12. When drawing a scale the above method of dividing lines into equal sections is often employed to find the small divisions for the end section. For example, when drawing a scale to represent feet and inches, like that shown in Fig. 6, the part between the left end and the figure *0* has to be divided into twelve equal sections, and these being small it is found often convenient to employ the above method of division. The process need not be again recapitulated, and the student will easily do it for himself by studying the

Fig. 6.

9 6 3	*0*	*1*	*2*	*3*

figure. It is to be noted that the cipher is placed at the end of the small divisions, and that when any measurement is made one leg will rest on the feet divisions and the other on the inch divisions, which will enable the distance to be read straight off. For example, if the distance was 2 feet 5 inches, one leg of the compasses would rest on the 2 foot division, while the other would point to five in the inch divisions.

Ex. 3. Construct a scale of 1 inch to the foot, to measure feet and inches.

Ex. 4. Construct a scale of $\frac{5}{8}$ inch to the inch, to measure inches and sixteenths of an inch.

CHAPTER III.

PROPORTIONAL LINES.

13. WHEN a line is given and another is to be found, bearing a certain proportion in length to the first, we can proceed to find that second line in the following way:—Suppose, for

Fig. 7.

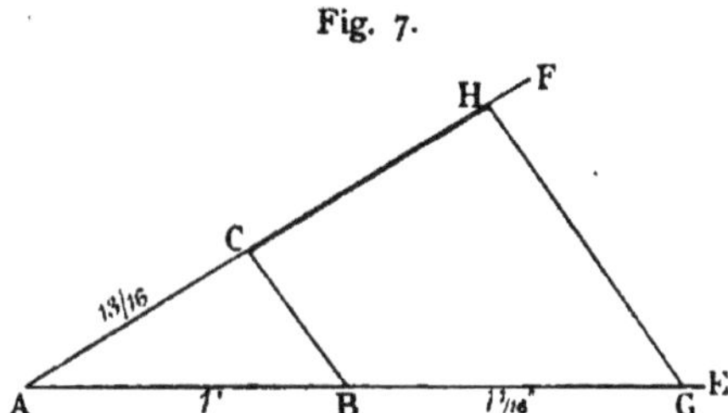

example, that the proportion of the two lines is to be as 1 inch : $1\frac{1}{16}$ inch—that is, the first given line, $\frac{13}{16}$ inch, is to bear to the second unknown line the proportion of 1 inch : $1\frac{1}{16}$ inch.

Draw A E horizontally and A F inclined to it at an angle of about 30°. Cut off from A E a part A B 1 inch in length, and along A F measure a distance A C $\frac{13}{16}$ inch in length. From B measure a distance B G $1\frac{1}{16}$ inch in length. Join B C, and draw from G a line parallel to B C and cutting A F. C H is the line required.

14. The whole thing may be put in another way thus:—

The first line A B is to the second line A C as the third line B C is to the fourth unknown line C H, or again the first line contains the second line as many times as the third line contains the fourth. Or thus

First proportional	:	Second proportional	: :	Third proportional	:	Fourth proportional
AB		AC		BG		CH

So C H, the unknown line, which is to be found, is called the fourth proportional.

Ex. 5. Find the fourth proportional to the lines $1\frac{1}{4}$, $1\frac{3}{4}$, and 2 inches.

Ex. 6. Find the fourth prportional to $1\frac{1}{2}$, $1\frac{3}{4}$, and $2\frac{1}{8}$ inches.

The proportion may be stated in the form of an equation; we have

$$\frac{CH}{AC} = \frac{BG}{AB},$$

and multiplying across, as we do in the solution of equations, and calling the unknown x, we have

$$x \cdot AB = AC \times BG$$

$$x = \frac{AC \times BG}{AB}.$$

15. This form of the problem gives us a means of finding by a simple construction the answer to complicated arithmetical fractions. For suppose the value of the fraction $\frac{1\frac{1}{4} \times 2\frac{1}{8}}{1\frac{5}{8}}$ is to be found. A C may be taken to represent $1\frac{1}{4}$; B G $2\frac{1}{4}$, and A B $1\frac{5}{8}$.

Ex. 7. Find the value of the fraction $\frac{1\frac{3}{16} \times 2\frac{1}{4}}{1\frac{5}{8}}$.

16. When the second line comes twice, the problem is sometimes called finding the third proportional.

Ex. 8. Find the third proportional to $1\frac{1}{4}$ and $1\frac{5}{8}$.

Ex. 9. Find the third proportional to $2\frac{1}{2}$ and $1\frac{3}{4}$.

17. We see that the first proportional multiplied by the fourth is equal to the second multiplied by the third.

The first and last terms of a proportion are often called the extremes.

The second and third the means.

18. Supposing the means to be equal to each other, the square of the means would be equal to the product of the extremes.

Ex. 10. Find a fourth proportional to 1 inch, $1\frac{1}{2}$ inch, and $1\frac{1}{4}$ inch.

Ex. 11. Find the value of $\frac{5^2}{3}$.

Ex. 12. „ „ $\frac{3^2}{2 \cdot 5}$.

Ex. 13. „ „ $\frac{(2 \cdot 5)^2}{4}$.

19. In a right-angle triangle, as A B C,

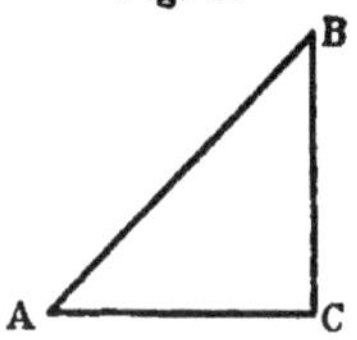

$$AB^2 = AC^2 + BC^2.$$
$$AB = \sqrt{AC^2 + BC^2}.$$

Fig. 8.

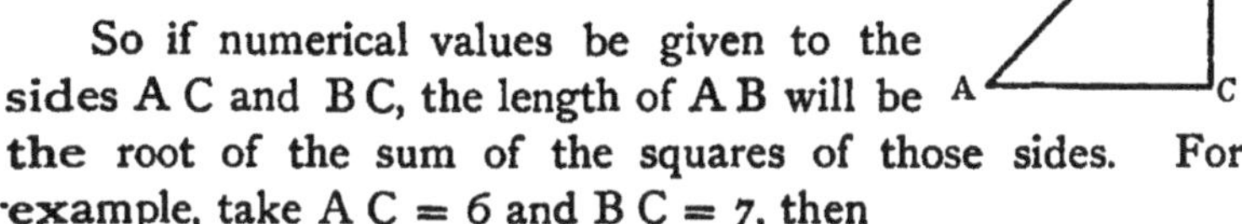

So if numerical values be given to the sides A C and B C, the length of A B will be the root of the sum of the squares of those sides. For example, take A C = 6 and B C = 7, then

$$AB = \sqrt{6^2 + 7^2}.$$

Ex. 14. Find the value of $\sqrt{4^2 + 3^2}$.

Ex. 15. „ „ $\sqrt{(3 \cdot 2)^2 + 2^2}$.

Ex. 16. Find a line to represent $\sqrt{\frac{2}{5}^2 + \frac{3}{4}^2}$.

20. If a line B D of a given length be drawn at right angles to A B, then

$$AD^2 = DB^2 + AB^2,$$

Fig. 9.

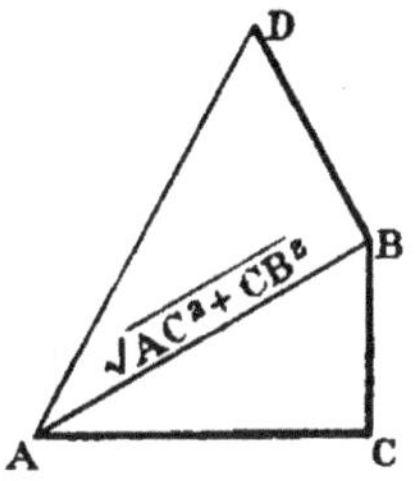

but

$$AB^2 = AC^2 + BC^2.$$

And inserting this value of AB^2 in the first equation we have

$$AD^2 = DB^2 + AC^2 + BC^2,$$

and taking the root of both sides we have

$$AD = \sqrt{DB^2 + AC^2 + BC^2}.$$

Ex. 17. Find the value of $\sqrt{4^2 + 3^2 + 2^2}$.

Ex. 18. " " $\sqrt{7}$

21. From Euclid we get that in the right-angled triangle ADC

Fig. 10.

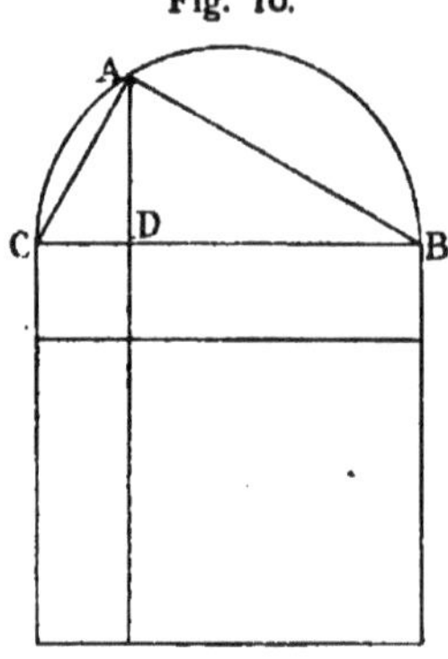

$$\begin{aligned}
AD^2 &= AB^2 - DB^2 \\
AD^2 &= AC^2 - CD^2 \\
\hline
2AD^2 &= (AB^2 + AC^2) - (DB^2 + CD^2) \\
&= CB^2 - (DB^2 + CD^2) \\
&= DB^2 + CD^2 + 2DBDE - (DB^2 + CD^2) \\
&= 2DB.DC \\
AD^2 &= DB.DC \\
DB &: AD :: AD : DC.
\end{aligned}$$

AD is therefore a mean between the lines CD and BD, the two sections of the diameter of the semicircle.

Ex. 19. Find a mean proportional between two lines $2\frac{1}{2}$ inches and $1\frac{1}{4}$ inch in length.

Ex. 20. Find a mean proportional between two lines 2 inches and 3 inches in length.

Ex. 21. One of the extremes of a proportion is 1 inch in length, and the mean $\frac{3}{4}$ inch, find the other extreme.

22. An easy method for finding the product of two numbers by geometry depends on the principle that the complements of a parallelogram about the diagonal are equal. That is, A B C D is equal to E D G F in area.

Fig. 11.

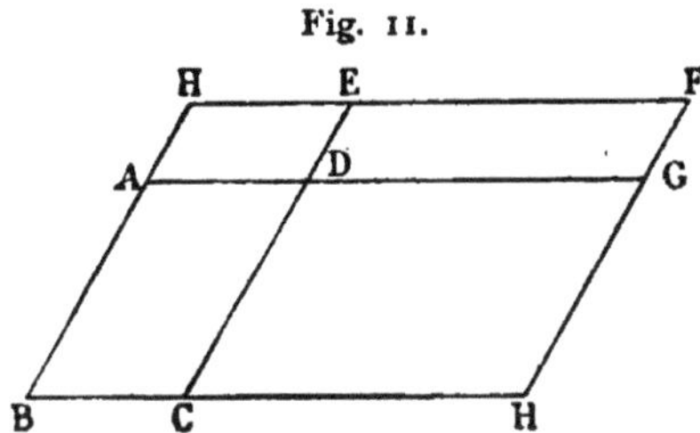

23. Suppose the product of 4 by 3 is to be found. A B = 4 B C = 3. Produce B A to H 1 unit further than A. Produce H D and B C until they meet, and complete the parallelogram.

$$\text{E D} \times \text{D G} = \text{A B} \times \text{B C} = 4 \times 3 = 12.$$

E D being 1, makes D G 12. Therefore the length of D G gives the answer.

Ex. 22. Multiply 4 by $2\frac{1}{2}$.
Ex. 23. Find the product of 3 by 2·25.
Ex. 24. " " 3·2 by 2·3.
Ex. 25. Find the quotient of 12 by $2\frac{1}{2}$.
Ex. 26. " " 13·25 by $3\frac{1}{4}$
Ex. 27. " " 10·3 by 5·2.

CHAPTER IV.

CONSTRUCTION AND DIVISION OF ANGLES.

24. An angle is the inclination of one straight line to another, and it is measured by the openness of the lines apart. We compare two angles, such as *a b c* and *e f g*, Fig. 12, by placing the

point f on b and laying the line $f\,e$ on $a\,b$, Fig. 13, and then observing whether $f\,g$ lies more distant from $b\,a$ and $f\,e$, or less distant. If nearer, the angle $g\,f\,e$ is less than $c\,b\,a$, if more distant, it is greater.

Fig. 12.

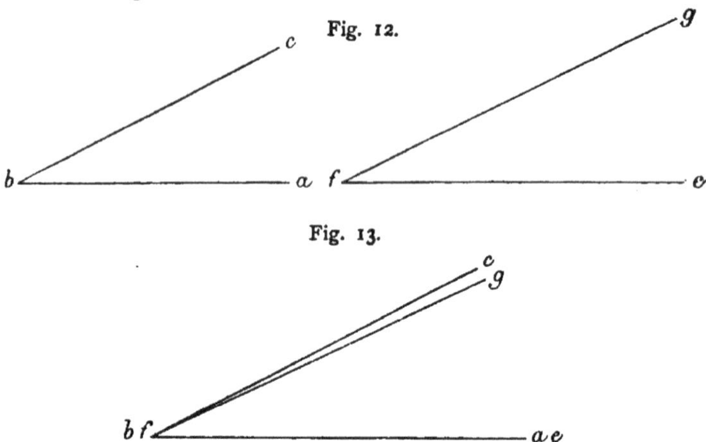

Fig. 13.

25. Angles are measured by taking a certain inclination as unity and seeing how many times the unit angle is contained in the angle under consideration. The unit angle which is always used while working problems in practical geometry is

Fig. 14.

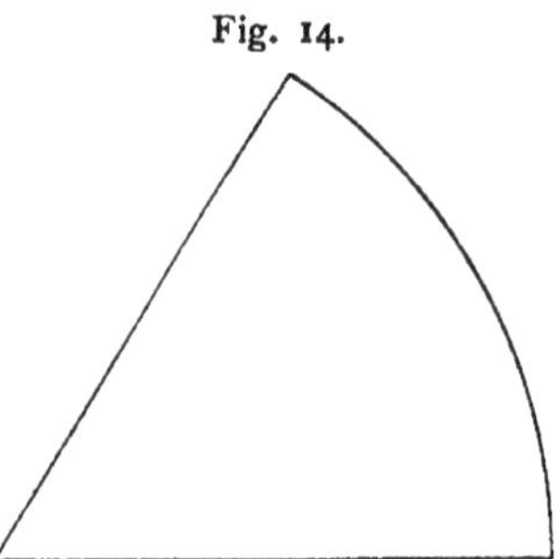

the ninetieth part of the right angle. But there is another unit angle used by scientific men, called the radian. The radian is the inclination of two straight lines which is subtended by an arc equal in length to the radius used for drawing the arc. For example, the angle, Fig. 14, has been drawn such that the real length of the arc, drawn about the angular point as centre, is just equal to the radius which was used for drawing the arc. This angle is the unit angle often used by scientific men; but we shall never use it in 'Mechanical Graphics.'

26. An angle is constructed and made equal to another, such as C B A, in the following way:—

Fig. 15.

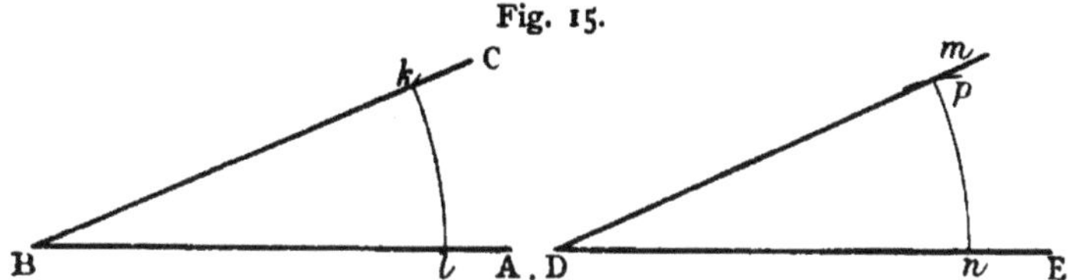

Draw any line D E.

With B as centre, and any radius less than B A, describe an arc cutting C B and B A; and with D as centre, and with the same radius, describe the arc *m n*.

Take a pair of dividers and measure the distance between the points *k* and *l*.

From *n* measure the same distance *m n*. Suppose *m* is the arc made by the other end of the dividers.

Fig. 16.

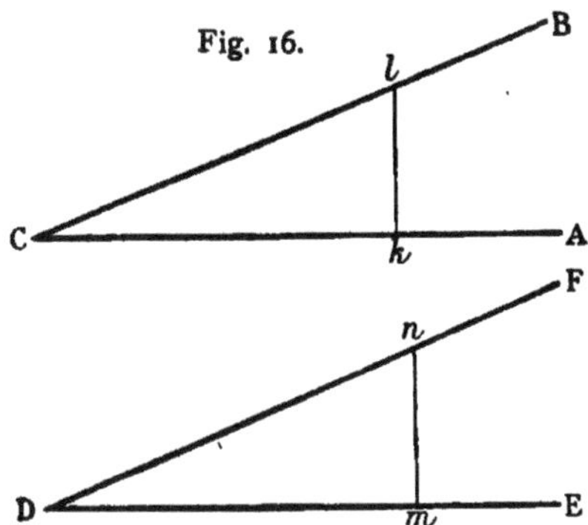

Draw a line through D and *p*; *p* D *n* will be equal to *k* B *l*, because the radii of the arcs are the same, and the chords of the arcs are equal in length.

27. We can solve the same problem in another way.

Take any point k in one of the lines containing the angle and draw from k a perpendicular to C A.

Draw any line D E.

Measure off a distance $d\,m$ from d equal to C k.

Draw $m\,n$ perpendicular to $d\,e$.

Measure $m\,n$ equal to $k\,l$.

Draw $d\,f$ through d and n and $f\,d\,e$ will be equal to $b\,c\,a$.

Ex. 28. Draw any two lines and construct an angle equal to it by both the above methods.

CHAPTER V.

DIVISION OF ANGLES.

28. VERY often when measuring angles we use what is called a protractor, a drawing of which is shown below, Fig. 17. Generally the semicircular one, Fig. 18, is made of horn,

Fig. 17.

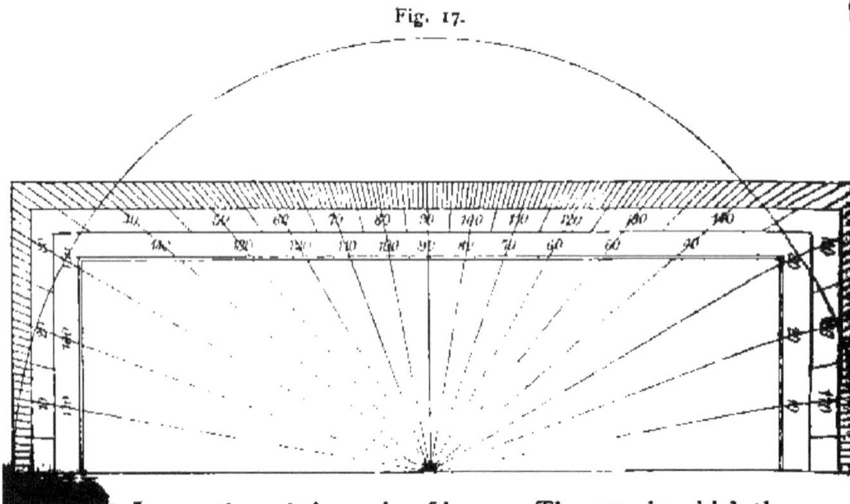

...ugh sometimes it is made of brass. The way in which the ...ngular scale has been constructed is quite obvious from ...lrawing. The rectangular is made of ivory or wood.

29. When an angle is to be constructed by means of the ivory or wooden protractor, we set about it in the following way. Suppose the line to be drawn is to start from A, Fig. 19,

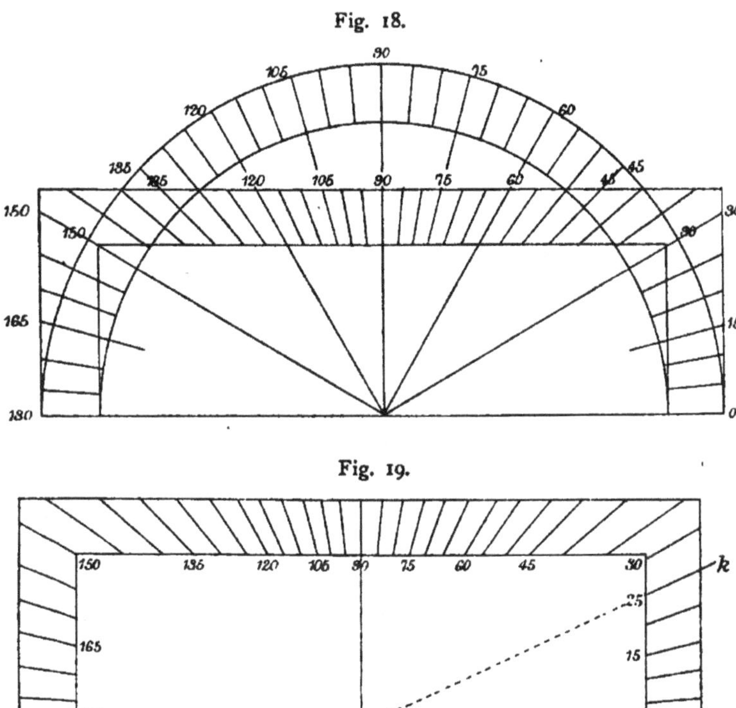

Fig. 18.

Fig. 19.

and to be inclined at 25° to A B. Lay the protractor on the line, and with the centre point coinciding with A, make a mark at the point 25°; remove the protractor and join A and *k*; *k* A will make an angle of 25° with A B.

30. There is still another method for constructing any given angle and it is done by means of the scale of chords. This method will be best understood after having explained the construction of the scale of chords.

To construct a scale of chords draw first two lines inclined at 90° to each other. Divide the arc A B into nine equal parts by means of the dividers. Take the length of the chord for 10° in the dividers and mark it from L along the line L M. Do the same with the chord for 20°, for 30°, and

Fig. 20.

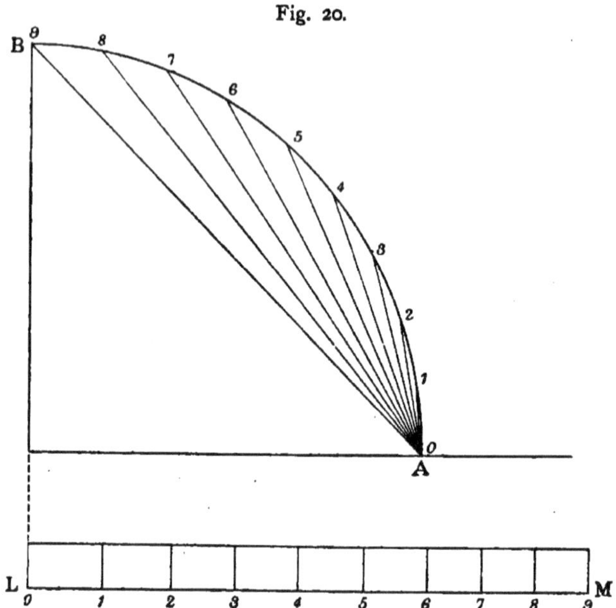

so on up to 90°, always measuring the distances from L. It will be observed that the chord for 60° is exactly equal to the

Fig. 21.

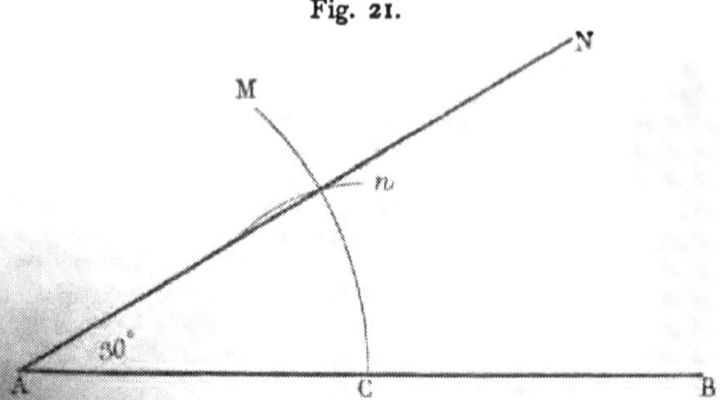

...sed for drawing the arcs. Now since this is the case ...ne has to do in constructing an angle of a given number of degrees on any line A B is to take the chord for 60° in the pencil compass and draw an arc about A as centre. Next take the chord of the given angle, say 30°, in the compasses, and mark the length of the chord by an arc *n* along the arc C M. Then join A and the point where the small arc N cuts the arc L M.

Ex. 29. Prick the given angle *c* on to your drawing paper and draw an angle equal to it on the line A B. (*a*) by the equal perpendiculars method and (*b*) by equal arcs method.

Fig. 22.

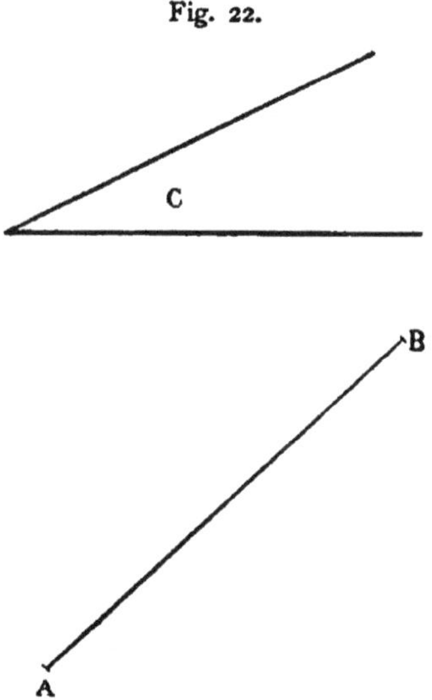

Ex. 30. Construct angles of 50°, 27°, 35° by means of the scale of chords and protractor, then apply the equal arcs method to see if you have got the same answer by both methods.

Ex. 31. On a base of 2 inches construct a triangle having one of the angles at the base 37°.

Ex. 32. Construct a triangle with one angle 40° and the sides containing the angle 2½ inches and 3¼ inches respectively.

31. Having shown how to construct an angle equal to any given angle or of a certain number of degrees, we will now

show how to divide an angle into equal parts. First comes the problem of how to bisect a given angle.

Fig. 23.

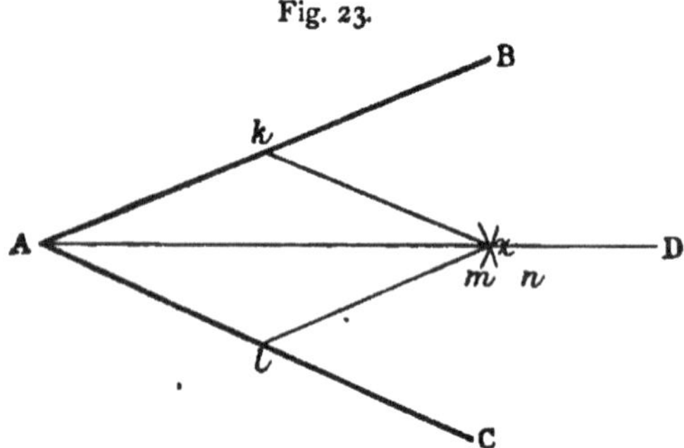

Suppose we are given an angle like B A C, Fig. 23, to bisect. Take pencil compasses, and with A as centre, cut A B and A C at any points *k* and *l*, using the same radius for

Fig. 24.

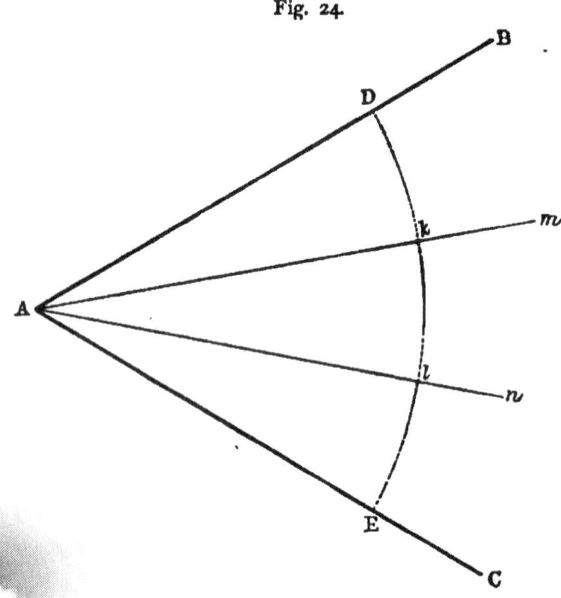

th *k* as centre, and with same radius describe an arc (*m*) h *l* as centre describe an arc (*n*). Join A and *z* the point of intersection of *m* and *n*. A D bisects the angle B A C.

The proof is very easy. Join *l* and *k* with *z*. In the two triangles A *k z* and A *l z* the sides A *k*, *k z*, are equal to the two A *l*, *l z*, and A *z* is common. Therefore the triangles are equal in every respect, and the angle *l* A *z* is equal to *k* A *z*.

32. The difficulty of dividing any angle into three equal parts which appears in plane geometry does not appear in practical geometry. The angle B A C, Fig. 24, is divided into three equal parts by describing any arc D E about A as centre, and dividing this arc into 3 equal parts by means of the dividers in the points of sections *k* and *l*, and by drawing lines through A *k* and A *l*. B A *m*, *m* A *n* and *n* A C are equal to each other.

In exactly the same way an angle may be divided into any number of equal parts.

When, however, the angle is a power of 2 it may be divided by a series of subdivisions. First it may be divided into two parts, and then each of those divisions again into two parts, and so on.

Fig. 25.

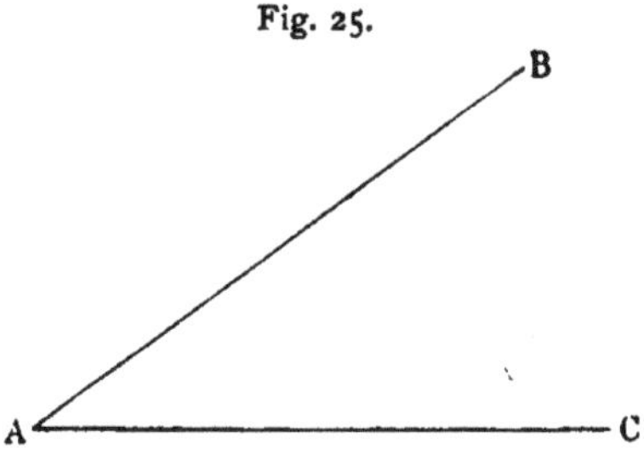

Ex. 33. Prick through this angle B A C on the drawing paper and bisect and trisect it.

Ex. 34. Divide 197° into 16 equal angles.

CHAPTER VI.

PROPERTIES OF THE CIRCLE AND OF THE INCLUDED TRIANGLES.

33. SINCE the angle in a semicircle is a right angle we can always get a triangle having a vertical angle of 90° by drawing a semicircle on the base. For example, suppose it is required to draw on A B, Fig. 26, a triangle A C B with vertical angle of 90°. On A B describe a semicircle and draw A C and B C to any point C in that semicircle.

Fig. 26.

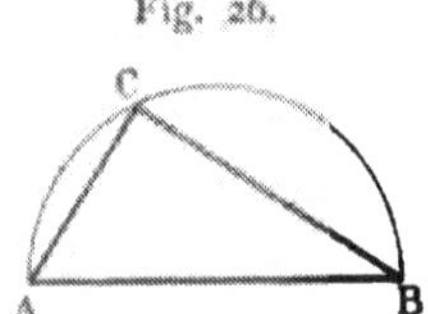

Ex. 35. On a base of three inches construct a triangle with vertical angle of 90°.

Now we can go a step further and make one of the sides and the base as well as vertical angle of definite dimensions.

FIG. 27.

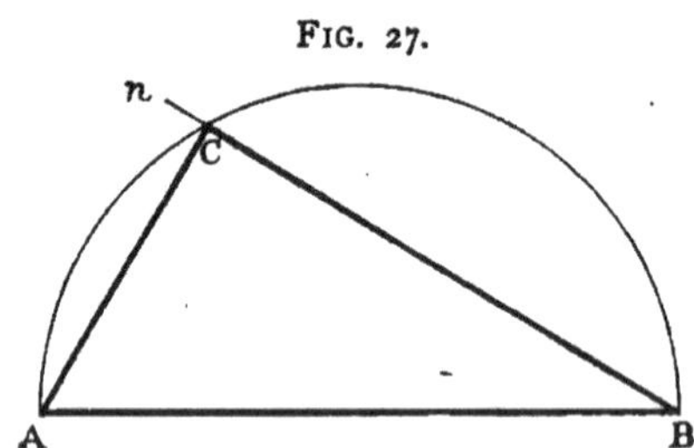

For suppose one side is to be 1 inch, with A as centre and radius 1 inch, draw an arc cutting the semicircle in C. A C B will be the triangle.

Ex. 36. On a base of $2\frac{1}{2}$ inches construct a triangle with rtical angle of 90° and one side 1 inch.

34. The angle at the centre of a circle is double of the gle at the circumference. In Fig. 28 the angle A E C is uble of the angle A B C. Therefore, if E F be drawn at [illegible] to A C, A E F will be equal to A B C.

Draw A D at right angles to the radius A E. Then

$$EAF + FAD = AEF + EAF,$$

and therefore

$$FAD = AEF$$
$$= ABC.$$

That is to say, if we are given the chord of a circle and the angle at the circumference, we can find the arc which contains that angle. For suppose we are given a chord $1\frac{1}{2}$ inch in length, and the angle subtended by that chord 45°, and it is required to find the circle circumscribing the triangle. Draw the chord A C $1\frac{1}{2}$ inch in length, draw A D making an angle of 45° with A C. Draw A E at right angles to A D. Bisect A C in F, and draw F E at right angles to A C. E is the centre of the circle. With E as centre and E A as radius describe the circle. Take any point B in the circumference and join B A and B C. A B C will be 45°, and the circle will pass through the points A, B, and C.

Fig. 28.

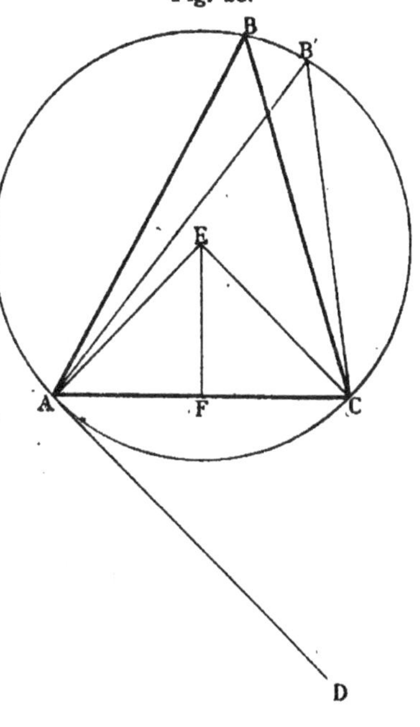

Ex. 37. A chord is 2 inches in length, and the angle at the circumference is 70°, find the circle whose circumference contains the ends of the chord and the vertex of the triangle.

Ex. 38. A chord is $1\frac{3}{4}$ inch long, and the angle at the circumference is 120°, describe the circle whose circumference contains the ends of the chord and the vertex of the triangle.

35. So with a triangle. If we get the base and the vertical angle we can draw the triangle. And because the angle at

the circumference is the same from whatever point we may choose to draw the lines containing the angle, if we are given the height of the triangle as well as the base and vertical angle we can draw it. For example, suppose A B, Fig. 29, is given as the base of a triangle, and the height is given as h, and the vertical angle as a.

Draw B A C = a. Draw A D at right angles to A C. Bisect A B in E and draw E F at right angles to A B.

Fig. 29.

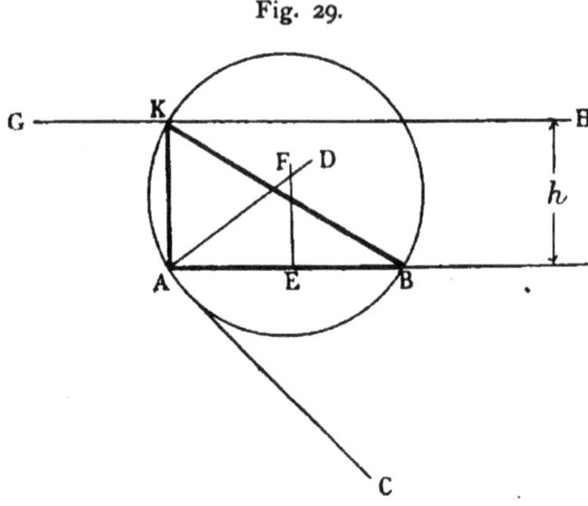

Describe a circle with centre F, radius F A. Draw G H parallel to A B and at a distance h from it, and let G H cut the circle in K. Join A K and K B. A K B is the triangle required.

Ex. 39. On a base of 3 inches construct a triangle with a vertical angle of 75°.

Ex. 40. Find a segment of a circle containing an angle 13°, and another 108°.

Ex. 41. On a base of $2\frac{1}{2}$ inches construct a triangle with a vertical angle of 63°, and one side $1\frac{1}{4}$ inches long.

Ex. 42. On a base 2·75 inches construct a triangle with vertical angle of 45°, and height of 1·3 inches.

Ex. 43. On a base of 2·9 inches construct a triangle with vertical angle of 109°, and height ·9 inches.

36. If we have a circle touching two lines, A B and A C, Fig. 30, and we draw another line, E F, touching the circle at H, then, seeing E H and E D are tangents to the same circle

$$EH = ED$$
$$AE + EH = AE + ED.$$

For the same reason

$$AF + FH = AF + FG,$$

adding

$$AE + EF + AF = AD + AG.$$

Sum of sides or perimeter = A D + A G, which being tangents = 2 A D

$$\therefore AD = \tfrac{1}{2} \text{ perimeter}.$$

Fig. 30.

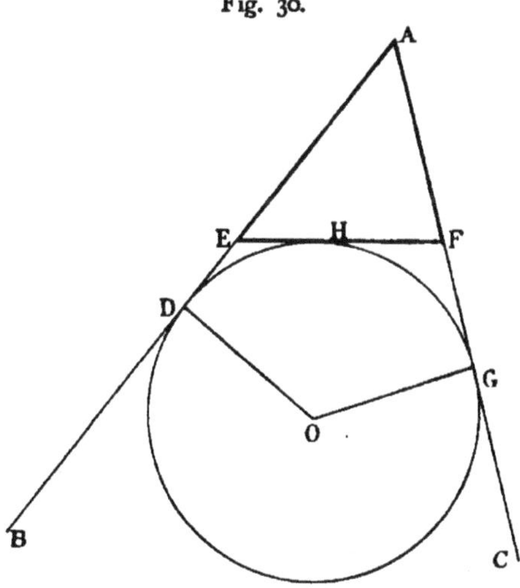

So that, given the perimeter, we can get the points D and G from which to erect perpendiculars for finding of the centre. For example, suppose the perimeter of a triangle is given as 4 inches, and it is required to construct the triangle. From any point A draw any two lines A B and A C. Measure off A D and A G each equal to half the perimeter 2 inches. From D and G erect perpendiculars. Describe a circle about O with O D as radius, and draw any line E F tangent to the circle. A E H is the triangle required.

Ex. 44. Construct a triangle, the sum of whose sides is 9 inches.

37. We can go a step further and construct a triangle which has the vertical angle defined as well as the perimeter. For in this case we can begin by drawing the two half perimeters inclined to each other at the given angle.

Ex. 45. The vertical angle of a triangle is 50°, its perimeter is 10 inches, construct it.

Ex. 46. The vertical angle of a triangle is 47°, its perimeter 11·25 inches, height 2½ inches, construct it.

Ex. 47. The vertical angle of a triangle is 64°, its perimeter 7·3 inches, height 1·75, construct it.

Ex. 48. A boy walks a distance of 10 miles, and his perpendicular distance from the starting-point is always either 0 or 2½ miles, and his return path makes an angle of 43° with his departure path. Draw a plan of the path in which the boy has travelled.

CHAPTER VII.

CONSTRUCTION OF POLYGONS.

38. ANY regular figure has its sides subtending equal angles at the centre of figure. For example, the sides of a square A B C D subtend right angles at the centre of figure O.

Fig. 31.

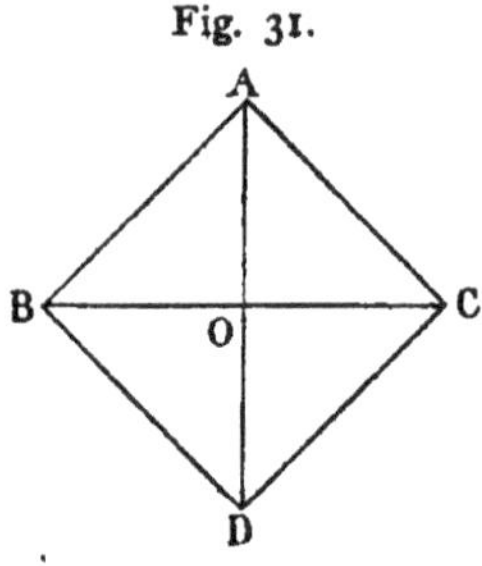

The side of a regular	triangle	subtends	120° or $\frac{360^\circ}{3}$	at centre.
"	square	"	90° or $\frac{260^\circ}{4}$	"
"	pentagon, or 5-sided fig.	"	72° or $\frac{360^\circ}{5}$	"
"	hexagon, or 6-sided fig.	"	60° or $\frac{360^\circ}{6}$	"
"	any polygon of n sides	"	$\frac{360^\circ}{n}$	"

39. This property enables us to draw a regular figure of any number of sides.

For suppose it is required to draw a pentagon of any length of side. Take any point A and with A as centre describe a circle with any radius. Step the dividers round

Fig. 32.

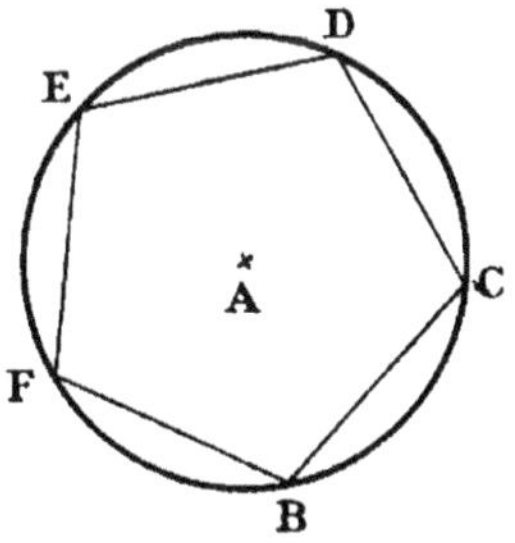

this circle five times exactly, by trial. Join the points of section. These lines B C, C D, D E, E F, and F B, are the sides of the regular pentagon.

Ex. 49. Draw an equilateral triangle.

Ex. 50. Draw a square.

Ex. 51. Draw a pentagon.

40. Now if we are given the length of the side of the polygon as well as the number of sides we can construct it

because we know that the angles C A B = C B A, and that the 3 angles

Fig. 33.

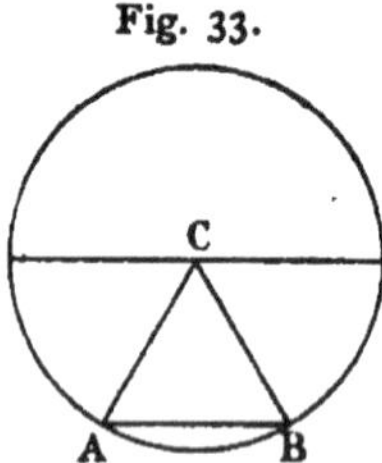

$$A C B + C A B + A B C = 180^\circ$$
$$A C B + 2 C A B = 180^\circ$$
$$C A B = \frac{180 - A C B}{2}$$

Given C A B we get the centre of a circle going round the polygon. And given the circle we can step round the circles.

Ex. 52. Describe a pentagon of 1½ inch side.

Ex. 53. Describe a hexagon of 2 inch sides.

Ex. 54. Describe a heptagon of 1⅓ inch sides.

Ex. 55. Describe an octagon of 1·75 sides.

CHAPTER VIII.

EQUAL AREAS.

41. ANY parallelogram between the same parallels A G and B C, Fig. 34, and on the same base as the rectangle A B C D, is equal in area to that rectangle.

42. This theorem enables us to draw a parallelogram equal to a rectangle on a given base and with side of any length, provided that side is not less than the height of the rectangle. For example, suppose the base B C of a rectangle is given as ½ inch and its height B A as 1 inch, and it is required to draw a parallelogram on the same base equal in area and with side 2 inches in length.

Draw the rectangle A B C D as required.

With B as centre and radius 2 inches, describe an arc cutting A G in E.

FIG. 34.

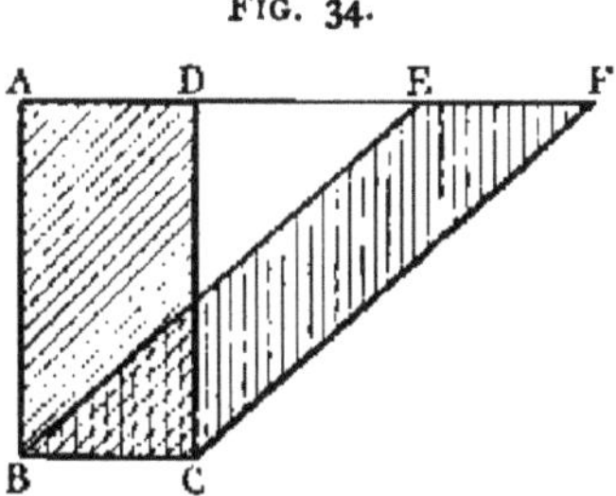

Draw C F parallel to B E. B C F E is the parallelogram required.

Ex. 56. Describe a parallelogram with perimeter 10 inches equal in area to a rectangle 2 inches × 3 inches.

Ex. 57. Describe a parallelogram having sides 3 inches × 5 inches equal to a rectangle of 12 square inches area.

Fig. 35.

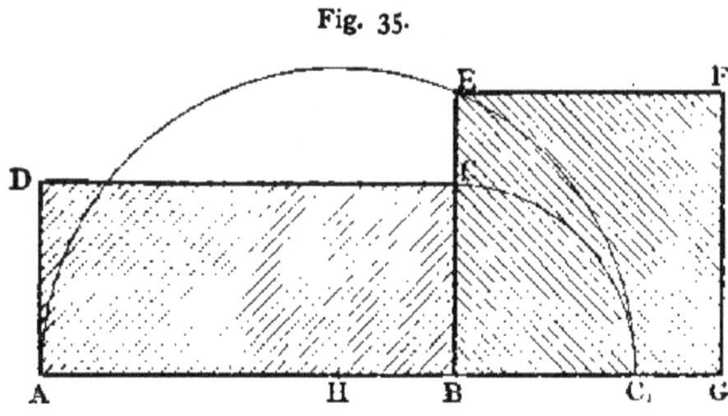

43. If the sides of a rectangle A B C D, Fig. 35, be laid end to end as shown by A B and B C, and if a semicircle be described on this whole line A C, and a perpendicular B E be raised to this line from B the point where the two lines meet, then the square on B E, that is the figure B E F G, is equal to the rectangle A B C D. (See 21, p. 10).

Suppose then the sides of a rectangle, A B and B C, are

given, and it is required to construct a square equal to it in area, it is proceeded with as follows :—

About B as centre and radius B C, describe an arc C C_1.

Bisect A C_1 in H and with H as centre and radius B C describe a semicircle.

Produce B C to E. The square on B E is equal to the rectangle.

Ex. 58. Construct a square equal to a rectangle 3 inches by $2\frac{1}{2}$ inches.

Ex. 59. Construct a square equal to a rectangle 10 inches in area.

Ex. 60. Construct a square equal in area to a parallelogram of 3 inch by $2\frac{1}{2}$ inch sides and having one angle 60°.

44. Conversely, a rectangle having one side any length we please can be found equal in area to any square. For, suppose the square A B C D is given, and it is required to construct a rectangle equal to it in area, and with one of its sides equal to B E.

Fig. 36.

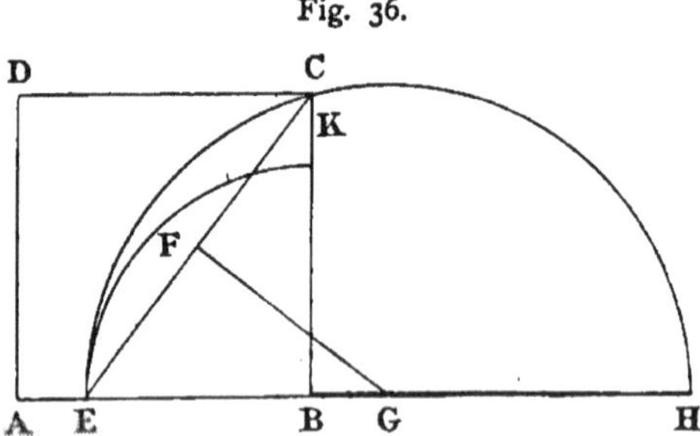

From B measure the distance B E.

Join E C and bisect it in F.

From F draw F G perpendicular to the line E C. The G is the centre of the semicircle described on the sides e rectangle laid end to end.

.bout G as centre and radius G E describe a semicircle. is the other side of the rectangle.

About B as centre and with B E as radius describe the arc and B H are the sides of the rectangle required.

Ex. 61. Construct a rectangle having one side 2 inches equal to a square 8 inches area.

Ex. 62. Construct a parallelogram one side $1\frac{1}{2}$ inch on angle 75° area equal to a square $\sqrt{5}$ inches side.

45. Sometimes the given side is 1 inch, or if the scale is not unity the side is taken unity. In that case we have

$$B\,E \times B\,H = \text{area of square.}$$
$$B\,E \text{ being one we have}$$
$$1 \times B\,H = \text{area of square.}$$

The side B H containing as many units of length as the square contains square inches. Or in other words, B H represents the area of the square when the other side of the rectangle is made unity.

Given then a square and required a line to represent its area, make one side of the rectangle equal in area to it, 1 inch, and the other side will represent the area of square.

Ex. 63. Find a line to represent the area of a square of $1\frac{1}{2}$ inch side.

Fig. 37.

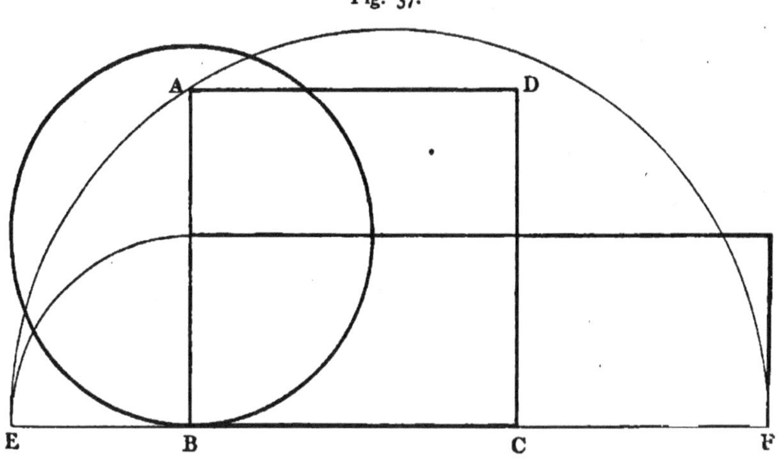

Ex. 64. Find a line to represent the area of a rectangle $1\frac{1}{4}$ inch × $2\frac{1}{8}$ inches.

46. Fig. 37 shows a square A B C D made equal in area

to a circle of 2 inches diameter. In working this problem B E is made equal the radius and B F equal to half the circumference of the circle—the product then being equal to $\pi r \times r = \pi r^2$. A semicircle is constructed on E F. The square on B A is equal in area to the circle.

CHAPTER IX.

REDUCTION OF FIGURES.

47. ANY triangle B D C, Fig. 38, between the same parallels, or of the same height, and on the same base or on an equal base to an isosceles triangle A B C, is equal to it in area.

Fig. 38.

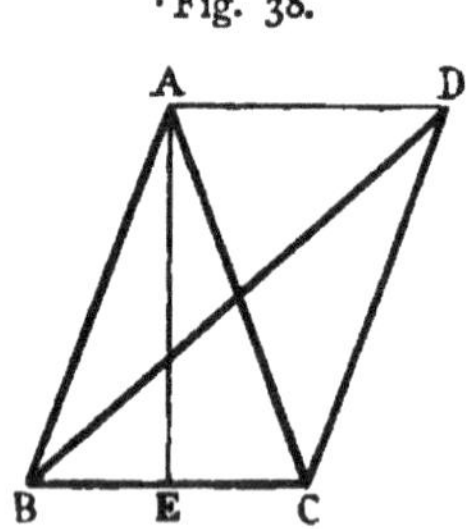

Suppose it is required to describe a triangle on a base ¾ inch in length and with one side 1½ inches in length, equal in area to an isosceles triangle on same base, and 1 inch high.

Draw a line B C ¾ inch in length.

Measure a perpendicular distance E A 1 inch in length.

Through A draw A D parallel to B C. With B as centre and radius 2 inches cut A D in D. Join B D and C D. B D C is the triangle required.

Ex. 65. Describe a triangle, base 2 inches, one side 5 equal in area to another triangle of the same base and 2½ inches.

On the same principle we can find a triangle equal in

area to any square. A line A B drawn parallel to the diagonal C D makes any triangle with base between the parallels C D and A B equal to C B D; C A D will be equal in area to C B D and therefore A C E will be equal in area to the square.

Fig. 39.

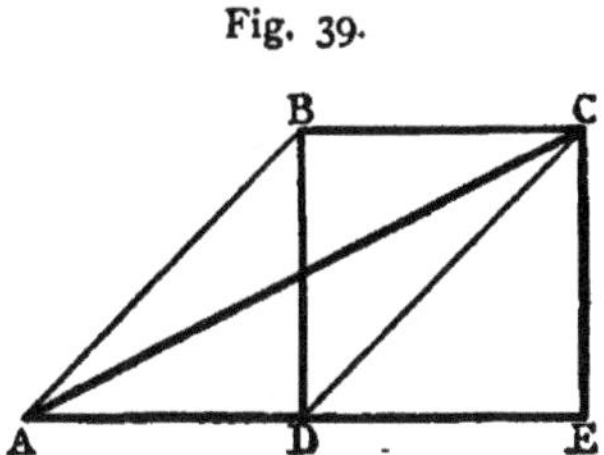

Ex. 66. Describe a triangle height 3 inches and equal in area to a square 9 inches area.

Ex. 67. Describe a triangle having two sides $2\frac{1}{2}$ inches, $3\frac{1}{2}$ inches, equal in area to another with sides 2 inches, $1\frac{1}{2}$ inches, $2\frac{1}{2}$ inches.

So with a pentagon. The line A F, Fig. 40, parallel to B E makes the whole F B C D equal to the pentagon, and the line C G, Fig. 41, parallel to B D will make the triangle F B G equal in area to F B C D, that is, equal to E A B C D.

Fig. 40. Fig. 41.

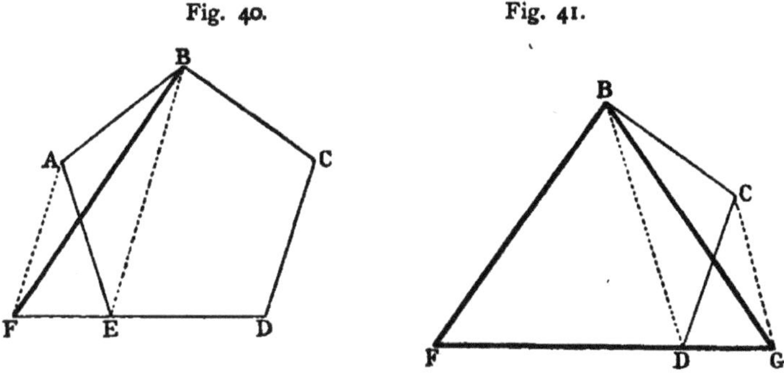

Ex. 68. Find a triangle equal in area to a hexagon, 1 inch side: then a rectangle equal to this triangle: then a square equal to this rectangle: and next a line to represent the area of the square.

Ex. 69. Find a triangle equal in area to a heptagon, 1 inch side: and a line to represent its area.

Ex. 70. Find a triangle equal in area to an octagon, $1\frac{1}{2}$ inch side: and a line to represent its area.

CHAPTER X.

THE CIRCLE AND ITS TANGENT.

49. A LINE drawn from any point A on the circumference of this circle at right angles to the radius is tangent to the circle.

Fig. 42.

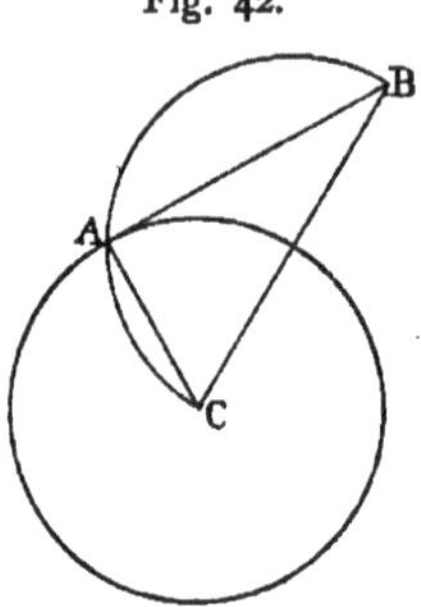

A tangent at a point in a circle is always at right angles to the radius at that point; hence, if we wish to draw a tangent to a circle from a point B outside that circle, a semicircle on C B will find for us the point where the tangent meets the circle.

Ex. 71. From any point on a circle 2 inches diameter draw a tangent.

Ex. 72. A string is pulled from a cylinder $2\frac{1}{2}$ inches diameter at an angle to the horizon of 30°: show the cylinder [illegible] string.

[illegible]3. Draw a tangent to a circle 2 inches diameter from [illegible] inches from the centre.

[illegible] Two pulleys hang on a wall at the same height

and 4 inches apart weights hang over the pulleys by strings, which are fastened to a point mid-way between the pulleys but 3 inches below their centres; show the pulleys and strings.

Fig. 43.

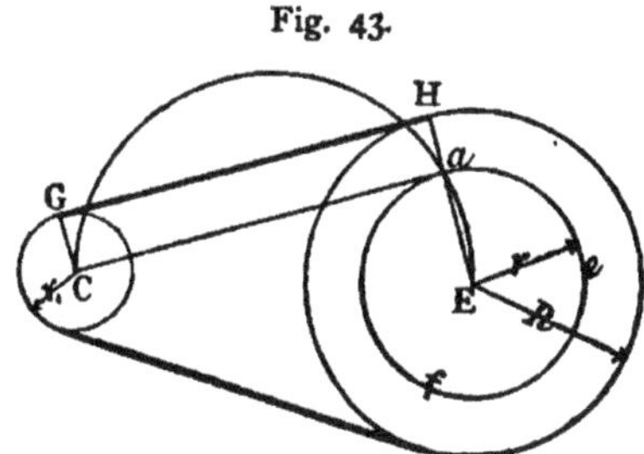

50. The tangent to the two circles Fig. 43 of unequal radii, will be parallel to the line C *a* drawn through the centre C of the smaller and tangent to the inner circle *a e f* whose radius is *r* = R — *r*.

Construct on C E the line of centres a semicircle. From C, the centre of the smaller, draw a line to *a*, the point where the semicircle cuts the circle within the larger.

Draw one radius through *a* and another radius through C at right angles to the tangent C *a*. G H is the tangent required.

There is another tangent on the other side of the circles, and another pair of tangents crossing the line of centres C E.

Ex. 75. Draw a tangent to two circles of 1½ inches and 2 inches diameter, with centres 3 inches apart.

Ex. 76. Draw a tangent to two circles of ½ inch diameter and 3 inches diameter, with centres 3 inches apart.

51. To find the cross tangents describe a circle of radius R + *r* about E as centre, Fig. 44.

Describe a semicircle about C E as diameter. Join *c* to *a*, the point where the semicircle cuts the outer circle about centre E. Join E *a* and draw the radius *c* G at right angles to the tangent C *a*.

G H is the tangent required.

J K, the other tangent, is found in the same way.

So four tangents have to be found before a complete solution of the problem is obtained.

Fig. 44.

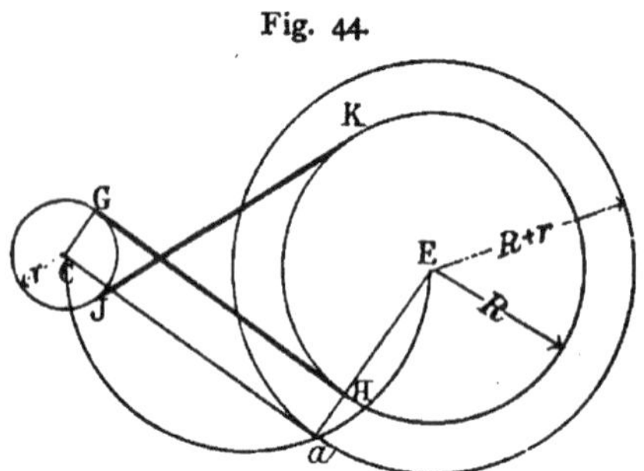

Ex. 77. Draw a tangent to two circles of 1½ inches diameter and 2 inches diameter, crossing the line of centres; centres 3 inches apart.

Ex. 78. Draw four tangents to two circles of 1·75 inch diameter and 2½ inches diameter, with centres 3½ inches apart.

CHAPTER XI.

THE CIRCLE AND ITS TANGENT—*continued.*

52. VERY often a circle has to be described between two lines which are inclined to each other. When the two inclined lines meet each other the construction is very simple.

For suppose A B and A C, Fig. 45, are the lines which meet at an angle.

Bisect the angle B A C with the line A D.

From any point E in A D drop a perpendicular on A C. With E as centre and the perpendicular E F as radius, [illegible]cle. This circle will touch the lines A B and [illegible]e the circle required.

[illegible]uppose the circle which has to be described

within and touching the lines is to be of a given diameter. Again let A B and A C, Fig. 46, be the two lines which meet.

Fig. 45.

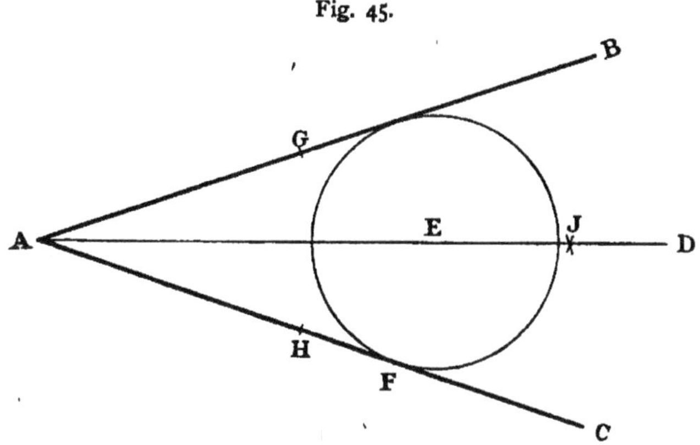

Draw a line D E at right angles to A C and measure from D a distance equal to half the given diameter.

Through E draw E F parallel to A C. F is the centre of the circle of given diameter, touching the two lines.

Fig. 46.

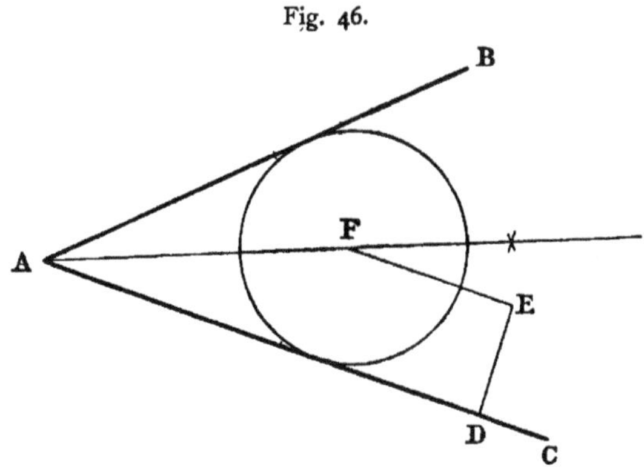

54. Suppose next the lines cannot be made to meet on the drawing paper. Take A B and C D, Fig 47, as the lines, and first find the line which bisects the angle between the lines.

From any point E in A B draw E F parallel to C D.
Bisect the angle B E F by the line E G.
From E draw a line E H at right angles to E G.
Bisect E H in J.

Fig. 47.

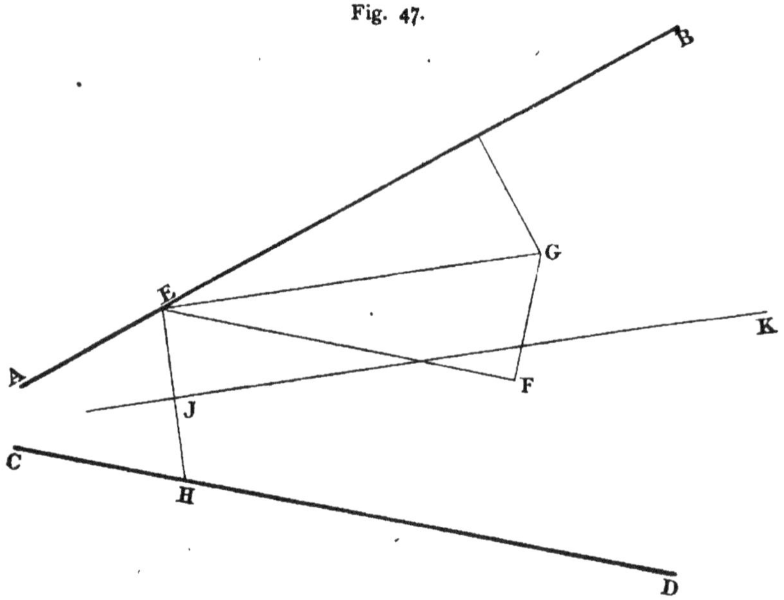

Through J draw a line J K parallel to A G. J K is the line required.

55. Let it now be required to describe a circle of given diameter touching two such lines.

Draw a line E F at right angles to A B from any point E in A B, and measure off E L equal to the radius of the required circle.

Through L draw a line L H parallel to A B. G H parallel to E L is the radius of the required circle and H is its centre.

Ex. 79. Draw any two lines making an angle of 63° from any point A and bisect them.

Ex. 80. Describe a circle of 1½ inch diameter touching the two lines referred to in last question.

Ex. 81. Draw any two lines at any angle, but such that

they do not meet on the drawing paper, and find the line bisecting them.

Ex. 82. Describe a circle 1¼ inch diameter touching the two lines referred to in the last question.

Fig. 48.

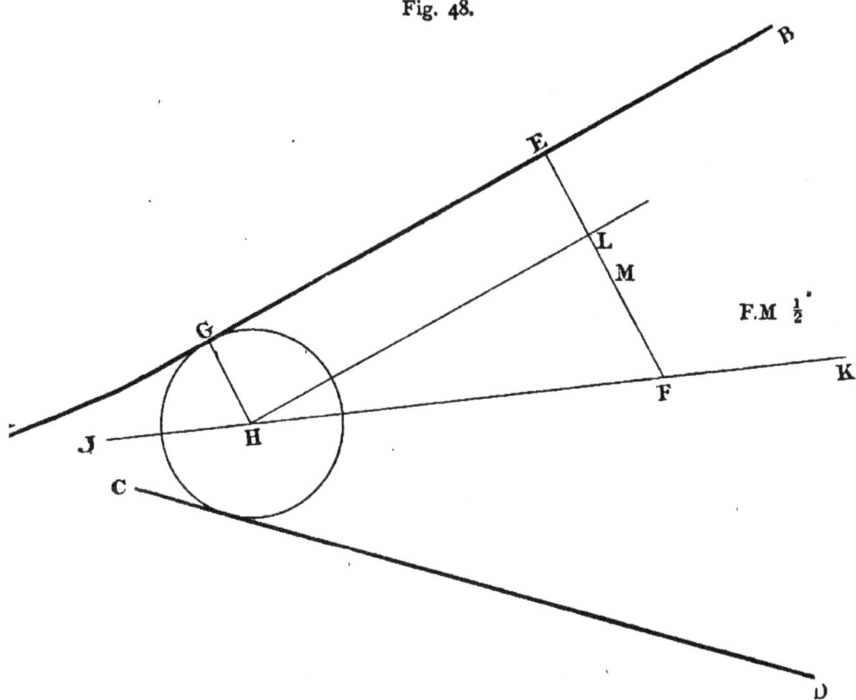

56. The tangents drawn from any point A to a circle are equal. So when a circle is given touching two lines we can by using this fact find a second circle to touch the two lines and the first circle.

Let A B and C D, Fig. 49, be the two lines, and G M L the circle. Draw a tangent M L from M the point where the circle cuts the bisector.

Measure off L N equal to L M.

Draw N O at right angles to A B. O is the centre of the required circle.

Ex. 83. Draw a second circle to touch the lines and circle referred to in Exercise 82.

57. It is often necessary when drawing machinery to describe a circle to touch two other curves. Draughtsmen

Fig. 49.

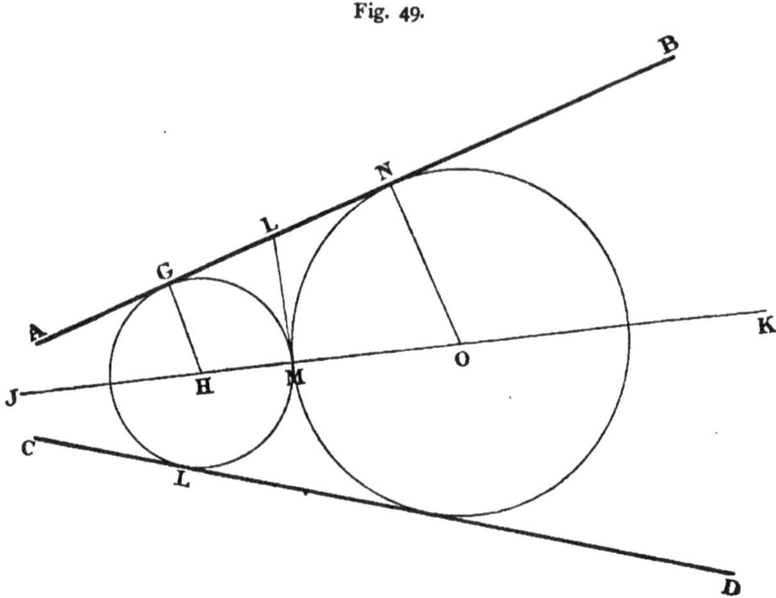

oftenest do this by finding the centre of third circle by trial; but it can be done by construction. Suppose A and B, Fig. 50, are the given circles of radii $r_{,}$ and R, and it is required to describe a circle of a given diameter, say $\frac{3}{4}$ inch, to touch both. Let r be radius of this circle.

With C as centre and radius equal to $r + r_{,}$ draw the arc D.

With $C_{,}$ as centre and radius $R + r_{,}$ draw the arc E. The intersecting point F is the same distance from circle B as it is from circle A. So F is the centre of the circle required.

58. Lastly suppose it is required to describe a circle to touch a given line and a given circle.

Take A, Fig. 51, as the given circle, and B C as the line, and D the point in the line where the required circle is to touch.

From D draw D E at right angles to B C, and equal to the radius of A. Join E F and make G F E equal to G E F.

Fig. 50.

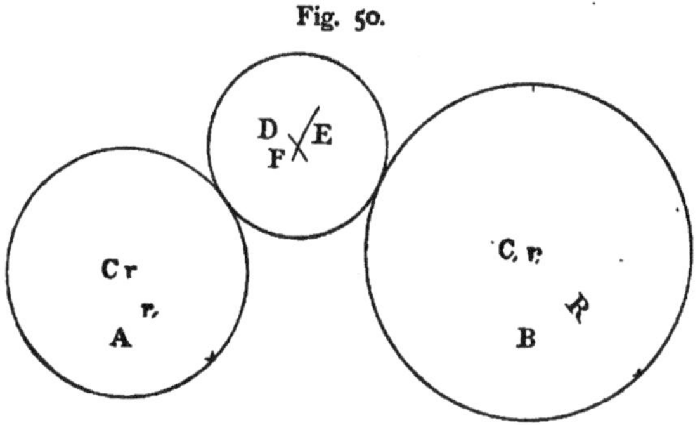

Fig. 51.

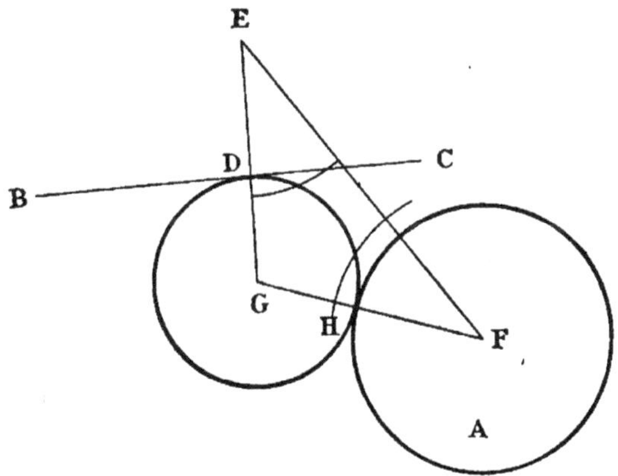

Then

G F = G E,

and by construction

H F = D E,

∴ G H = G D.

And G is the centre of a circle which touches the line at D and the given circle A.

Ex. 84. Two circles of 1 inch and 1½ inch diameter have their centres 2 inches apart, describe a third circle of 2 inches diameter to touch the first two circles.

Ex. 85. Describe a circle to touch a given line A B C at the point B, and a circle $1\frac{1}{2}$ inch diameter with its centre at a perpendicular distance of 1 inch from A C and $\frac{3}{4}$ inch perpendicular distance to the right of B.

Mechanics have often to lay off a certain distance, called

Fig. 52.

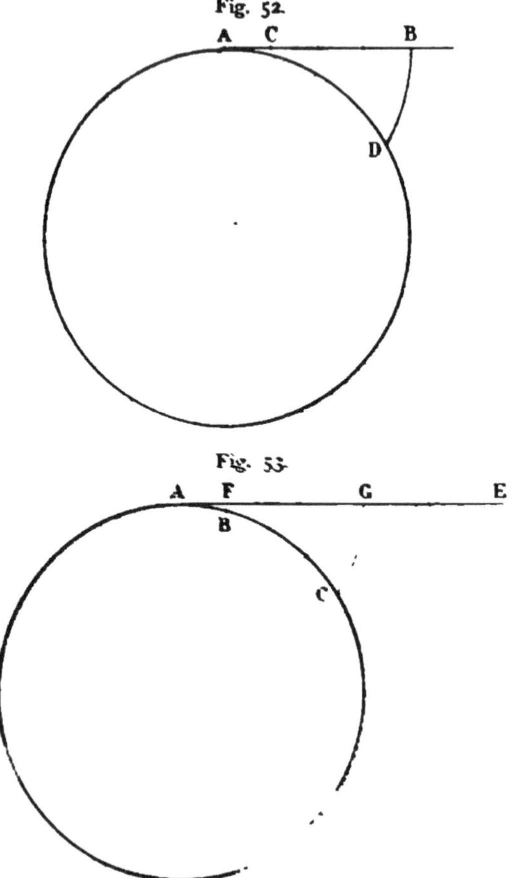

Fig. 53.

the pitch of teeth, along a circle called the pitch circle. This problem resolves itself into one of setting the length of a given straight line A B Fig. 52. along an arc of a circle, or finding an arc of a curve equal in length to a given straight line.

Measure off a distance A C, Fig. 52, equal in length to one-fourth of A B, and with C as centre, and C B as radius. Describe an arc B D. The arc A D is equal to the line A B.

Conversely, it is often found necessary to find the length of a given arc by construction, as when finding the length of wrapping connections, that is when the length of the cord which goes round a pair of pulleys is required. Suppose the length of the arc A C, Fig. 53, is wanted. Divide A C into four equal parts; draw a tangent at A, and with A as centre, and radius equal to the chord A B; describe an arc cutting the tangent in F. With F as centre, and F C as radius, describe the are C G. A G is the distance equal to the length of the arc.

Ex. 86. Find the length of the arc subtending an angle of 60° in a circle of 2 inches diameter.

SECTION II.

ORTHOGRAPHIC PROJECTION.

CHAPTER XII.

POINTS.

59. THE position of a point situated in space with respect to its height above a horizontal plane may be shown by marking a point immediately behind it on a vertical plane. For example, the height of the point A, Fig. 54, above the horizontal plane is clearly shown by the point *a'* at the end of a

Fig. 54.

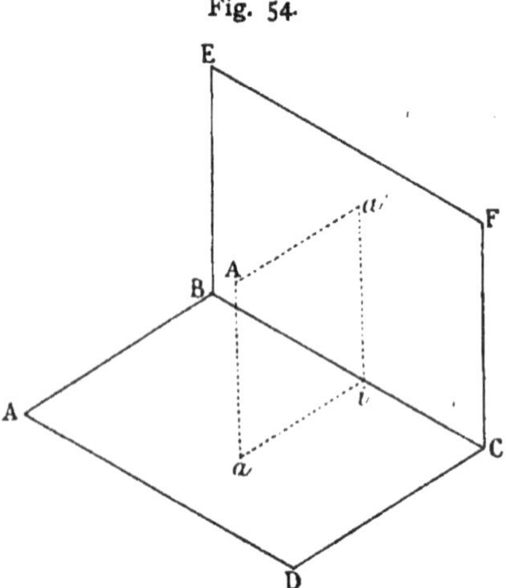

perpendicular from A to the vertical plane E F C B. The point *a'* is called the vertical projection of A. So the point *a* the horizontal plane shows the distance of the real point A front of the vertical plane. The point *a* is called the plan.

In this way the position of the point A, with respect to both the vertical and horizontal planes of proportion, is fixed.

If, then, a point A be a certain defined distance in front of the vertical plane, and also a certain defined distance above the horizontal plane, a person informed of these distances can place a point—his pencil-point for example—under exactly the same conditions with regard to two similar planes of projection. And, further, he could represent his pencil-point on his vertical and horizontal plane by dropping perpendiculars from it to them, and thus represent it.

On the other hand, if he could do this with respect to a point of whose position he had been informed, he could without a word being spoken or a line written to him, understand where a point would be if its plan and elevation were represented to him on paper, as explained above. The points he would see would be *a'* and *a*, and in his mind's eye he would see A stand out in space in front of the vertical plane and above the horizontal plane. *a' i* would show him the height above the horizontal plane; *a i* the distance in front of the vertical plane.

For convenience paper is usually carried about in a portfolio, so it becomes necessary to flatten the plane E F C B

Fig. 55.

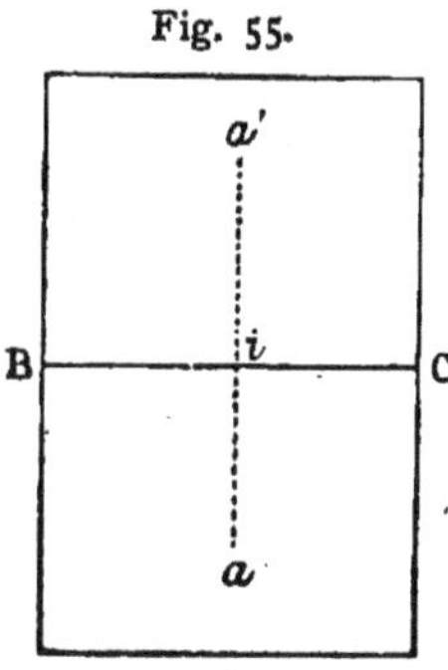

until it is on a level with A B C D; but this does not alter our line B C, nor the line *a' i* which represents the height of the point A.

We see then, that, although the whole paper is flat, we may still represent the position of a point A by letting a horizontal line represent the line where the vertical and horizontal planes meet, taking care to mark off the proper distance from that line: *a' i* to represent the height, and *a i* to represent the distance in front. The distances *a i* and *a' i* will be at right angles to B C. *a* is called the plan; *a'* the elevation; sometimes *a'* vertical projection; *a* horizontal projection.

Ex. 87. A point A is 2 inches in front of the vertical plane and 1 inch above the horizontal plane.

Ex. 88. A point B is 3½ inches in front of the vertical plane and 2½ inches above the horizontal plane.

Ex. 89. A point C is in the vertical plane and 2 inches above the horizontal plane.

Ex. 90. A point D is in the horizontal plane and 2 inches in front of the vertical plane.

Ex. 91. A point E is in the vertical plane and in the horizontal plane.

CHAPTER XIII.

LINES.

60. THE plan and elevation of a horizontal line, the position of whose extremities are given, can also be shown.

Fig. 56 shows such a line A B, at right angles to V.P. and parallel to H P; and Fig. 57 shows its orthographic projection, *a b* the plan, and *a b* the elevation.

Fig. 56 shows a horizontal line D C, parallel to V.P.; and Fig. 57 shows how it looks in orthographic projection.

Ex. 92. A line C D 3 inches long is parallel to H.P. and at right angles to V.P.

Ex. 93. A line A B 2·5 inches long is parallel to V.P. and to H.P.; its distance from H.P. is 1·5 inches and in front of V.P. 2·5.

Ex. 94. A line E F 2·75 inches long is parallel to V.P., and at right angles to H.P.

61. The line may be parallel to one plane and not parallel

Fig. 56.

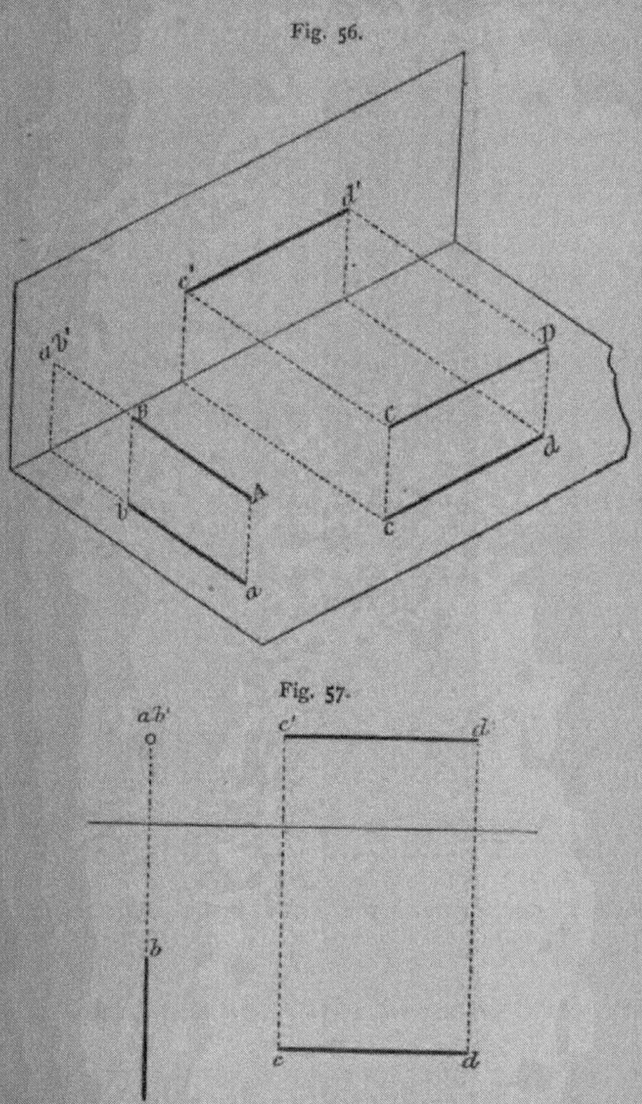

Fig. 57.

to the other. Such a line is shown in Fig. 58. G H is parallel to V.P., but not to H.P. In such a case the distance of the line from V.P. is generally given, and the heights of its ends

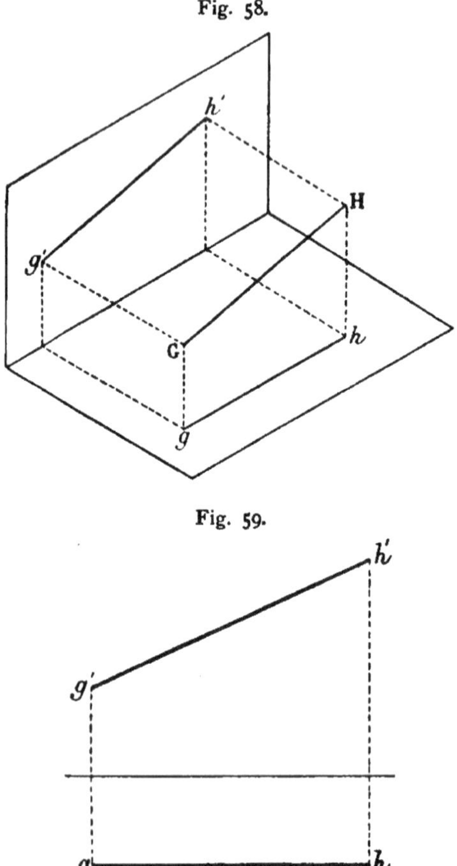

Fig. 58.

Fig. 59.

from H.P. and its true length, or the length of its plan, may be given. Take the following example :—

Ex. 95. A line G H parallel to V.P. has G $\frac{1}{2}$" above H.P. and H $1\frac{1}{8}$" above H.P. The plan is $1\frac{1}{2}$ inches in length, the distance in front of V.P. is $\frac{1}{2}$".

Begin by measuring a distance of $\frac{1}{2}$ inch in front of $x\,y$,

...fore take any point *g*. Draw from *g* a line ... From *g* measure a distance *h* $1\frac{1}{8}$ ins.; *g h* ... Mark from *g* along the projector *g g'* the point ... above *x y*, and *h'* $1\frac{1}{8}$ ins. high; *g' h'* will be the ... projection.

Next, suppose the true length of the line is given in... of the plan. For example, take another line A B under ... the same conditions as the last, only in place of the ... the "plan measures $1\frac{1}{8}$ ins.," read the true length of the ... $1\frac{1}{16}$ inches."

Now this is an important case, because we cannot now ... the plan before the elevation, and it therefore illustrates ... necessity of considering with what projection we must ... The line is parallel to the vertical plane, and therefore ... true length is shown by the vertical projection.

Begin, then, with any point *a'*, Fig. 60, $\frac{1}{2}$ inch above *x y*. ... next a horizontal line *m n* 1 inch above *x y*. As the ... *b'* is 1 inch high it must be somewhere in this line.

Fig. 60.

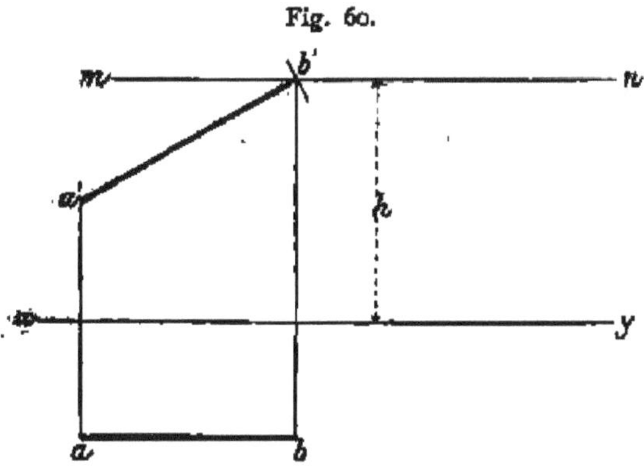

... take *a'* as centre, and with $1\frac{1}{16}$ inches as radius, ... an arc cutting *m n*. The point of intersection of the ... arc will be 1 inch high and $1\frac{1}{16}$ inches distant from ... point is *b'*, the vertical projection of the other end ... line.

... plan *a b* can now be easily found by projecting down

the points a' b'. Plan a b will lie between the projectors and parallel to V.P., and at a distance of $\frac{1}{2}$ inch in front of x y.

63. Fig. 61 shows a line parallel to H.P., and with its ends

Fig. 61.

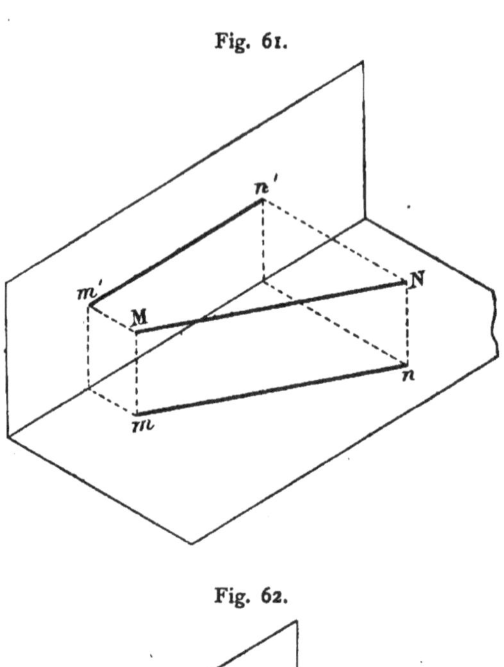

Fig. 62.

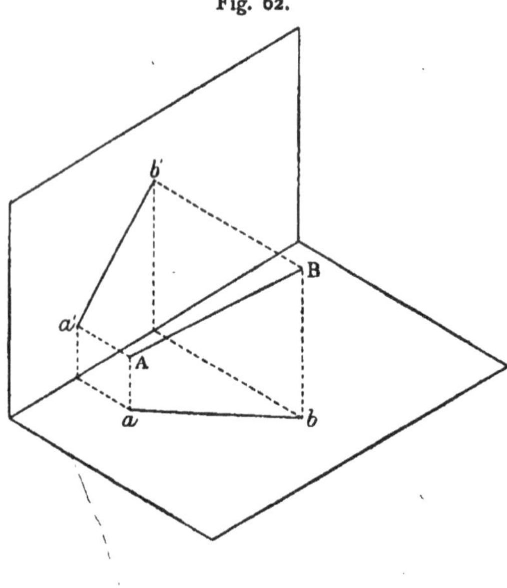

at given distances from V.P. In this case, as in the last, the length of plan may be given, or the length of the elevation. But the problem and its solution is of exactly of the same nature as the last, only the H.P. in this case corresponds to the V.P. of last case.

The last case is that in which the line is parallel to neither plane of projection, and a picture of such a line is shown in Fig. 62.

In such a case the distances of the ends are given from the planes of projection, and the length of the plan or elevation may be given.

Fig. 63 shows how it would appear in orthographic projection. Figs. 64 and 65 show lines not parallel to either plane of projection, but in other positions.

Fig. 63.

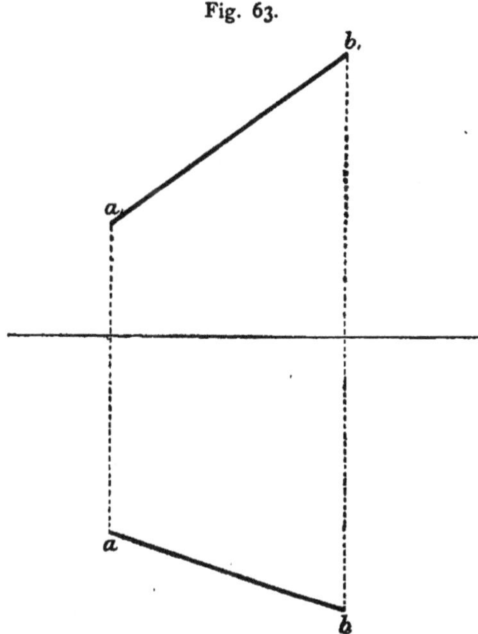

Ex. 96. A is 1 inch in front of V.P. and B is 2 inches. The line is parallel to H.P. and 1¼ inch high. The elevation is 1½ inch in length.

Ex. 97. C is ¾ inches in front of V.P. and 1 inch above H.P. D is 1½ inch in front of V.P. and 1⅝ inch above H.P. The plan is 1¼ inch long.

Ex. 98. Draw the projections of the same line when the elevation is 1½ inch in length.

Fig. 64.

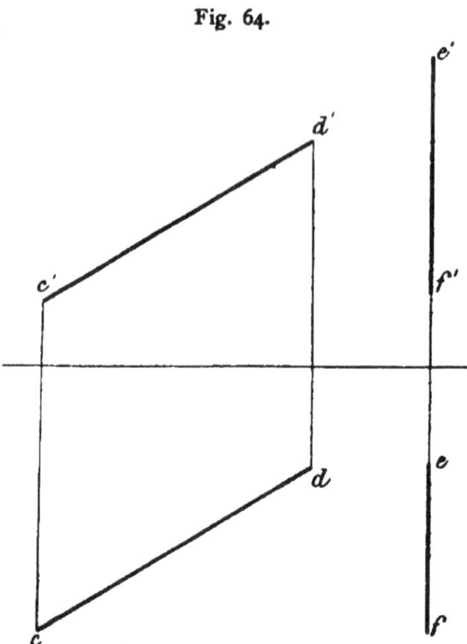

Ex. 99. A line I J parallel to H.P. has I 1¼ inch in front of V.P. and J 2¾ inches in front of V.P. The elevation is 2½ inches long.

Ex. 100. A line I J 2 inches long parallel to H.P. has I 1¼ inch in front of V.P. and J 2½ inches in front of V.P.

Ex. 101. A line K L 3 inches long parallel to V.P. has K 1¼ inches high and L 2¼ inches high.

Ex. 102. A line M N has M 1 inch in front of V.P. and 2 inches high, N 2 inches in front of V.P. and 1 inch high. Length of plan is 3 inches.

CHAPTER XIV.

OTHER VERTICAL AND HORIZONTAL PLANES.

64. THERE may be any number of vertical planes. If A is the ordinary horizontal plane, and B the ordinary vertical plane, then there may be another vertical plane with its intersecting line $x_{,,}$ $y_{,,}$. These vertical planes are often called auxiliary planes. They are often introduced for the purpose of getting a particular projection, such as the vertical projection which gives the real length of a line. Suppose, for example, A is a point in space, and that its plan is *a* and elevation *a'*, Fig 65, as usual. To find the vertical projection

Fig. 65.

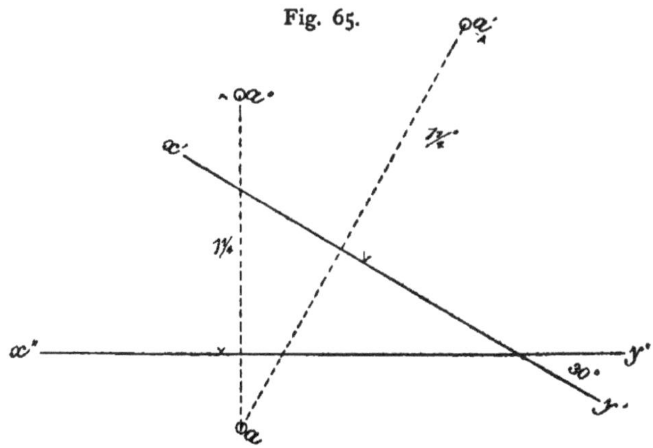

of A on the new plane draw a projector from *a*, the plan, to $x' y'$, and then deal with the new vertical projection of the point just as if the new $x y$ were the old. So a point will be represented on the two auxiliary vertical planes in the way shown in the sketch. The point *a* is shown, in plan and elevation, with reference to the first $x_{,,}$ $y_{,,}$, as in all the cases we have up to the present considered. But in the second case the drawings of the projectors of A are drawn at right angles to $x' y'$. The perpendicular distance of a'' from $x'' y''$ is equal to the perpendicular distance of a' from $x'' y''$. That is, the lengths are each $1\frac{1}{4}$ inch as marked.

Ex. 103. A point A is 1 inch high and 2 inches in front of the vertical plane, show its elevation on a vertical plane inclined at 45° to the original vertical plane.

Ex. 104. A point is $1\frac{3}{4}$ inch high and $1\frac{1}{2}$ inch in front of the vertical plane; show vertical projections of it on two vertical planes inclined at 30° and 40° to the original vertical plane.

65. Now we can deal in exactly the same manner with plans. When it is convenient and gives an advantage we make new plans of things in quite different positions. A point may be drawn in different plans, as shown in sketch.

A is projected with reference to $x, y,$ as usual, and another plan is taken from the elevation a' on the under side

Fig. 66.

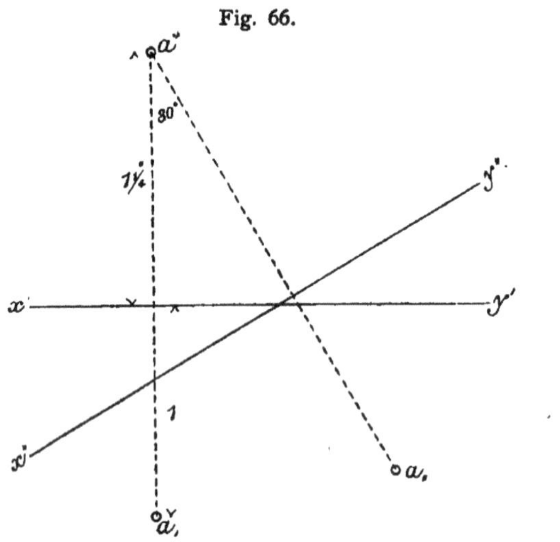

of $x'' y''$. The distance of the second plan $a_{,,}$ from $x'' y''$ is the same as the distance of $a_{,}$ from $x_{,} y_{,}$. That is, the distances are each 1 inch. Observe also that the elevation has the dash at the top of the right-hand side of the letter, while they are situated at the bottom of the right side of the plans.

CHAPTER XV.

PROJECTIONS OF PLANE FIGURES.

66. MANY interesting problems occur in the projection of planes, especially when they are given in curious positions, and when it becomes a difficult question to determine whether to begin with the vertical plane first, or to seek a new vertical and horizontal plane with which to begin.

67. Suppose, for example, we get such a problem as the following. A square of 1 inch side has its plane horizontal and two sides parallel to V.P., the nearer being $\frac{1}{2}$ inch distant from V.P. Begin by measuring a distance of $\frac{1}{2}$ inch in front of V.P., and from this point draw a line parallel to xy and 1 inch long; on this line construct a square. This will be the

Fig. 67. Fig. 68.

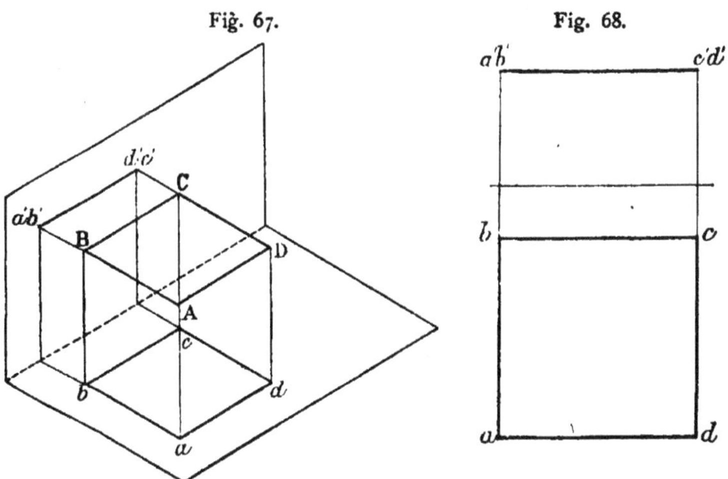

plan of the square. As no specific height is given let us suppose that this is $\frac{9}{16}$ inch. The line a' b' c' d' $\frac{9}{16}$ inch high, lying between the projectors and parallel to xy, will represent the vertical projection. Fig. 67 shows the picture of the drawing. Fig. 68 is the orthographic projection.

68. If a rectangle is given as parallel to V.P. 1½ inch in front, two sides parallel to H.P., and the nearer ¾ inch above it; then Fig. 69 shows the picture of the projections, and the

Fig. 69.

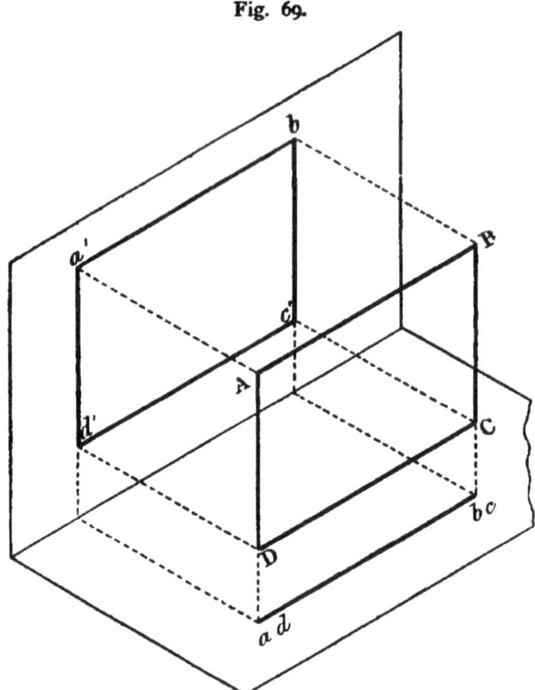

orthographic projection of a square under same conditions is got thus :—

Measure any point *d'* at a distance of ¾ inch above ***xy***. From it draw a horizontal line *d' c'* correct length, and construct a square *a' b' c' d'* on the upper side of it. Draw the projectors *d', a,* 'and *c' b*, making *a c* 1½ inch in length. ***a d c b*** is the plan of the plane.

Ex. 105. A square 2 inches side has its plane horizontal, and two sides parallel to V.P.

Ex. 106. A square 2·5 inch side has one diagonal parallel to V.P., the plane of the square is horizontal.

Ex. 107. The same square has two sides perpendicular to

V.P., and one side ½ inch above H.P., draw the plan and elevation.

Ex. 108. The same square has one diagonal vertical; plane of square perpendicular to V.P.

Ex. 109. An equilateral triangle 2 inch side has one side vertical; plane of triangle at right angles to V.P.

Fig. 70.

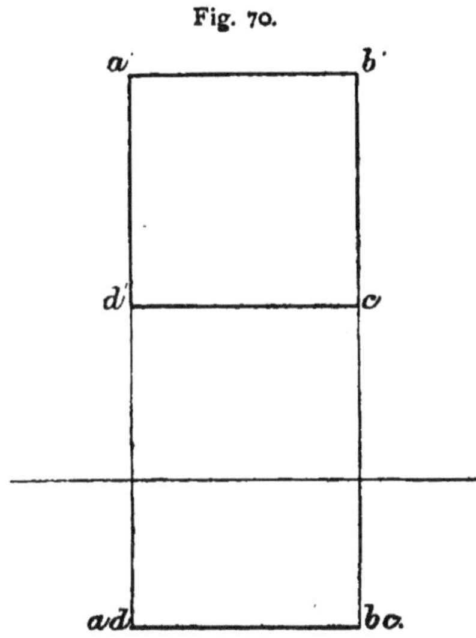

Ex. 110. A circle 2·5 inches diameter has plane parallel to V.P.

Ex. 111. A hexagon 1 inch side has one diagonal vertical and plane parallel to V.P.

Ex. 112. An octagon has two sides at right angles to H.P., and its plane is parallel to V.P.

CHAPTER XVI.

PLANE FIGURES INCLINED TO THE CO-ORDINATE PLANES.

69. THE planes of surfaces such as squares, triangles, and circles are not always parallel to one of the planes of projection. Sometimes they are inclined. When they are so it becomes a question what projection must be drawn first. Take for example the case of a square, with its plane at right angles to V.P., and inclined at 30° to H.P. Fig. 71 shows a picture of such a square inclined to the horizontal plane in this way.

The square is drawn by beginning with the vertical projection Fig. 72. Suppose the height of the lowest side is

Fig. 71. Fig. 72.

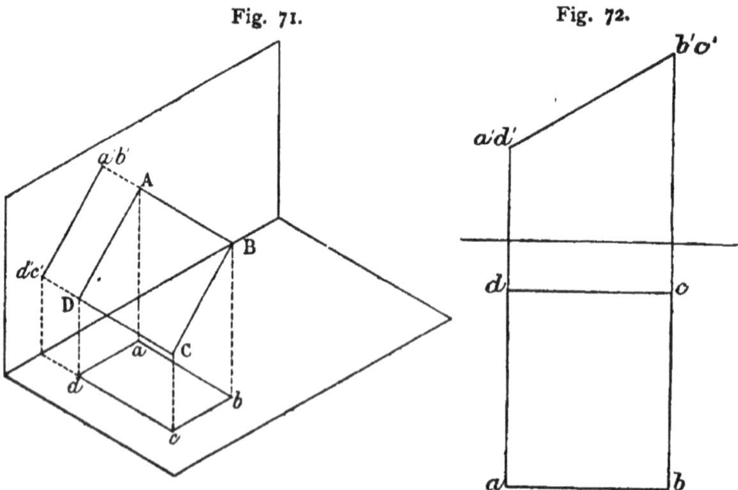

given as ½ inch above the horizontal plane. Measure a distance of ½ inch above $x y$, and draw from that point a line making an angle of 30° to the horizontal. Mark off a distance equal to the length of the side of the square 1 inch. This line will be the vertical projection of the square.

Draw projectors from the two ends and measure off the

distance, which the nearest side is in front of V.P. (½ inch). Make *a d* 1 inch in length, and draw from *a* and *d* two lines

Fig. 73.

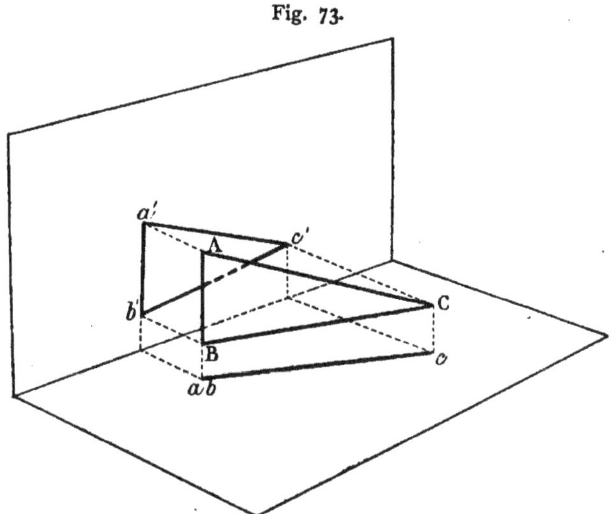

parallel to *x y* between the projectors. Complete the square by joining *b c*.

70. Sometimes the plane of the thin surface is at right angles to the horizontal plane, and inclined to the vertical plane. In such a case it will be found necessary to draw the plan first, as the elevation is foreshortened. And sometimes it is necessary to have an auxiliary drawing of the surface as in the following case. Fig. 74 shows a picture of an isosceles triangle 1 inch base; sides 1 $\frac{3}{16}$ inches, with its base at right angles to H.P., and its plane at 30° to V.P.

Before beginning to draw the plan and elevation, describe the triangle A B C, and as this triangle is only for purposes of construction it may be inked in with red (crimson lake). Next from any point *a* draw a line inclined at 30° to *x y*, and measure off a distance *a c* equal in length to C *d*. This line will be the plan of the triangle, and the point *b a* may be taken to represent the base.

From *a* draw a projector, and from any point *b* above *x y* in the projector, measure off a distance *b' a'*, equal to the length of the base. Bisect the base and draw a perpendicular

Fig. 74.

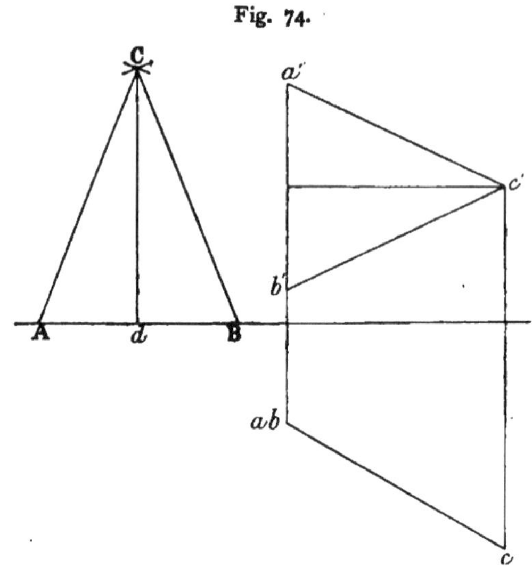

to *a' b'*; this will be the middle line of the triangle, and will contain the vertex *c'*. From the plan *c* draw a projector. This line will contain the vertical projection of *c*. The vertex *c'* will be where the middle line and the projector intersect.

71. Take next a circle 2 inches diameter with its plane inclined at 30° to H.P. Draw any line *a' b'*, Fig. 75, at an angle of 30° to *xy* and measure off a distance of 2 inches. This line will be the vertical projection of the circle. Find by projection the plan *a b* of this line *a' b'*. Bisect this line in *o* and draw through *o* a line at right angles to *a b*.

Construct on *a' b'* a semicircle and take points *c' d' e' f' g'* in the line *a' b'*. Draw a projector from *c*. It is next required to find what lengths to lay off on this projector on each side of the centre line *a b*. What is the distance through the circle at the point *c'*? Evidently it is twice *c'* 1. So lay off on each side of *a b* the distance 7 *l* and 7 *c* each equal to *c* 1. At 8 lay off the distances 8 *k* and 8 *d* each equal to *d'* 2, and so on.

Then carefully draw through the points found a curve by means of a French Curve. This curve is an ellipse.

Ex. 113. A square 2 inches side is inclined 30° to H.P., and has two of its sides at right angles to V.P.

Fig. 75.

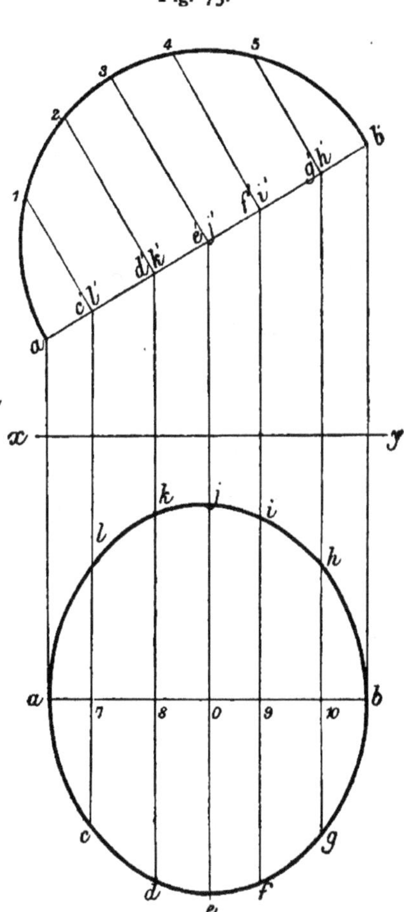

Ex. 114. The diagonal of same square makes 60° with V.P., and the other diagonal makes 90 with H.P.

Ex. 115. The base of an isosceles triangle 3 inches side 1 inch base is horizontal, its plane is inclined 30° to H.P.

Ex. 116. A hexagon has one side on H.P., its plane is at right angles to H.P. and 45° to V.P.

CHAPTER XVII.

PROJECTION OF SOLIDS.

72. SOLIDS can also be shown in plan and elevation on the two planes of projection. Fig. 76 shows a picture of a cube with two faces parallel to H.P. and two parallel to V.P. The plan is shown on the horizontal plane, and is the figure seen when

Fig. 76.

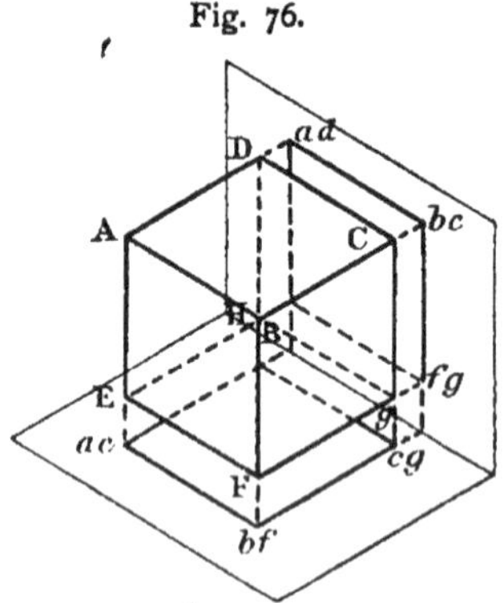

the cube is looked at from above, every point being looked at in a direction at right angles to the horizontal plane. The elevation is also shown on the vertical plane, and is the figure seen when the cube is looked on from the front, every point being looked on in a direction at right angles to the vertical plane.

The cube A B C D E F G H, shown in Fig. 76, has its plan *a e*, *b f*, *c g*, *d b*, as shown on the horizontal plane, and *a' d', b' c', f' g' e' h'* in the vertical plane. These projections are both squares.

73. The orthographic projection of the cube may be proceeded with in the following way. Draw a square to represent the plan of the cube, Fig. 77, constructing the square on a line parallel to *xy* and at the given distance from V.P.,

Fig. 77.

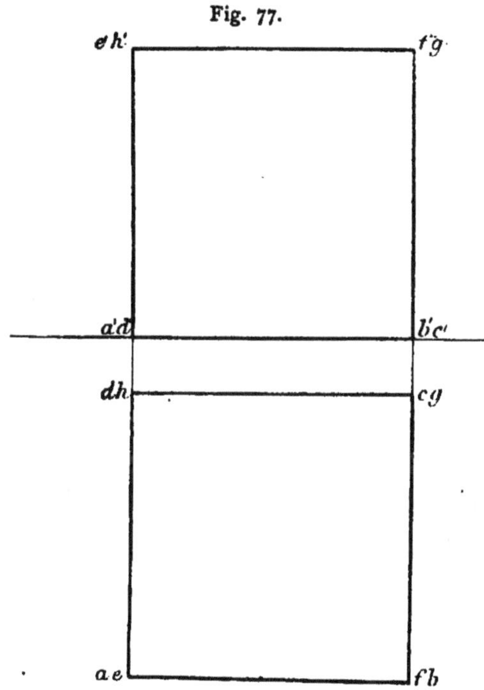

and of a length 1½ inch equal to the edge of the cube. Letter the bottom face of the cube *a b c d* and the top face *e f g h*. Each corner of the square will in this way have two letters, for they really represent vertical straight lines, each end of which has a letter for its name.

Draw next projectors from *c* and *d* to *xy* and join the intersection with *xy*, *a' b'*. On *a' b'* construct a square. This square represents the vertical projection of the cube. The point *a' d'* will represent the straight line *a d*, and each corner will represent a horizontal straight line. The height of $e' f' g' h'$ will of course be equal to the height of the cube.

74. Fig. 78 shows a case where the sides of the cube are at 45° to the vertical plane. It is begun by drawing any line at

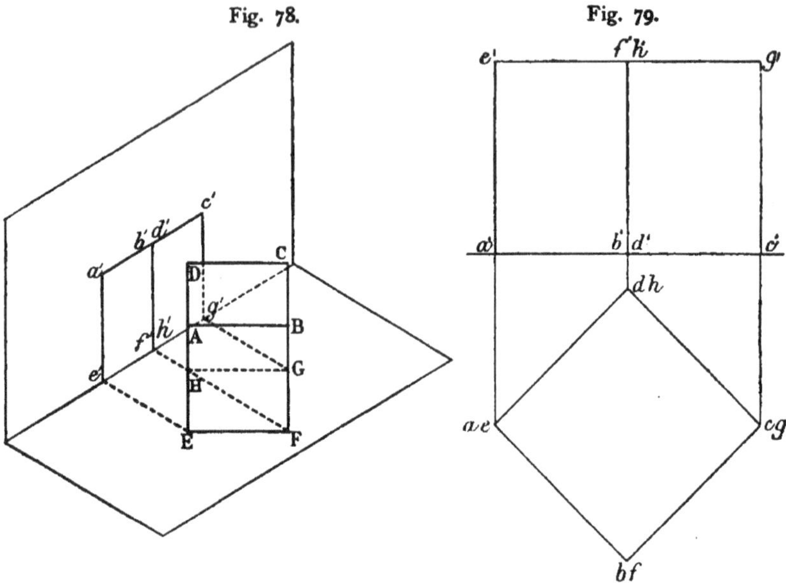

45° to xy, measuring off the length of the edge of the cube on that line and on it constructing a square. Letter this square $a\, b\, c\, d$, and suppose it to represent the bottom face of the cube. Letter the top face $e f g h$, and draw projections from all the corners to xy. First draw a projector from a. The point a is on the ground, so its vertical projection will be in $x y$. The point e has the same plan as a, but it is the height of the cube higher. So measure a height above a' equal to the height of the cube. This point is e'. The other points f', g', and h', are got by projection from their plans in the same way.

75. Fig. 80 shows the picture and Fig. 81 shows the plan and elevation of a pyramid of square base 1-inch side, with two sides of base at 45° to V.P. It is constructed by drawing a square to represent the base, and drawing four lines $a\, b$, $a\, c$,

Fig. 80.

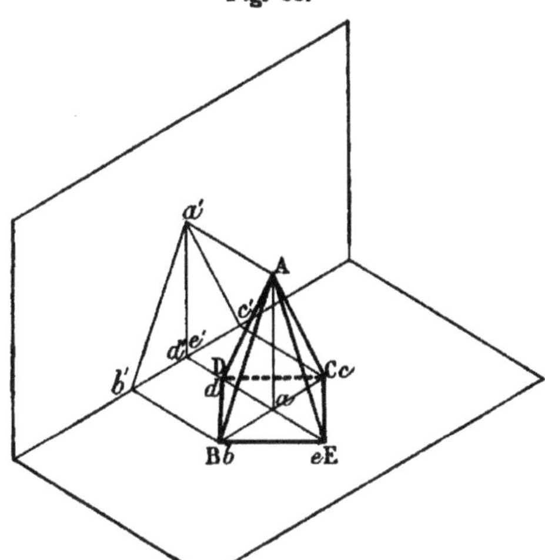

Fig. 81.

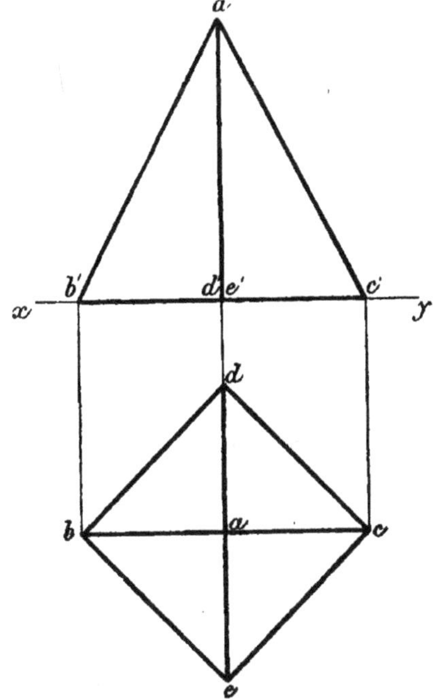

a d, and *a e* from the middle to represent the slant edges of the pyramid. The vertical projection of the base is in *x y*, and is easily found. The vertical projection of the apex is in the projector drawn from *a*, and is the length of the axis above *x y*.

76. A tetrahedron is a solid having four equal equilateral triangles for sides. The easiest position for drawing the tetrahedron is when it stands on one face, with one side of that face at right angles to V.P. Suppose the length of the edge of the tetrahedron is given and a plan and elevation are required. Draw a line *b c* (Fig. 82) at right angles to *x y*, measure off the length of the edge of the tetrahedron, and on

Fig. 82.

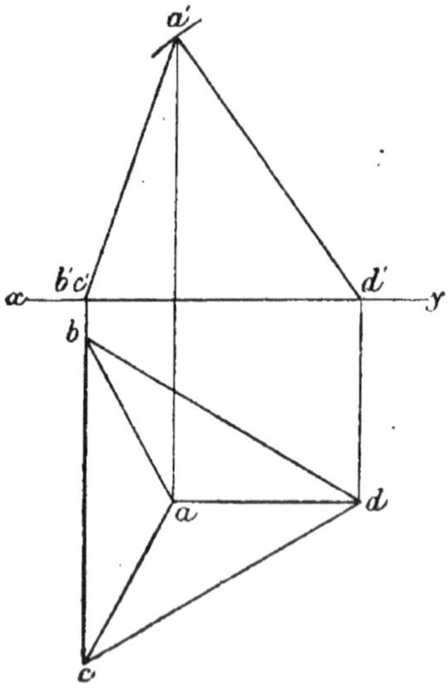

it describe an equilateral triangle *b c d*. The plans of the slant edges of the solid will bisect the angles of the base, so draw *c a*, *b a*, and *d a* bisecting the angles of the triangular base. Find the vertical projection of the base *b′ d′ c′*. They will be in *x y*. From *a* draw a projector, and with *d′* as centre and radius equal *b c* describe an arc cutting the projector from *a*. The point of section is *a′* the apex.

Join *b' c'* and *a'* and *a' d'*; the line *a' d'* represents an edge; *a' b' c'* represents a face.

Ex. 117. Draw the plan and elevation of a cube of 2 inches edge, standing with one face on H.P. and two faces inclined at 30° to V.P.

Ex. 118. Draw a hexagonal prism; base 1 inch side, and long edge 2½ inches, standing on one end, and with two long faces at right angles to V.P.

Ex. 119. Draw a pentagonal pyramid standing on its base, with one side of base at right angles to V.P.; length of axis 2½ inches, side of base 1 inch.

CHAPTER XVIII.

SOLIDS WITH FACES INCLINED TO CO-ORDINATE PLANES.

77. As in the projection of surfaces, it is sometimes found necessary to draw the elevation first, so it is necessary often when drawing solids to draw the elevation first. For example, take the cube, Fig. 83, standing on one edge at right angles to V.P., and with one side inclined at 30° to H.P. A line *a' b'* is first drawn, making an angle of 30° to *xy*, and a length *a' b'* is measured off from the intersection with *xy* equal to the length of the edge of cube. On this line a square is constructed, and this square represents the elevation of the cube. The square is then lettered; *a' e' g' c'* being the front face, and *d' h' f' b'* the back. Projectors are drawn from the corners of the square, and the points *d h f b* in the plan taken in a line parallel to *xy*. The point *c* will be in front of this line a distance equal to the length of the edge, and *g*, *a* and *e* will be the same; *d a* in the plan will be a dotted line, because it is not seen from above.

78. Fig. 84 shows a pyramid standing on one side of base, which is inclined to H.P. at an angle of 45°. Here the base

is drawn in the given position in the V.P., and the vertical projection of the pyramid constructed on the base.

The plan is projected from the elevation. Draw a projector from *a' b'* and from any point in the projector measure off a distance *a b* equal to the length of the side of the base of

Fig. 83.

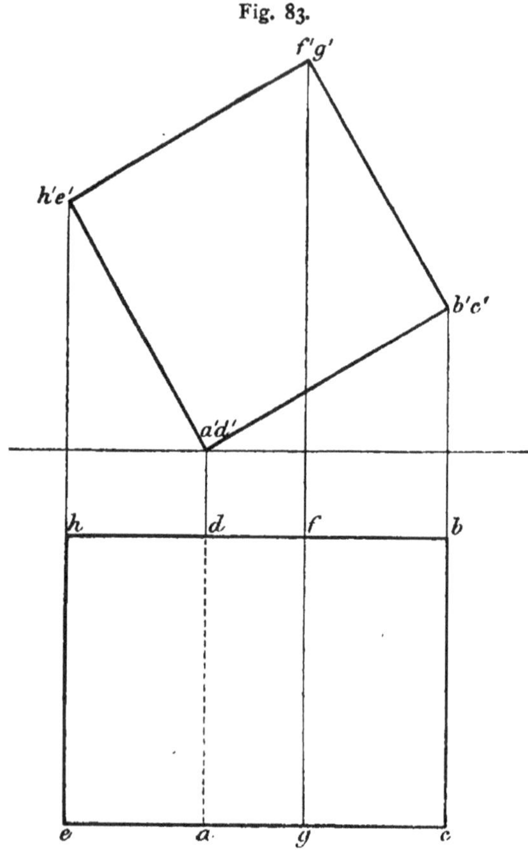

the pyramid. Draw *a c* and *b d* parallel to *xy*. The points *d* and *c* are found in the projector from *c' d'*. *a b c d* is the plan of the base of the pyramid, and *a b* not being seen from above will be dotted.

Bisect *a b*, and from the point of bisection draw a perpendicular. From *e'* draw a projector. The intersection of the perpendicular and projector is the point *e* in the plan.

Join *e a*, *e d*, *e c*, and *e b*, to represent the edges of the pyramid in plan.

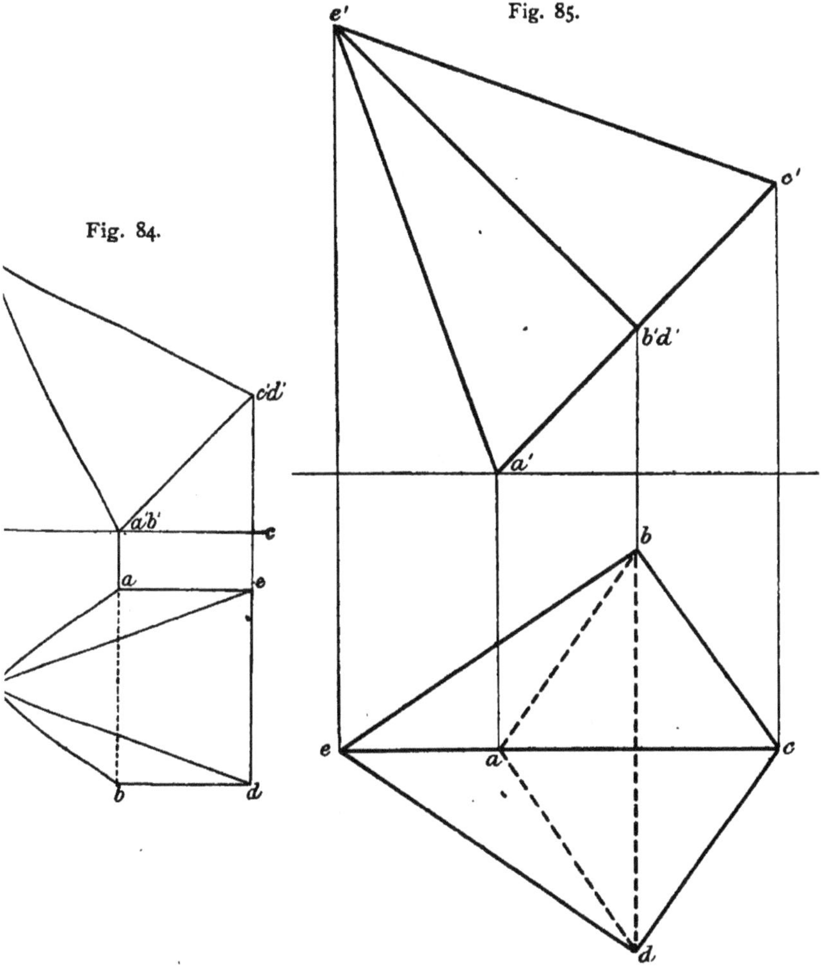

Fig. 85.

Fig. 84.

79. Fig. 85 shows the projections of a pyramid standing on one corner, and with one diagonal of base at right angles to V.P., while the base itself is inclined at an angle of 45° to

H.P.; axis parallel to V.P. The construction is exactly similar to the last.

Ex. 120. Draw the plan and elevation of a tetrahedron with one side of base at right angles to V.P., and opposite edge inclined at 30° to H.P. Length of edge 2 inches.

Ex. 121. Draw a cylinder; diameter of base 2 inches, length of axis 3 inches, and with axis parallel to V.P. and inclined 60° to H.P.

Ex. 122. Draw plan and elevation of a cone; diameter of base 2½ inches, length of axis 3 inches, with axis parallel to V.P. and inclined to H.P. at an angle of 45°.

CHAPTER XIX.

SOLIDS AND AUXILIARY PLANES.

80. It is sometimes necessary to draw an auxiliary figure to enable one to get the projections. A case of this kind occurs in finding the projections of a hexagonal prism lying on one long face, and with its long edges parallel to V.P., Fig. 86.

If the length of axis and side of end be given, the side of the plan can be found; but *a d*, the distance across corners of hexagon, cannot be found unless a hexagon be drawn of the same size as the end of the prism. In the elevation *b′f′* is the distance across the flats of the hexagon. The other parts are easily obtained. Sometimes the end view is taken as another elevation, as it is in figure, and the plan is obtained by projection from this elevation, or auxiliary elevation.

Ex. 123. Draw the projections of a hexagonal prism lying on one of its long sides, and with one of its long edges inclined at 30° to V.P., side of base 1 inch, long edges 3 inches. See 81.

Ex. 124. Draw the projections of same prism when it

stands on one long edge at 60° to V.P., and with its two adjacent faces inclined equally to H.P. See 82.

81. The plans and elevations of solids in given extraordinary positions are often found by drawing the projections

Fig. 86.

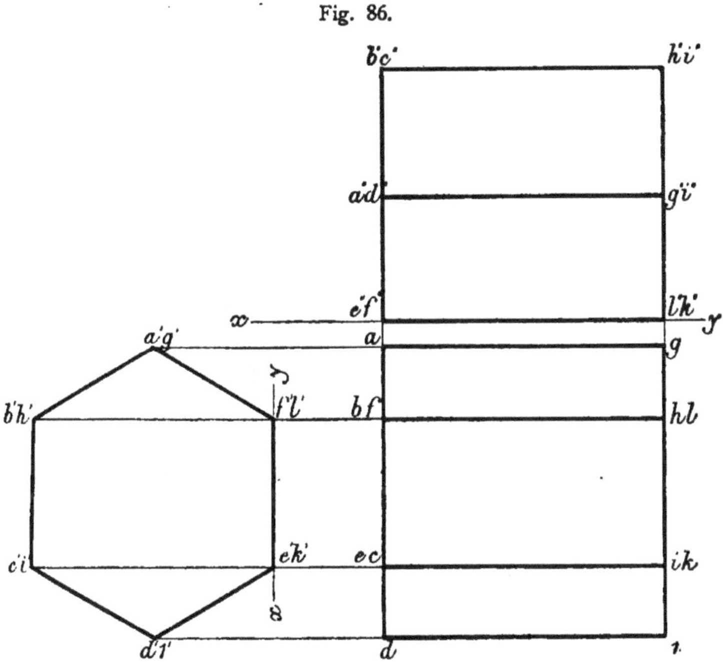

of the solid first in an easy position, and then, by continued projections from these on auxiliary planes, the required projections are obtained.

Take for example the prism referred to in 80 lying on one long face and with its long edges making an angle of 30° to V.P.

First draw an end view of the prism with one side inclined at 60° to xy, as in Fig. 87, then draw any line $a'a$ making an angle of 30° to xy. Measure anywhere along this line a distance ag equal to the length of the edge of the prism. From a draw a line at right angles to ag, and equal in length to *a' d'*. Project *b f h l* and *c e k i* from *b' f' h' l'* and *c' e' k' i'*. Draw *g i'* parallel to *a d*, *b h* and *e i* parallel to *a g*. This completes the plan. Carefully letter the plan, one end having

Fig. 87.

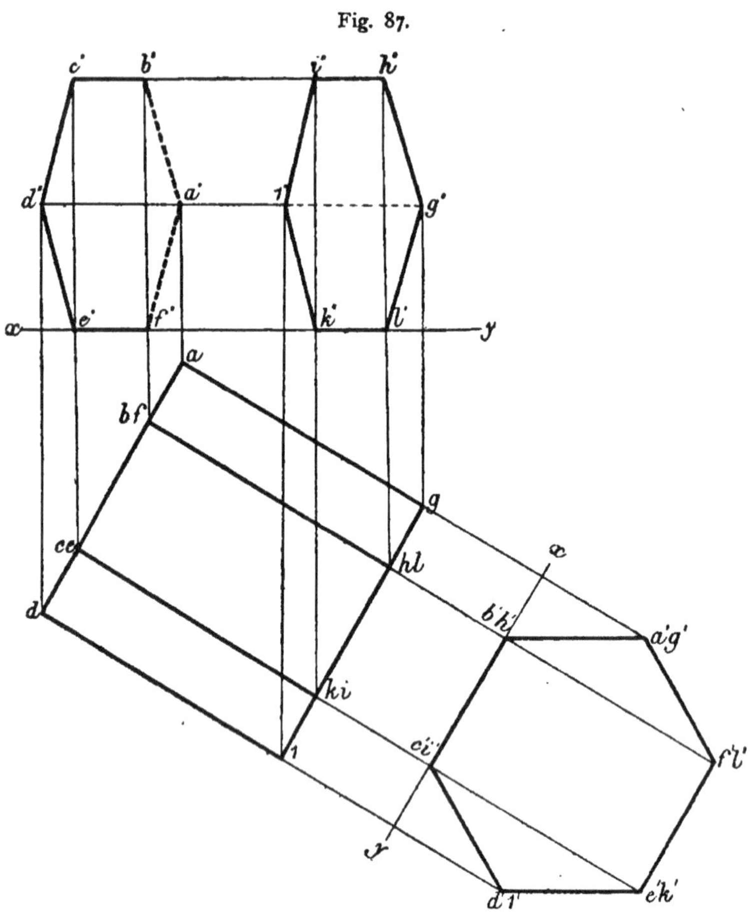

the letters *a b c d e f* at its corners, and the other end having the letters *g h i* 1 *k l* at its corners. Note that *e* and *f* are on the ground, *d* and *a* are at a height equal to half the distance across flats, and *c* and *b* are at a height equal to the distance across flats.

To find the elevation on the original $x y$, first draw a projector from g; g is half way up, so mark off a distance above $x y$ equal to half $d' f'$. Letter it g''. Then take l and draw a projector; l is on the ground. Where the projector from l cuts $x y$ mark l''. The point k is also on the ground. Where the projector from k cuts $x y$ mark k''; j is half way up and same height as g''. On projector from j mark j'' same height as g'' above $x y$. The point i comes next, and is at a height equal to the whole distance across flats. Mark on projector from i a distance equal to $f' b'$ above $x y$. Letter it i''. Last comes h at same height as i. Mark the point on projector from h at same height as i. Join $g'' h''$, $h'' i''$, $i'' j''$, $j'' k''$, $k'' l''$, and $l'' g''$. They will be all full black lines; for looking from the front the whole face $g h i j k l$ is seen.

In the same way find the points $a'' b'' c'' d'' e'' f''$ and join them. They are all seen, and therefore represented by full black lines, with the exception of $b'' a''$ and $a'' f''$ at the back of the solid. These two lines must be drawn dotted, as shown.

Next join the long edges. All of them are seen with the exception of $a'' g''$ at the back. The line $a'' g''$ is dotted.

84. Fig. 88 shows a cube standing on one edge with one face inclined at 30° to H.P., and four edges at 30° to V.P.

The projections are got by first drawing a line $b f$, making an angle of 30° to V.P., and marking on this line a distance $b f$ equal to the length of edge of cube. If a paper cube is taken and placed into such a position with respect to the inclined planes that it fulfils the conditions required, it will be observed that the vertical projection of the cube on a new vertical plane parallel to the ends of the cube which are at right angles to H.P., will be a square. Begin, then, with this vertical projection. For this purpose draw another $x, y,$ at right angles to $b f$. The vertical projection of $b f$ on this new $x y$ will be the point marked $b' f'$ on the ground. From b' draw $b' c'$ at 30° to $x, y,$, and equal in length to $b f$ the edge of the cube; on $b' c'$ construct a square. This square represents two faces of the cube, the back and front. Letter the front face *a' b' c' d'*, and the back face *e' f' g' h'*.

To find the plan of the cube, draw through the points *b* and *f* two lines, *a c* and *e g*, at right angles to it. These two

Fig. 88.

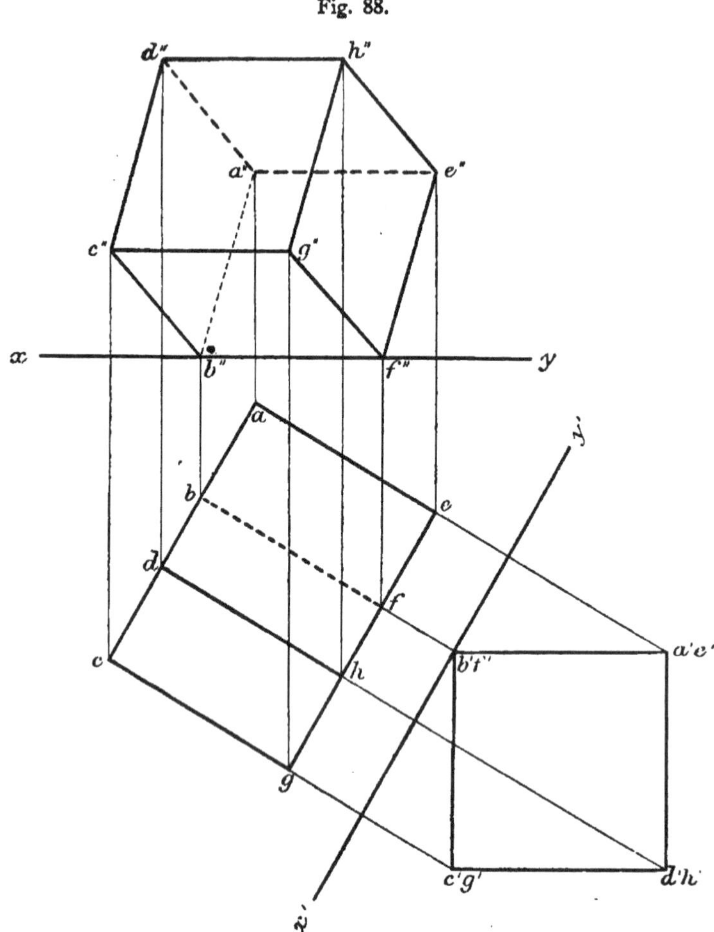

lines will contain the plans of two faces, as will be seen if the small model is again looked at from above. From *a' e'* draw a projector, *a e* will be one edge. Projectors from the other corners of the square will find the other edges *b f*, *d h*, and *c g*. If the model be looked at again it will observed that the edge *b f* cannot be seen, and must be dotted.

Begin the elevation on the original vertical plane by finding the points on the nearest face *e f g h*. From *e* draw a projector. The height of e'' above *x y* will be equal to the height of e' above $x_1 y_1$. So mark up this height and letter the point e''. Draw projectors from *f h g* and measure their heights

Fig. 89.

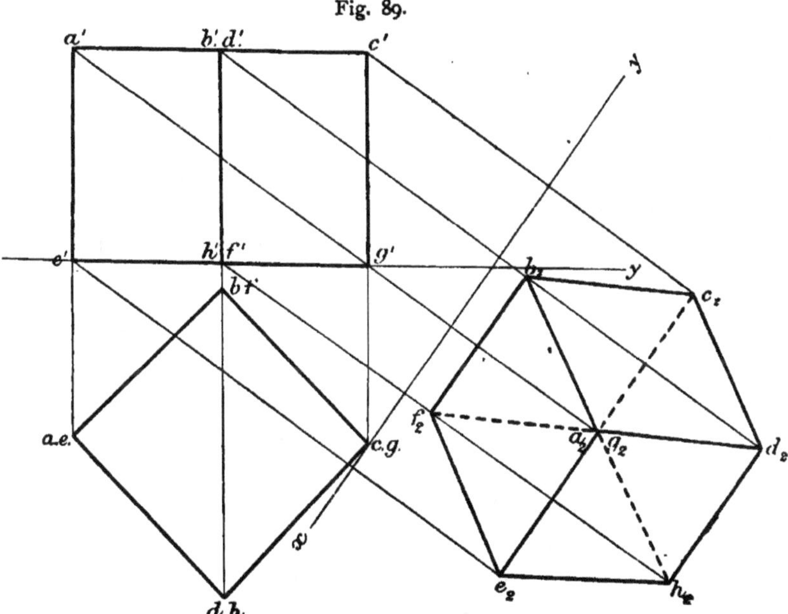

above *x y*. The elevations g'' h'' f'' will be at exactly the same heights above *x y* as g' h' f' above $x_1 y_1$. Join e'' f'' g'' h''. They will be all full black lines, for they are all seen.

In the same way find a'' b'' c'' d'' by drawing projectors from *a b c d* and measuring their heights above *x y*, equal to the heights of a' b' c' d' above $x_1 y_1$. Join a'' b'' c'' d''. If the model be again looked at from the front in the direction of the original vertical plane, it will be observed that d'' a'', a'' b'', and a'' e'' are not seen, and must be made dotted lines.

Ex. 125. Draw the plan and elevation of a pyramid of square base, standing on one side of base; side of base 2 inches, axis 2½ inches; has two sides of base at 45° to V.P. and base itself at 30° to H.P.

Ex. 126. Draw a pentagonal prism; side of base 1½ inch, axis 2½ inches, with one side of base at 30° to V.P. and axis inclined at 45° to H.P.

Ex. 127. Draw a cylinder; diameter of base 2 inches, axis 3 inches, with ends inclined at 30° to V.P. and axis at 45° to H.P.

Ex. 128. Draw a cone; diameter of base 2¼ inches, axis 3 inches, with base inclined at 30° to V.P. and axis inclined at 45° to H.P.

83. Sometimes the projections of solids are obtained by taking a new plan from a simple vertical projection.

Take, for example, the case of a cube, Fig. 89, standing on one corner with diagonal vertical. To obtain the projections of the cube when thus situated, simply draw a cube standing on one face with one diagonal of horizontal face parallel to V.P. In this way the diagonal of the solid $a' g'$ is got parallel to the V.P., and its true length is shown by its vertical projection. If the diagonal $a' g'$ is looked down on in the direction of a' to g' its plan will be a point, and it will therefore be standing at right angles to a new H.P., supposed to be at right angles to $a' g'$. Draw then an $x_, y_,$ at right angles to $a' g'$ and show a plan of the solid on it. From e' draw a projector and measure a distance from $x_, y_,$ equal to the distance of c from the original $x\ y$. Mark this point c_2, not c'', for it is a plan not an elevation. In the same way find the points $b_2\ d_2\ f_2\ h_2$ and e_2 by drawing projectors and measuring distances from $x_, y_,$ equal to the distances of $b_, d_, f_, h_, e_, a_,$ and g from $x\ y$. This will give a new plan. If the model be looked at when put in this position, it will be observed that the edges $c_2\ g_2$, $f_2\ g_2$, and $h_2\ g_2$ cannot be seen, and must be represented by dotted lines.

CHAPTER XX.

PLANS AND ELEVATIONS OF SOLIDS.

84. FIG. 90 shows another solid whose projections have been found by the same method. It was required that one long edge of the pentagonal prism should be at right angles

Fig. 90.

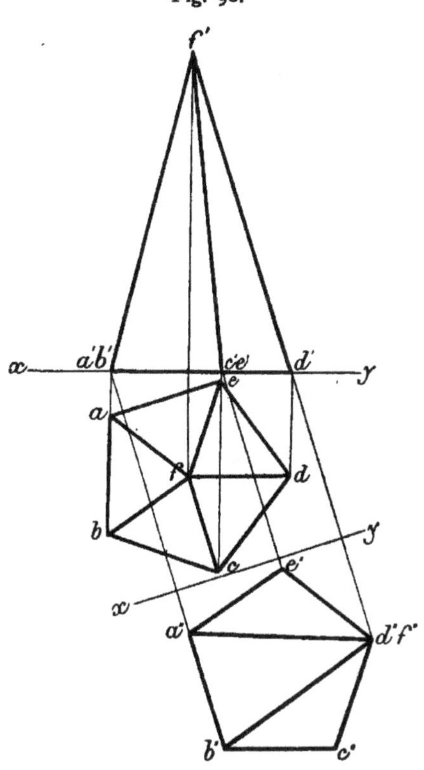

to H.P. Simple projections of the solid were taken, the vertical plane being parallel to the particular edge, and then a plan was projected from this vertical projection with an *x y* at right angles to the edge.

Ex. 129. Show a plan of a tetrahedron of 2 inches edge standing on one edge which is at right angles to V.P., and with one adjacent face inclined at an angle of 30° to H.P.

Ex. 130. Show plan of a hexagonal prism, base 1¼ inch side, length of axis 3 inches, standing on one side of end, and with axis making an angle of 60° with H.P., and with its plan inclined at 45° to V.P.

Fig. 91.

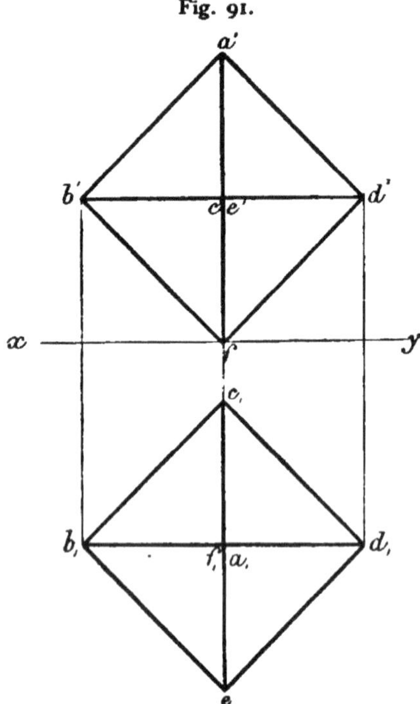

85. It is sometimes necessary to use more than one auxiliary plane, as in the case shown in Fig. 92, where it is required to draw the plan of an octahedron standing on one face.

An octahedron is a solid with eight faces, equilateral triangles, and with three axes at right angles to each other. Fig. 91 shows an octahedron in plan and elevation, and it has been drawn when the lengths of the axes have been given as data.

In Fig. 92 the same construction has been used for finding

Fig. 92.

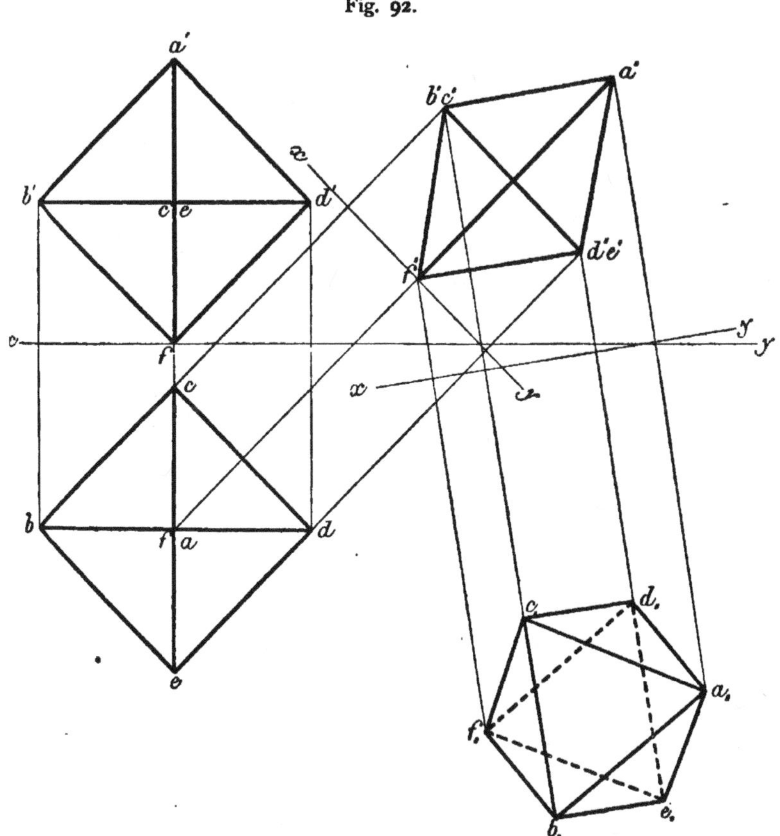

the plan *a b c d e f* and the elevation *a' b' c' d' e' f'*, and next a vertical plane *x y* has been taken at right angles to one of the faces, so as to have that face, *f'' d'' e''*, represented on the new vertical plane by a line. From this vertical projection another plan is taken on a plane parallel to the face $f''d''e''$. So an xy is drawn parallel to $f''d e''$, and the distances of the points $a_{,,}$ $b_{,,}$ $c_{,,}$ $d_{,,}$ $e_{,,}$ $f_{,,}$ in the required plan from $x_2 y_2$ are equal to the distances of the points in the other plan $a\,b\,c\,d\,e\,f$ from $x_{,}$ $y_{,}$.

Ex. 131. Draw plan and elevation of a tetrahedron of 2 inches edge with one side of base parallel to V.P., and these projections show a plan of the solid lying on another face.

Ex. 132. Draw the plan of a cube 2 inches edge standing on one edge, so that its two faces shall be equally inclined to H.P.

Ex. 133. Draw the plan of a tetrahedron 2 inches edge, so that one slant side shall be vertical.

Ex. 134. Draw the plan of a cone standing on its vertex, base 2 inches diameter, axis 3 inches, making angle 60° to H.P.

Ex. 135. Draw the plan of an octahedron 1 inch edge, standing on one face.

Ex. 136. Draw plan of a cube 2 inches edge, with one diagonal vertical.

Ex. 137. Draw the plan of a hexagonal pyramid, base 1½ inches side, axis 3 inches long, with slant edge vertical.

Ex. 138. A cube has one edge on H.P. and at right angles to V.P. and two faces making 30° to H.P., edge of cube 2 inches.

Ex. 139. A tetrahedron has one edge in H.P. and at right angles to V.P. and the adjacent face 45° to H.P., edge 2 inches.

Ex. 140. Same tetrahedron has one edge in V.P. at right angles to H.P. and the adjacent face at 20° to V.P.

Ex. 141. Show elevation of a square 2 inches side with two sides horizontal and its plane vertical, on a vertical plane inclined to first vertical plane at an angle of 20°.

Ex. 142. A cube 2 inches edge stands on H.P. Show elevation on a V.P., making 60° with the old vertical plane.

Ex. 143. A tetrahedron 1½ inches edge stands on H.P. Show elevation on a V.P. inclined at 20° to one side of base.

Ex. 144. A cube has one edge in H.P., making an angle of 30° with first V.P., one adjacent face makes 20° with H.P. Show an elevation on a V.P. at right angles to edge in H.P., edge 2 inches.

Ex. 145. A tetrahedron 2 inches edge has base inclined at 20° to H.P. and one side of base inclined at 30° to V.P.

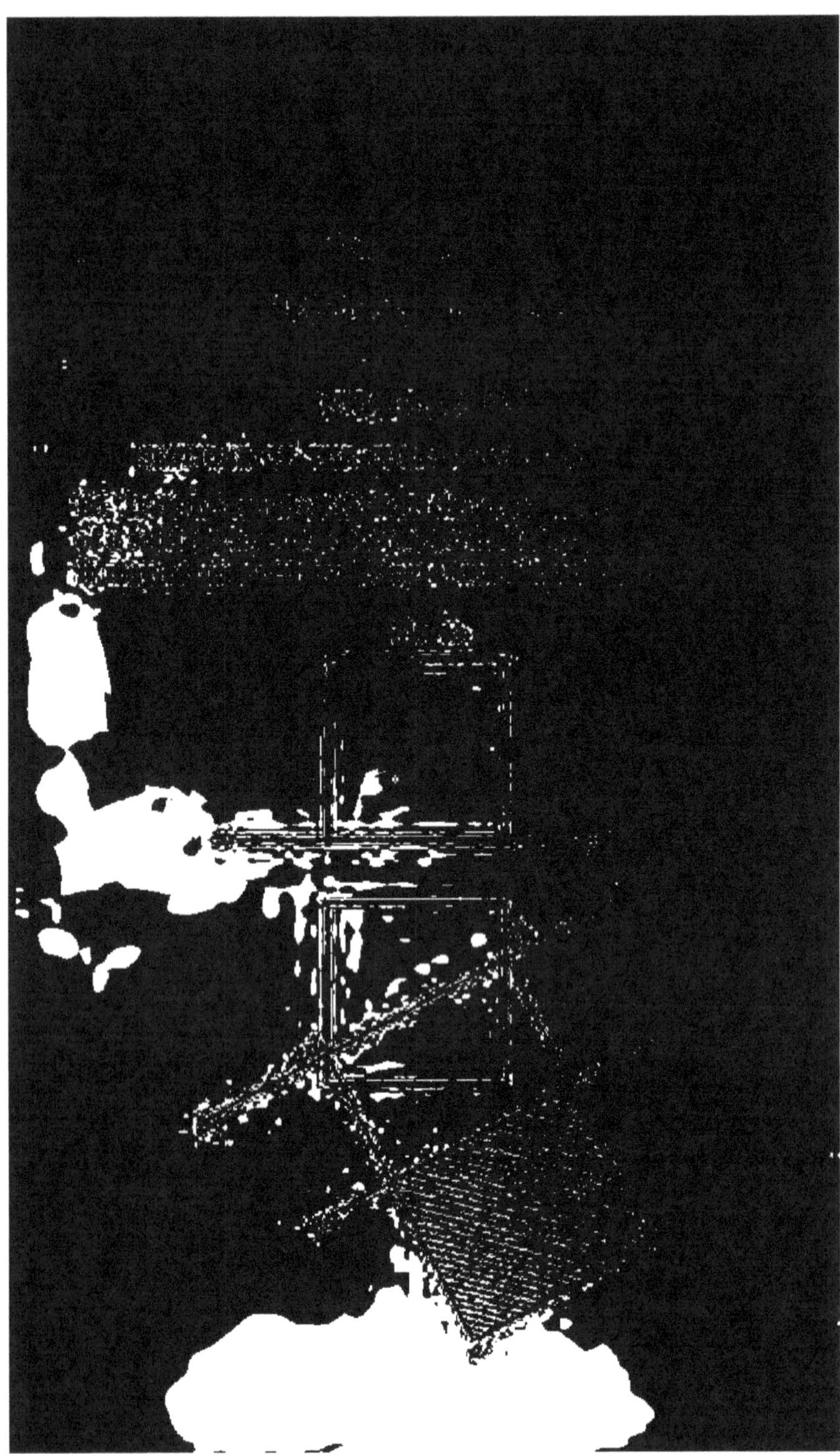

plane of the section. Take any line *x, y,* parallel to A B, as the ground line of this new elevation which is to show the true shape of this section. Draw through the points *a b* projectors, and from *x, y,* measure up a distance equal to the height of the cube. *a' b' c' d'* is the section of the solid. It may be coloured in by a thin wash of sepia.

Fig. 94. Fig. 95.

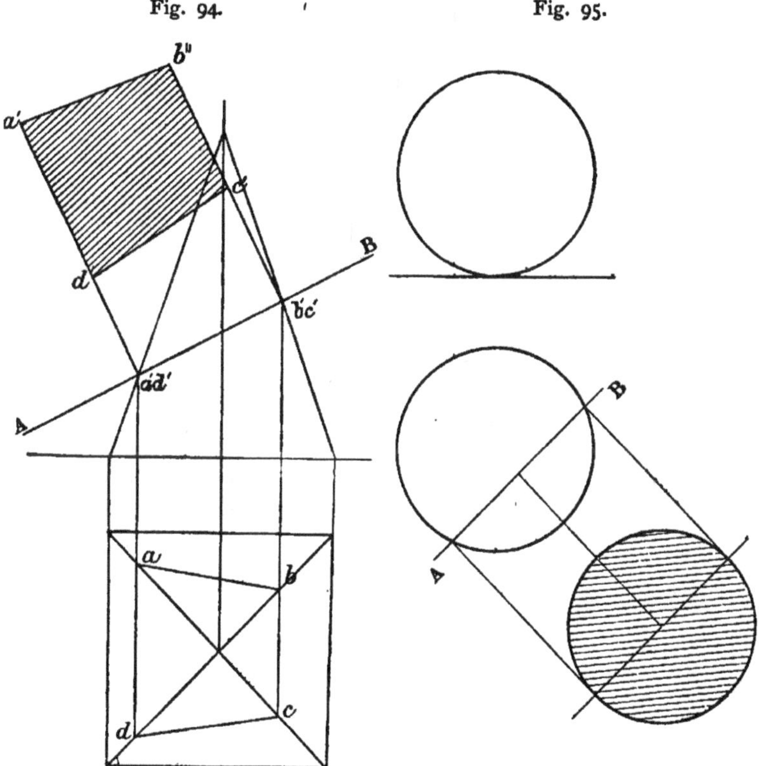

Ex. 146. A cube $1\frac{1}{2}''$ edge stands on one face with two sides inclined at 30° to the V. P.; the nearest edge to the V. P. is $\frac{1}{2}$ inch in front of it; find the shape of the section made by a vertical plane parallel to V. P., and $1\frac{1}{4}$ inches in front of V. P.

87. Take next the pyramid, Fig. 94, and let it be required

to find the shape of the section made by the plane A B, which is at right angles to the V. P., but inclined to H. P.

Take an $x y$ parallel to A B. In this case it will be convenient to take A B as the $x y$; $a' b'$ will show the length

Fig. 96.

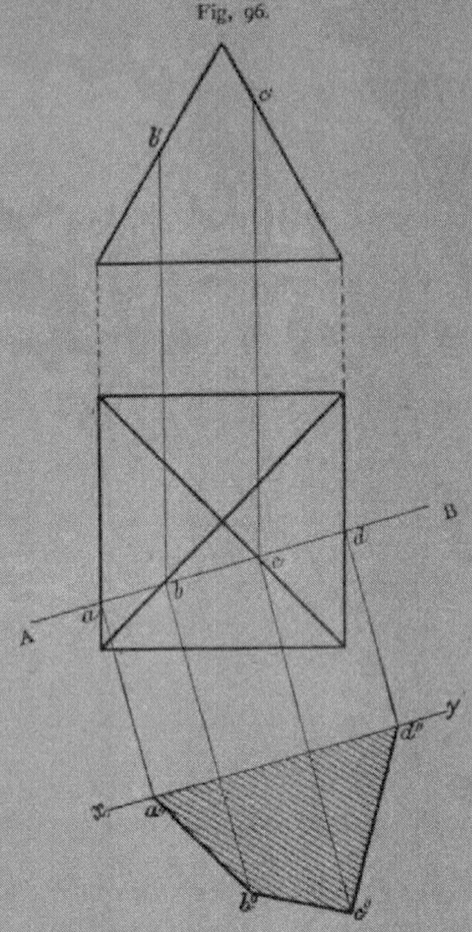

of the section along the middle line. The line $a d$ on the plan will show the distance through the solid at the point a' on the elevation, so along the projector from a' measure $a' d''$

equal to *a d*. Measure also *b' c'* equal to *b c*; *a' b' c' d'* is the section.

88. Take next A B, another section of the same solid, Fig. 96, but this time let the section be at right angles to H.P. and

Fig. 97.

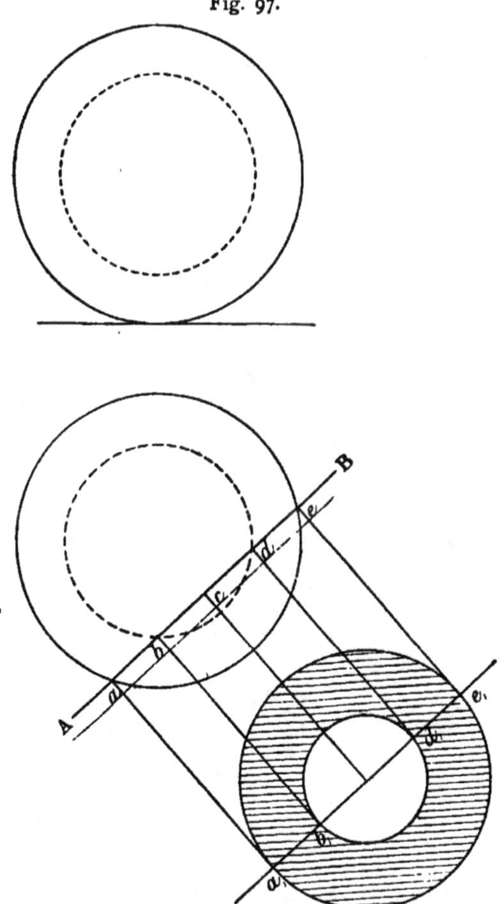

inclined to V. P. Draw *x, y,* parallel to A B, and draw projectors from the points *a b c d* where the plane of section cuts the edges of the solid. The height of *a* on the new elevation is nothing, so it will be shown by *a''*. The height of *d* is the same,

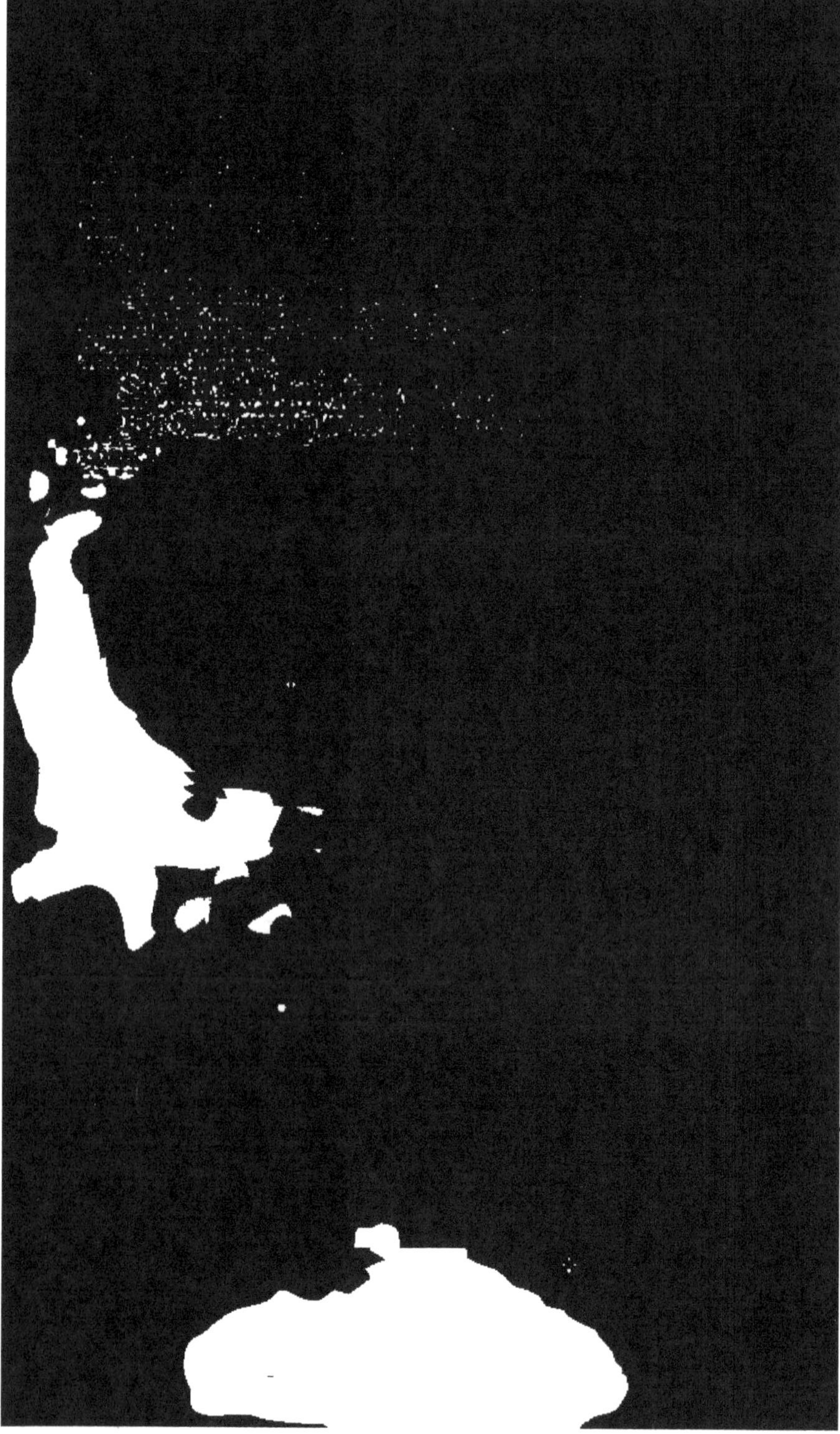

SECTION IV.

CURVES.

CHAPTER XXII.

SECTIONS OF THE CONE.

90. IF a cone be taken and cut across from one slant side to the other slant side, the section of the cone cut in this way is called an ellipse. The curve marked ellipse is such a

Fig. 98.

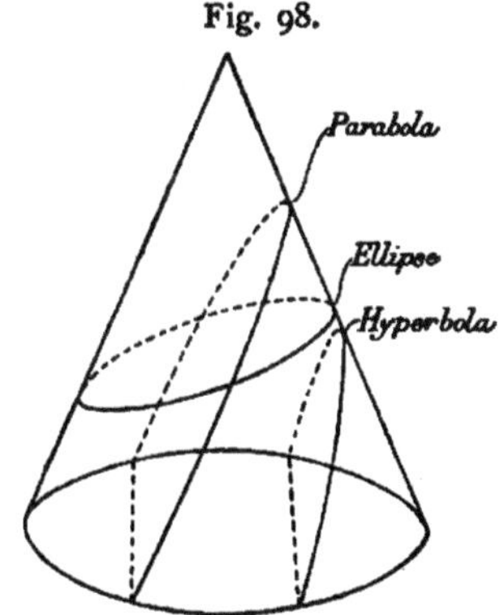

section. If, however, it be cut in such a way that the angle which the section makes with the axis is less than the angle which a slant side makes with the axis, then that section is called an hyperbola. The curve marked hyperbola is such a section. When the section neither makes a greater angle than the slant side with the axis, as is the case with the ellipse, nor makes a less angle than the slant side with the axis, as is done by the section called a hyperbola, but is inclined just at the same angle, then this section is called a parabola. It is a limiting ellipse, and also a limiting hyperbola. The parabola is one limiting case of the ellipse, the other is when the section is at right angles to the axis, and the section is then a circle.

91. The line down the middle of any of the curves which divides them into two symmetrical parts is called the axis of the curve.

The ellipse can be divided symmetrically in two ways, and it has therefore two axes. One of the dividing lines, the longest possible line which can be drawn across the curve, is called the major axis, as *a b*, Fig. 99; the other axis is the shortest possible line which can be drawn across the curve, and is called the minor axis, as *cd* of the same figure.

CHAPTER XXII.

THE ELLIPSE.

92. TAKE first a section such as A B, Fig. 99, which cuts both slant sides of the cone. Divide the vertical projection of the section into any number of parts such as 1, 2, 3, 4, 5. Some discretion will be required in making these divisions; it will be found best to make the divisions shorter at the ends than in the middle of the line.

Through 1 draw a line at right angles to the axis, and on it construct a semicircle. Draw 1 1′ parallel to the axis. 1 1′ is half the distance through the cone at the point 1, and is therefore half the width of the section at that place. Draw any line $x' y'$ parallel to the section, and from 1 draw a line at right angles to $x' y'$. On each side of $x' y'$ set off a distance on this line equal to 1 1′. Go through exactly the same construction for points 2, 3, 4, 5, *a*, and *b*. Through the points so found, draw a curve by means of a French curve. This curve will be found to be an ellipse.

93. But it will always be found easier to use the following construction for describing an ellipse. Let A B and C D be the major and minor axes. On A B and C D describe circles These circles are generally called auxiliary circles, and they will be referred to as such in future.

Fig. 99.

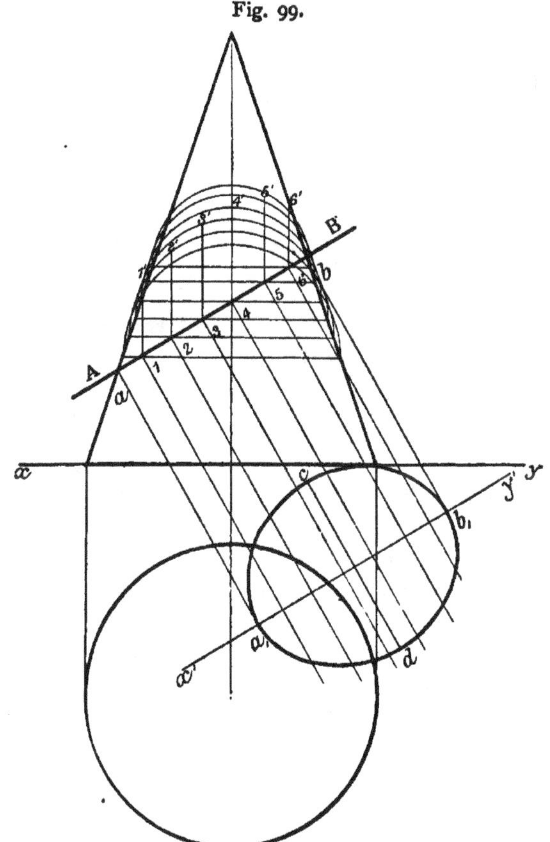

Draw any lines as radii from the centre. Drop perpendiculars from the points where they cut the outer circle and horizontal lines from the points where they meet the inner circles. The meeting points of these lines are points in the ellipse. The curve is drawn through the points by means of a French curve.

97. For example take the major axis 2½ inches and the minor axis 1½ inches, construct the ellipse.

Set off any line A B 2½ inches in length, bisect it in *o*, and set off C D equally on each side and at right angles to A B.

Fig. 102.

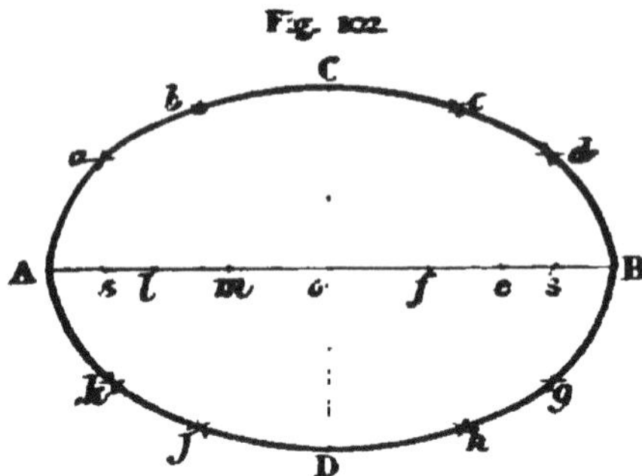

With C as centre and A *o* as radius find the foci *s s*. Divide *s o* in some such way as shown in figure, and with A *e* as radius and S and S, as centres describe arcs *a k d g*. Then, with the other part of the major axis *e* B as radius and *s s* as centres, describe arcs cutting the former four. The four intersections of the four sets of arcs will give four points in the ellipse.

Next, with A *f* as radius and *s s* as centres, describe another set of four arcs, and with the other part B *f* of the

Fig. 103.

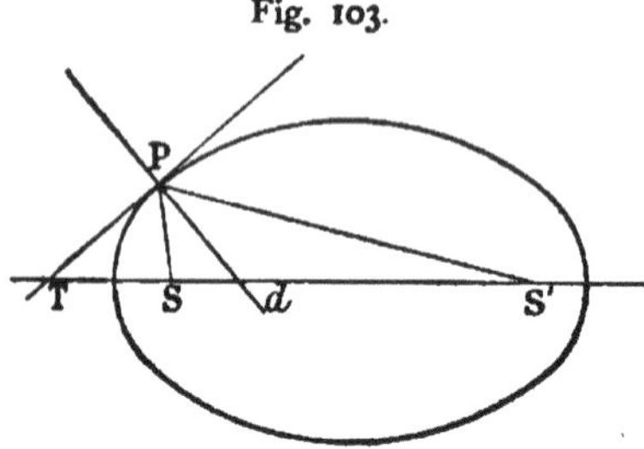

major axis, and with the same centres describe arcs cutting the last. This gives another set of four points in the ellipse. Through the twelve points draw the curve, and be careful not to make A B angular points.

Ex. 148. Construct an ellipse by this method. Major axis $3\frac{1}{4}$ inches, minor axis $2\frac{1}{2}$ inches.

98. A tangent can be drawn at any such point as P, Fig. 103, by bisecting the angle S P S, and drawing from the point P, a line P T at right angles to P *d*. This line, perpendicular to the tangent at the point P, is called the normal to the point P.

Fig. 104.

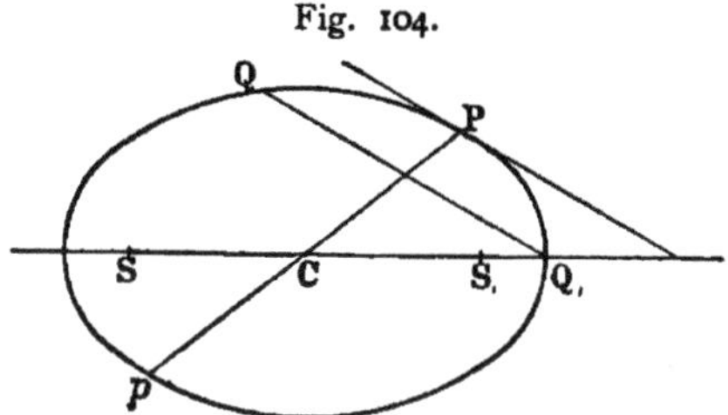

99. If any line such as P C *p*, Fig. 104, be drawn across the ellipse, and passing through the centre, that line is called a diameter; and any other line Q Q, drawn through the ellipse, parallel to the tangent at P, is called the diameter conjugate to P C *p*.

CHAPTER XXIII.

THE PARABOLA AND HYPERBOLA.

100. THE PARABOLA.—It has been stated before, that the parabola is that section of the cone which is parallel to a generating line, and is that particular section which divides the ellipse sections from the hyperbolic sections.

Take any line *x y*, Fig. 105, and by projection find the figure A B C. The same construction used for the ellipse applies here. B is called the vertex.

101. When a diameter and the distance of the vertex is given another construction may be conveniently used.

Produce the axis EC, Fig. 106, to D making C D = E C and join A D and D B. Divide A D and D B each into four equal parts and mark them as shown. Join 1 1, 2 2, and 3, 3 and draw a curve having these lines as tangents. This curve is the parabola.

Fig. 105.

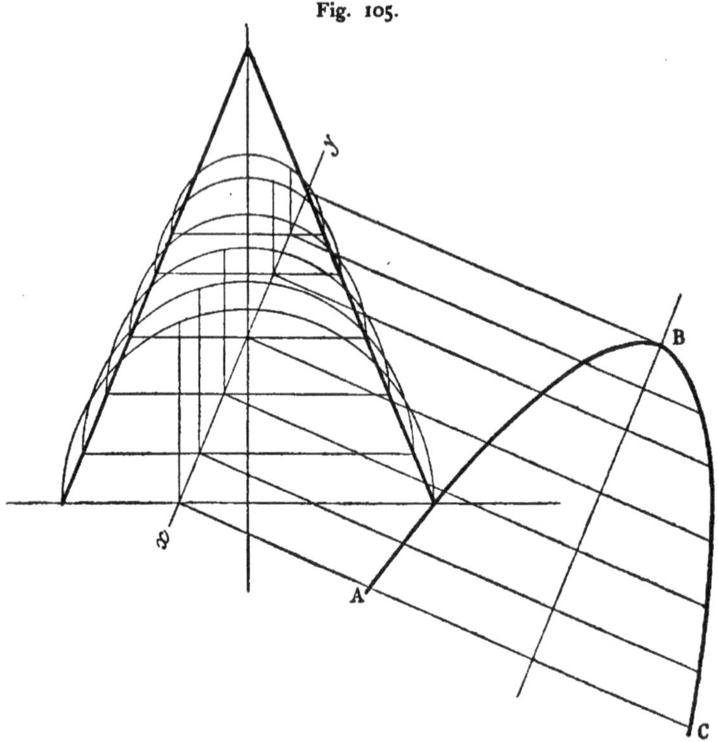

Ex. 149. Construct a parabola, given that the diameter is 3 inches and length of tangent at widest part of curve is $3\frac{1}{2}$ inches.

102. Another method is this: divide half the ordinate E 4 into four equal parts as shown, Fig. 107, and the depth also into four. Then draw radiating lines from A to 1 2 3 as shown, and vertical lines through 1 2 3. The intersections of the corresponding lines are points in the parabola.

The tangent at any point P, Fig. 107, of the parabola is found by dropping a perpendicular P N on the axis and producing N A to T; making A T = A N. T P is the tangent.

103. The Hyperbola.—To construct a hyperbola when given an ordinate o 4, the vertex A and the end of the major axis H, Fig. 108. Draw o 4 parallel to A o and divide the ordinate

Fig. 106. Fig. 107.

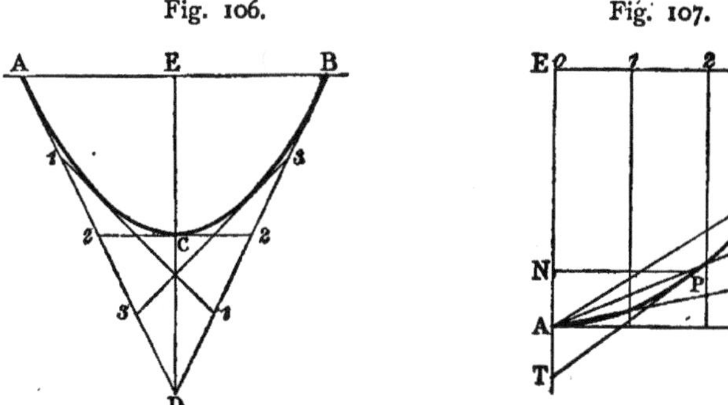

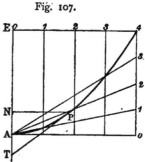

o 4 and the perpendicular 4 o each into four equal parts and mark them as shown. The points in the curve are where the corresponding radiating lines cross.

Fig. 108.

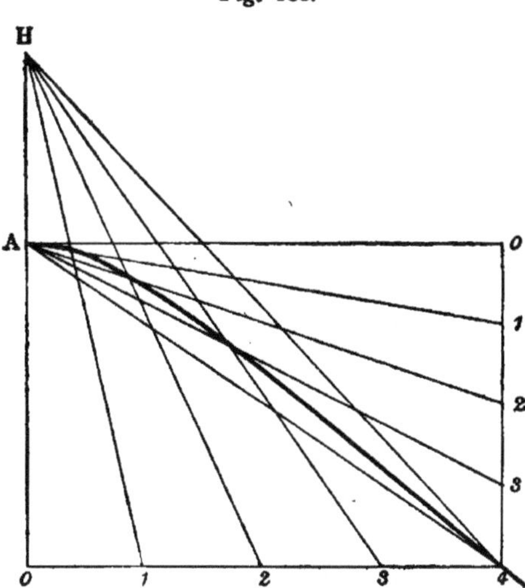

104. This curve may also be looked at from another point of view. When two shafts which are not parallel and do not meet, are to be connected by gearing, so that one drives the

other, it is found necessary to connect them with a pair of wheels of a peculiar shape. The nature of the action of the two wheels is such that there is always one straight line on the surface of the one inclined to its axis, in contact with a similar line on the surface of the other inclined to its respective axis. It follows, of course, that the surface of each wheel is generated by a line at a certain distance from the wheel and inclined to its axis.

105. The meaning is best shown by a projection. Suppose that *c′ c′* and *c c*, Fig. 109, are the projections of an axis of this kind, and *a′ b′* and *a b* the projections of the line which is to generate the surface, then it will be found that as *a b* revolves about *c c*, always keeping at the same distance from it and at the given angle, it generates a solid whose section down the axis is an hyperbola.

Fig. 109.

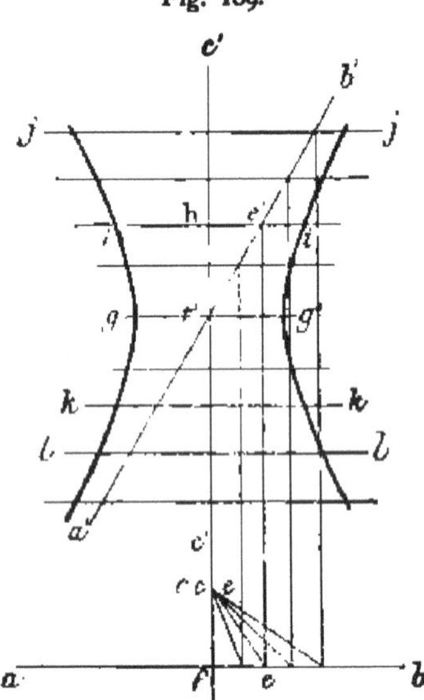

The point *f* will give the points *g′ g′*, for the point *f* in the line *a′ b* will come to *g′* and *g′*, when it comes into the plane of the paper in the course of its revolution. Take next a point *e*. The distance of *e* from the axis when it comes into the plane of the paper in the course of its revolution will be *c e*. Find the vertical projection *e' e*, and draw a horizontal line through it, and measure off the distances *h i h i*, each equal to *c e*—*i i* are two points in the curve ; other points are obtained in the same way.

CHAPTER XXIV.

THE CYCLOID AND ARCHIMEDEAN SPIRAL.

106. THE cycloid is a curve traced by a point in the circumference of a circle as the circle rolls along a straight line.

Fig. 110

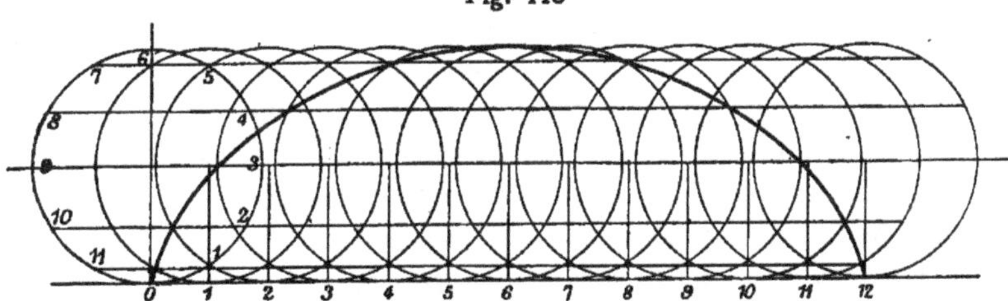

If the circle roll along the straight line until it has completed one revolution it will have travelled from 0, Fig. 110, a distance equal to the circumference of the circle. Lay off this distance along the line 0, 12, having first got its length by calculation. Divide the circle 0 8 4 into twelve equal parts, and the horizontal line 0 12 into twelve equal parts. As the circle rolls along, the point 1 in the circle will come on 1 in the straight line, and when 1 is on 1, 0 will have risen as high as 1.1, so draw a circle with 1 as its bottom point, and draw through 11 a horizontal line, and find where this horizontal line cuts the circle. The point of intersection of the horizontal 11, 1 and circle on 1, is a point in the cycloid. On 2, describe a circle, and find where the horizontal line through 10 cuts it. That point is another point in the cycloid. Proceed to find other points by drawing horizontal lines through 3 4, &c., and circles standing on 3, 4, 5, &c., and draw a curve through the joints thus found by means of French curves.

Ex. 150. Draw a cycloid with a generating circle of 1½ inch diameter.

Ex. 151. Draw a cycloid with a generating circle ¾ inch diameter.

Ex. 152. Draw the curve generated by a point within the generating circle. Radius of circle 1 inch, distance of generating point from centre ½ inch. This curve is called an inferior trochoid.

Ex. 153. Draw the curve generated by a point ½ inch without a circle 1½ inch diameter rolling along a straight line. This curve is called the superior trochoid.

Ex. 154. Draw a curve generated by a point on the circumference of a circle 1 inch diameter rolling on a circle 3 inches diameter. This curve is called the epicycloid.

Ex. 155. Draw the curve generated by a point on the circumference of a circle 1 inch diameter rolling within a circle 4 inches diameter. This is the hypocycloid.

107. A peculiar case of this last is when the diameter of generating circle is equal to the radius of the enclosing circle; the curve then becomes a straight line.

The student should try a case of this kind.

108. The cycloid is used by engineers for obtaining the curves for teeth on racks. The epicycloid and hypocycloid for teeth on wheels. And the peculiar case spoken of above, where the diameter of generating circle is equal to the radius of enclosing circle, is used for obtaining the shapes of radial teeth.

109. Another important curve is that used as a template for shaping cams which have to give a reciprocating piece a uniform rate of motion. It is described in the following way. Suppose the projection of the shaft on which the cam is fixed is shown, and *d*, Fig. 111, shows the thickness of the metal of the boss. Let *a b* represent the length of stroke. Divide *a b* into six equal parts, and, beginning at *a b*, divide the circle into 12 equal angles with radial lines *cj*, *ci*, *cb*, &c., as shown.

Suppose the curve to begin at the point *f* and the reciprocating piece to be touching it there. When the curve has moved through an angle of 30° the reciprocating piece will have travelled out from the centre by a distance equal to $\frac{1}{6}$ *ab*.

Fig. 111.

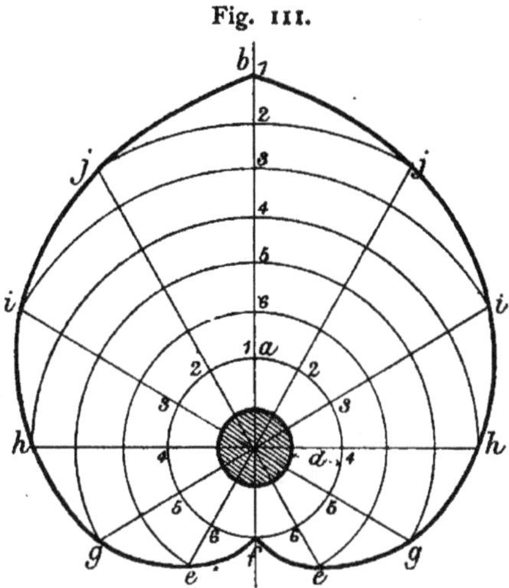

To obtain this point, take *c* as centre and radius *c* 6; describe the arc *e* 6 *e*; *e e* will be points in the curve. Next, with *c* as centre and radius *c* 5, describe the arc *g* 5 *g*; *g g* will be points in the curve, and so on. When the curve has been carefully drawn through the points it has the shape of a conventional heart, as shown. Sometimes this curve is called the archimedean spiral.

CHAPTER XXV.

ANTIFRICTION BEARING.

ANOTHER important curve is the antifriction curve, which is used where there is an end thrust of a revolving spindle to be taken.

110. In the case of an ordinary foot-step, such as that shown

in sketch, Fig. 112, the work consumed by friction at any such little surface as *a* will depend on the pressure on the surface and the space passed through by the surface in a given time. For, as is well known, work is pressure through space, and the pressure here is the resistance which the little surface offers to being moved. In one revolution the little surface moves through a space equal to the circumference of the circle of which r is the radius. The work done in a revolution, in moving the surface *a*, will be the pressure $\times$ $2\pi r$ = pressure $\times 2\pi r$. Now take an exactly equal surface much nearer to the centre, and exactly the same kind of thing happens there, only the space passed through is not so great in the second case.

Fig. 112.

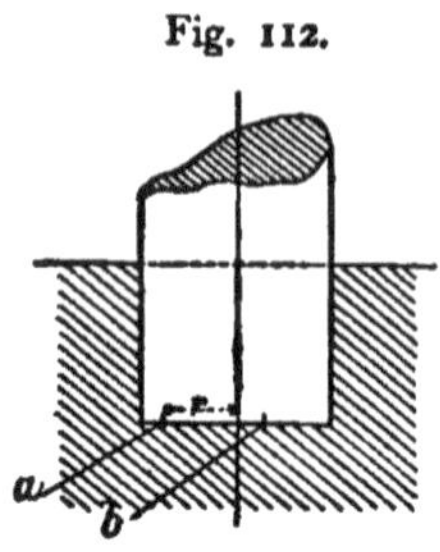

Work done at second surface = pressure $\times 2\pi \times p$,

111. So the work done and lost by the friction at the outer surface is much greater, greater because the radius is greater, than the work done at the inner surface. In the last sentence it was said that the work was lost; but this is not quite true. For it is converted into heat, and this heat and the rubbing injures the surface, the rubbing and injury being in proportion to the work converted into heat. Of course the outside part of the bearing shown above, gets more quickly injured, because the rubbing and the heat developed is greatest there.

112. Should two equal forces, as P P, Fig. 113, act on the back of two wedges, one being a very sharp wedge, the other a blunt one, and a triangle be drawn to represent the balanced external forces acting at the wedge, such a triangle *c d e* represents the force P, and the forces acting on the sides of the wedge which balance P, and it is seen that the side *c d*, which represents the force acting at right angles at the side in both cases, is much greater in the case where the wedge is very thin. The pressure, then, on the side of the wedge which has little inclination to the pressure, is greater than the other.

113. In the case of a bearing of the shape shown in sketch,

Fig. 114, the same condition of things exists. At places like *a* the pressure per square inch of surface is much greater than at places like *b*, because the inclination of the surface at *a* to the

Fig. 113.

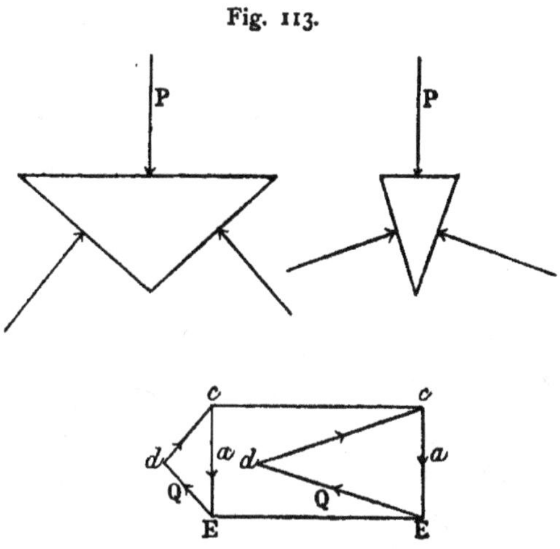

vertical is much less than at *b*. But the circle through which a square inch of surface at *b* has to travel during every revolution of the shaft, is much greater than the distance through which a

Fig. 114.

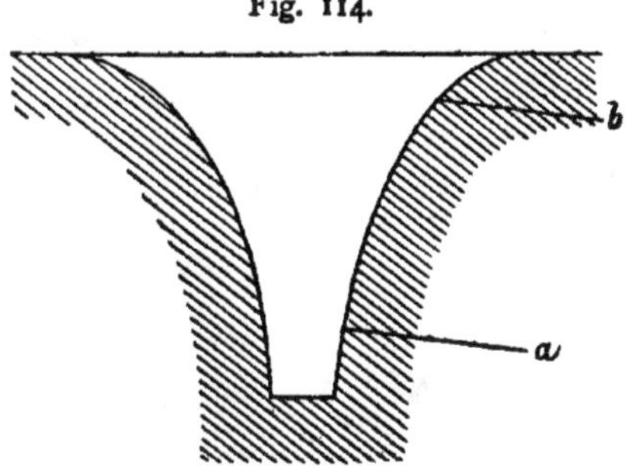

square inch of surface at *a* has to travel, because the radius is much greater in the one case than in the other. So although the pressure at *a* is greater than at *b*, the distance travelled is less.

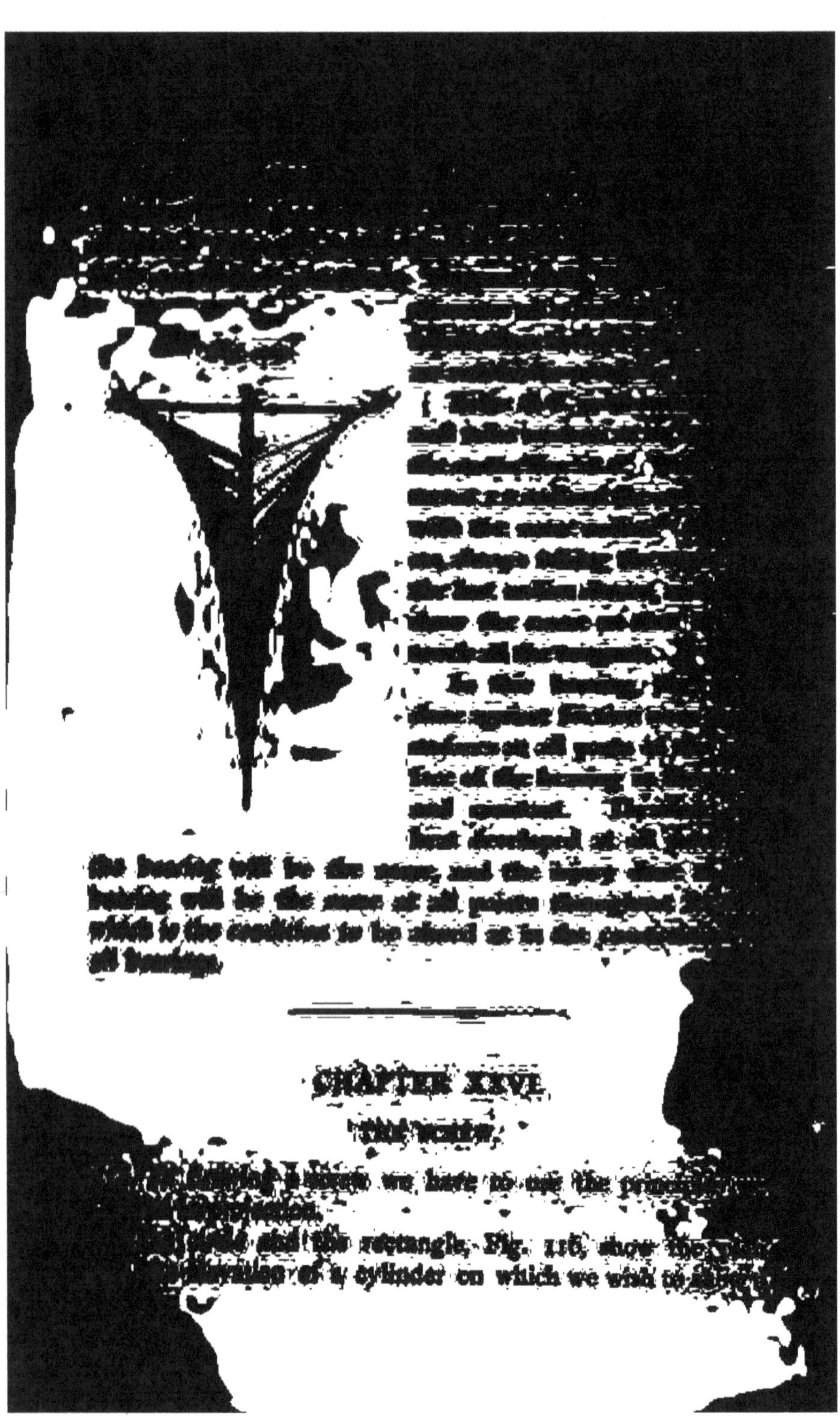

[illegible] and constant. [illegible] heat developed at all [illegible] the bearing will be the same, and the injury [illegible] bearing will be the same at all points throughout [illegible] which is the condition to be aimed at in the [illegible] all bearings.

CHAPTER XXVI.

THE WORM.

[illegible] we have to use the principles [illegible]

[illegible] and the rectangle, Fig. 116, show the [illegible] drawings of a cylinder on which we wish to [illegible] square-threaded screw. Suppose the outside upper edge of the screw to commence at *a'*, it will go round the cylinder, and when it gets back to the same generating line it will have

Fig. 116.

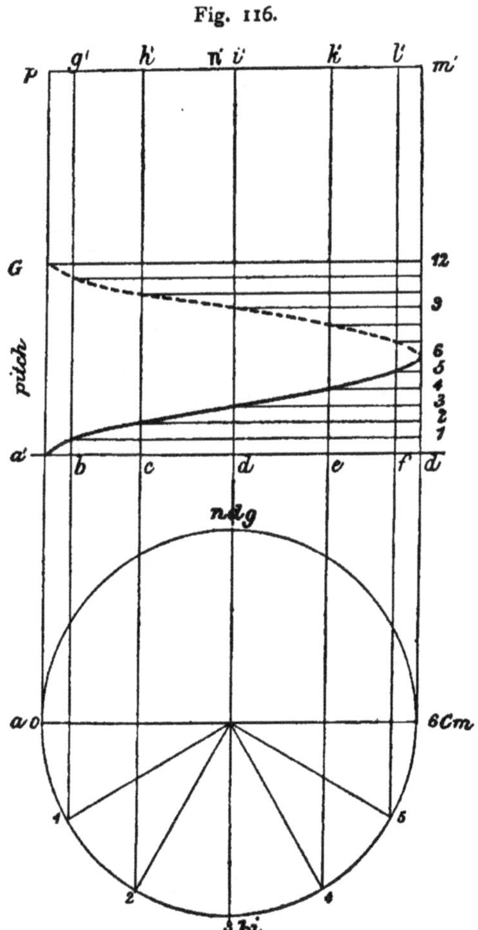

risen to G, a height equal to the pitch. In rising to the point G, it will have risen through equal heights for equal horizontal angles moved through.

Looking at the plan we see that a small body going

[illegible] of this by [illegible] [illegible] travelling point has [illegible] have them through [illegible] three-sixths, and so on. To [illegible] it will be found convenient [illegible] not by a geometrical method [illegible] dividers graduated by a screw [illegible] do this division with the great[illegible] possible. If you find, after step[illegible] your dividers, that there is an [illegible] the point of the compasses and the [illegible] your compasses and step it off again.

116. As the pitch is the rise of [illegible] of the thread, the student must be care[illegible] in going across from one side to the [illegible] is but half the pitch.

117. A square thread is generally [illegible] and the opening is the same width as the [illegible] the curve of the bottom edges of the thread [illegible] plan 1, 2, 3, etc., with a diameter equal [illegible] bolt at the bottom of the thread, and take [illegible] them as in the case of the outside edge [illegible] thread on the elevation of the screw can [illegible] cutting a piece of thin pear-tree wood, [illegible] when placed on the paper it just correspo[illegible] sections of the vertical and horizontal con[illegible] between *a* and *d*. Such a shape is called a [illegible]

118. To make things clearer, and to ena[illegible] better to understand the construction of a screw [illegible] draw out two screws; one square-threaded [illegible] pitch, and a V-threaded screw of half-inch pitch [illegible] diameter outside measurement.

Draw first *b a* and *c d* (page 104), two verti[illegible]

represent the outside of the elevation of the screw, and from a point *e* and radius 2 inches describe the semicircle 0 3 6 to represent half plan. Measure up the line *d*, 1.2', 1 inch, that is the pitch, and divide it into twelve equal parts. Mark them as shown. Now if a point travels up the outside edge of the screw, it will rise equal heights for equal horizontal angles moved through. Divide 0 3 6 into six equal angles by the lines *e* 1, *e* 2, *e* 3, etc.

Draw projectors from 1, 2, 3, etc. When the point is above 1, it will be in the projector above 1, that is its elevation will be somewhere in 1 *f*. But it will have risen through a height just one sixth of half pitch, that is one sixth of *d* 6'. The point will therefore lie in the horizontal line drawn from 1'. So when the point has come to 2, it will lie in the projector 2 *g*, and as it will have risen through two sixths of *d* 6, it will lie in the horizontal line drawn through 2'. The curve *a h* 6', will be the vertical projection of the outer edge of the bottom of the thread,

The upper outer edge of the thread will be parallel to this and half inch higher, so mark a distance *a k* half inch high. Apply the template used for drawing *a h* 6' to *k* 12', and draw a curve. This curve will be the upper edge of the thread.

In the same way, draw all the curves *l m n o*, etc., parallel to each other.

Measure *ap* half inch, and with *e* as centre, and *eq* as radius describe the semicircle *q* 3_2 6.

Find the curve *p h r* by exactly the same process as that adopted for obtaining the curve *a h* 6', and draw *s t v*, and the corresponding curves above that parallel to *p h r* and by means of the same template.

Some parts of the curves are dotted. The student will observe that the dotted lines are the parts of the edges which are not seen.

To construct the V-threaded screw, draw *a b c d*, page 118, to represent the outside of the cylinder on which the screw is to be cut.

Mark off the pitch *a l* and *o*, 12'. Divide this into twelve

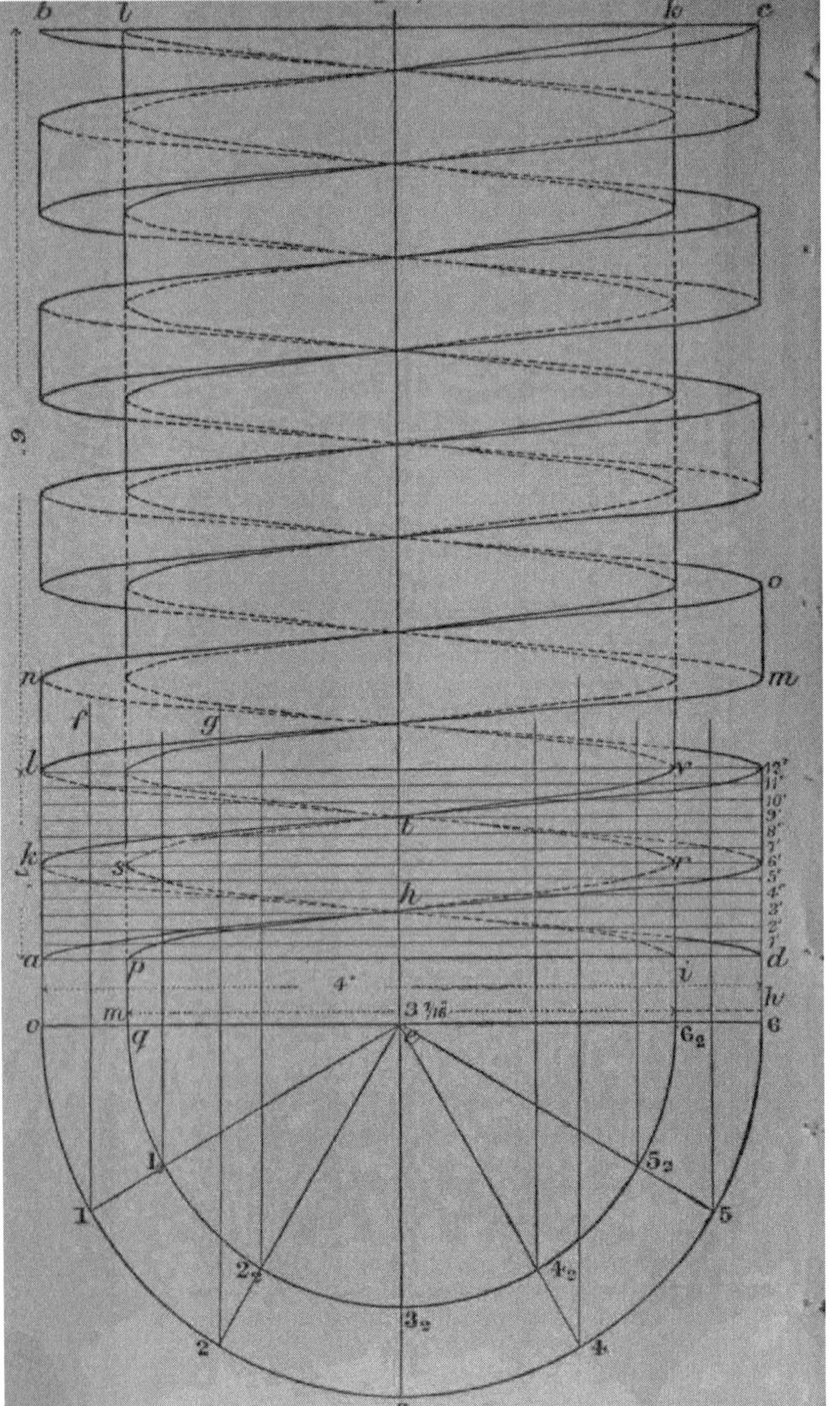
b
l
k
c
o
n
m
f
g
l
v
12'
11'
10'
9'
8'
7'
6'
5'
4'
3'
2'
1'
t
k
s
r
h
a
p
i
d
4'
h
m
3 1/16
o
q
e
6₂
6
1₂
5₂
1
5
2₂
4₂
3₂
2
4
3

equal parts, and through the divisions draw horizontal lines. About *e* describe a semicircle 4 inches diameter, and divide this into six equal angles. Draw projectors from 1 2 3 4 5, and find the points of intersection with the corresponding horizontal lines. Through these points of intersection, draw the curve *a h* 6', by means of a template constructed to coincide with the intersecting points.

Draw the other curves *l t f*, etc., parallel to this one, and by means of the same template.

From *l*, draw a line with the 30° set square, and from *a* the same. These lines will meet in *g*, and make the angle *l g a* 60°, which is rather more than the 57° of Whitworth's design.

Draw a projector *g k*, and from *e* as centre, and radius *e k* describe the semicircle *k* 3_2 5_2, and draw projectors from them. Find the intersection of these projectors with the corresponding horizontal lines, beginning this time at 6'. Then by means of a template draw a curve *g m n* through the points thus found. Draw *p q*, etc.; parallel to *g n*, and by means of the same template. The upper V's and curves are mere repetitions of the first.

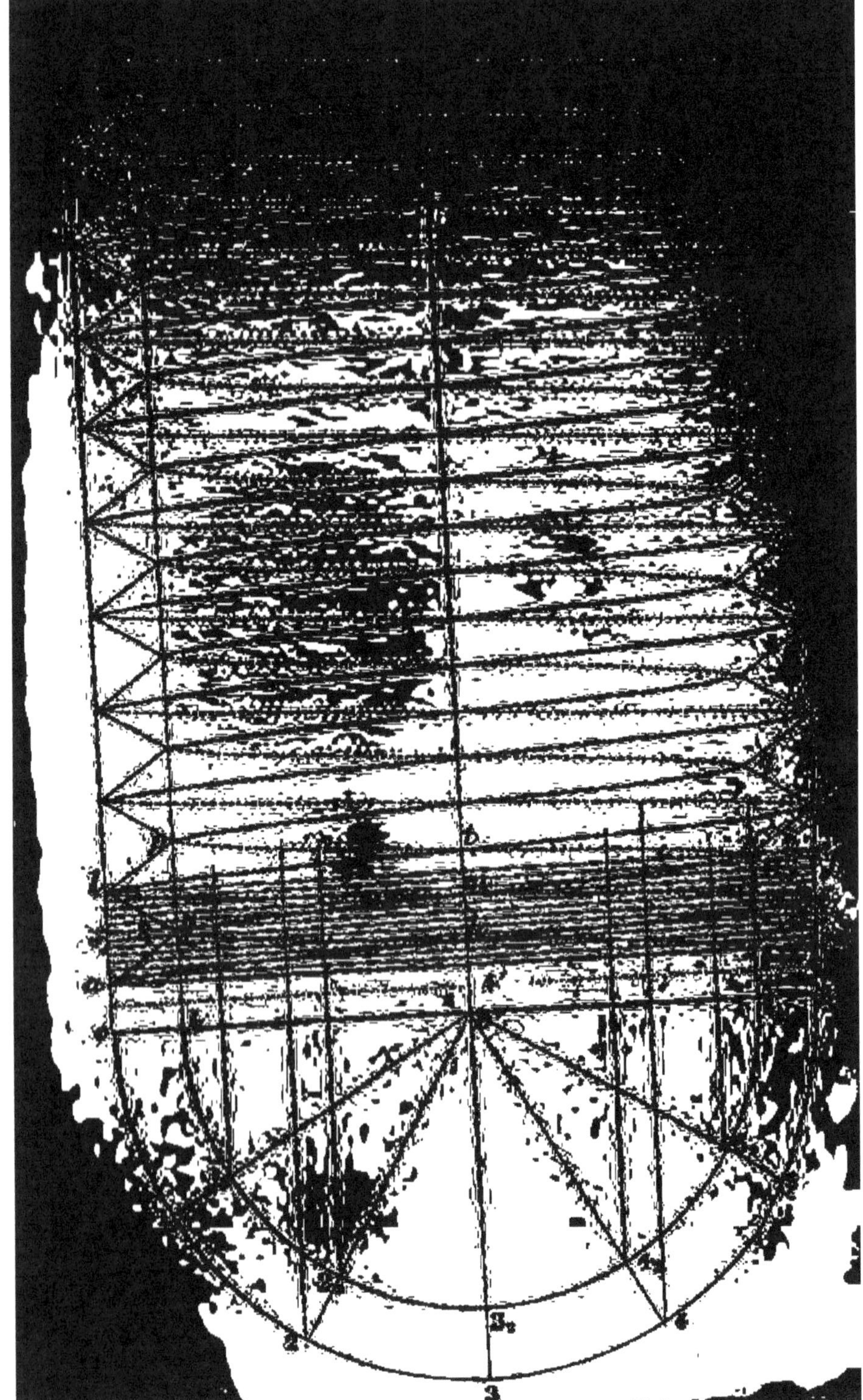

SECTION V.

TRACES OF LINES AND PLANES.

CHAPTER XXVII.

TRACES OF LINES.

119. A LINE AB, shown in picture, Fig. 119, parallel to the vertical plane and inclined to the horizontal plane will, if produced, cut the horizontal plane in a point. That point, it

Fig. 119.

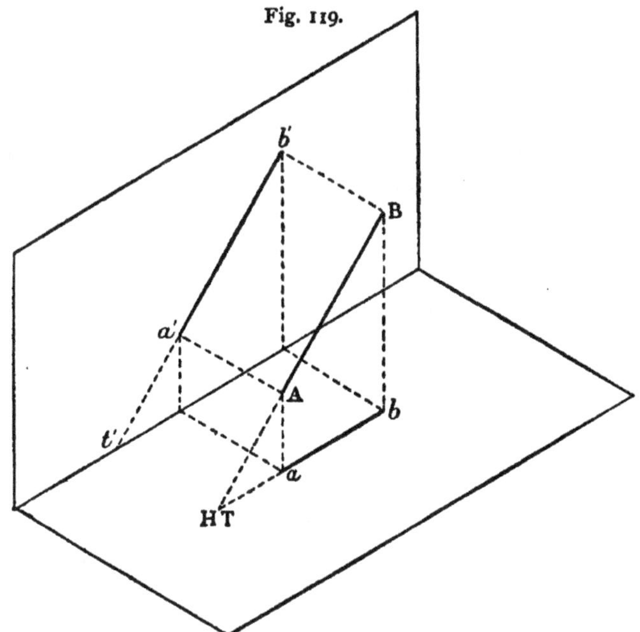

is evident, will lie in the plan produced and just opposite the point where its vertical projection meets xy. This point is called the horizontal trace of the line.

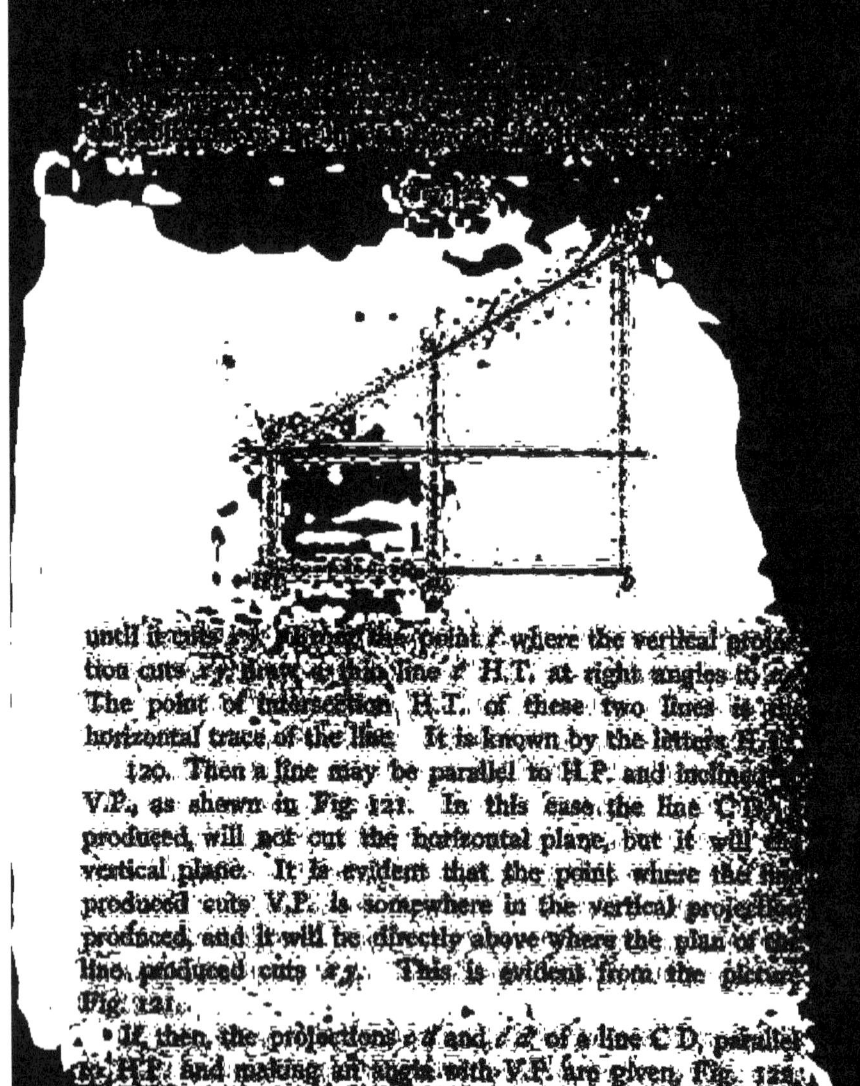

until it cuts xy. [illegible] the point t where the vertical projection cuts xy. Draw [illegible] line t H.T. at right angles to xy. The point of intersection H.T. of these two lines is the horizontal trace of the line. It is known by the letters H.T.

120. Then a line may be parallel to H.P. and inclined to V.P., as shewn in Fig. 121. In this case the line C D, produced, will not cut the horizontal plane, but it will cut the vertical plane. It is evident that the point where the line produced cuts V.P. is somewhere in the vertical projection produced, and it will be directly above where the plan of the line produced cuts xy. This is evident from the picture, Fig. 121.

If, then, the projections cd and $c'd'$ of a line C D, parallel to H.P. and making an angle with V.P. are given, Fig. 122, and the vertical trace is required, produce cd the plan to t, [illegible] and $c'd'$ the elevation to V.T. Draw a vertical line [illegible] and find where it cuts $c'd'$ the vertical projection produced. That point V.T. where the vertical line from t meets the vertical projection produced, is the vertical trace. It is known by the letters V.T.

121. When the line is inclined to both planes of projection, as shown in Fig. 123, it will have both a vertical trace and a horizontal trace.

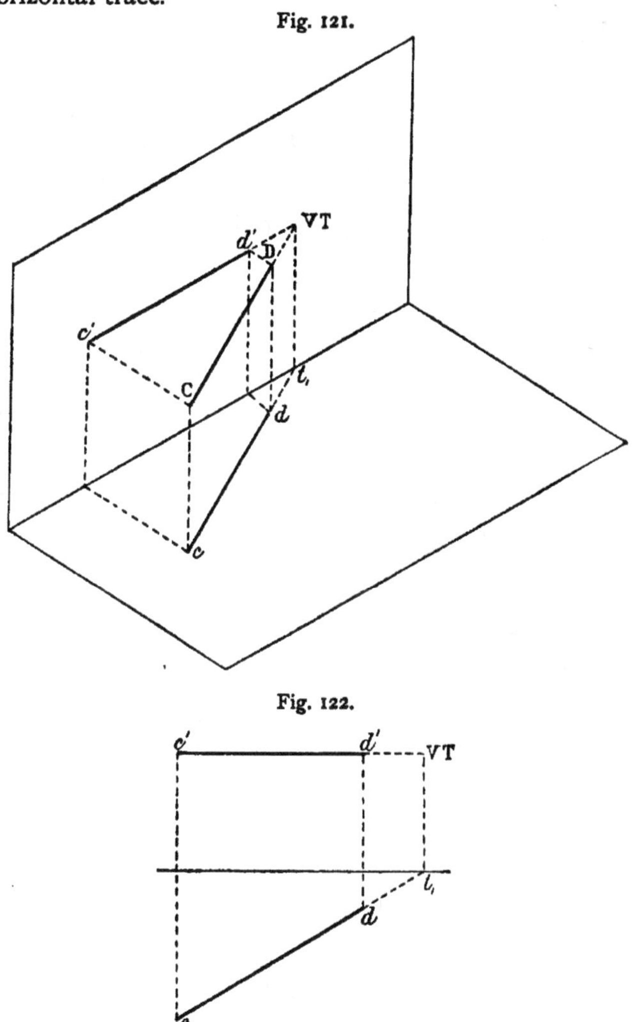

Fig. 121.

Fig. 122.

It is evident from the figure, that the horizontal trace will be somewhere in the plan of the line produced, and that the point where the elevation produced meets xy is the elevation

[illegible]

Fig. 124.

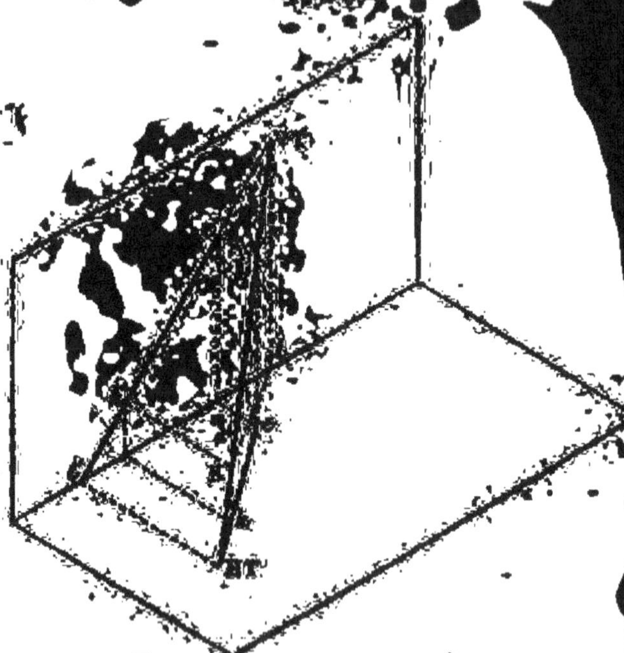

Suppose, then, it is required to find the traces of a line [illegible] when its projections [illegible] and [illegible] (Fig. 124) are given. Produce [illegible] until it cuts xy in [illegible]. Through [illegible] draw a vertical line; produce [illegible] until it cuts this vertical line. The point [illegible] is the horizontal trace.

[illegible] produce [illegible] until it cuts xy in [illegible], and through [illegible] draw [illegible]. Produce [illegible]. The point where [illegible] intersects [illegible] vertical line through [illegible] is the vertical trace.

[illegible] 126. A line A B parallel to V.P. 1¼ inch in front has A

1 inch high, and B 2 inches high. The plan of the line is 1·25 inch long. Show the horizontal trace of the line.

Ex. 157. A line C D has C 1·25 inch high and 1 inch in front of V.P., and D ·25 inch high and 2 inches in front of V.P. The plan is 2 inches long. Find the H.T.

Fig. 124.

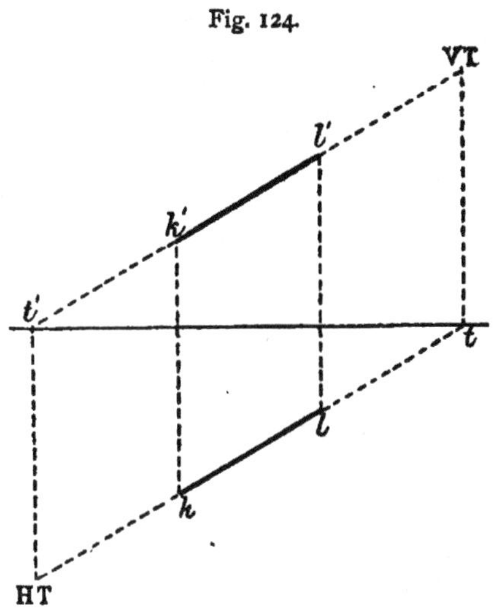

Ex. 158. A line E F parallel to H.P. ½ inch high has E 1½ inch in front of V.P., and F ½ inch in front of V.P. The true length of the line is 1·75 inch long. Find its vertical trace.

Ex. 159. A line G H has G ½ inch in front of V.P., and ¼ inch high, and H 1·25 inch in front of V.P., ¾ inch high. The plan of the line is 2 inches long. Find its V.P.

Ex. 160. Find both traces of line, Ex. 157.

Ex. 161. Find both traces of line in Ex. 159.

Ex. 162. Find the true length of C D, Ex. 157.

Ex. 163. Find the true length of G H, Ex. 159.

Ex. 164. Find the true length of the diagonal of a cube 1 inch edge.

Ex. 165. Find the true length of the diagonal of a cube, 1½ inch edge.

[illegible]

[illegible] plane [illegible] planes used. It is often [illegible] to [illegible] which contains two lines which intersect, and [illegible] that plane by the lines where it cuts both planes [illegible] tion. For example, take the lines A B and A C [illegible] in A. Suppose a plane or stiff piece of paper [illegible]

Fig. [illegible]

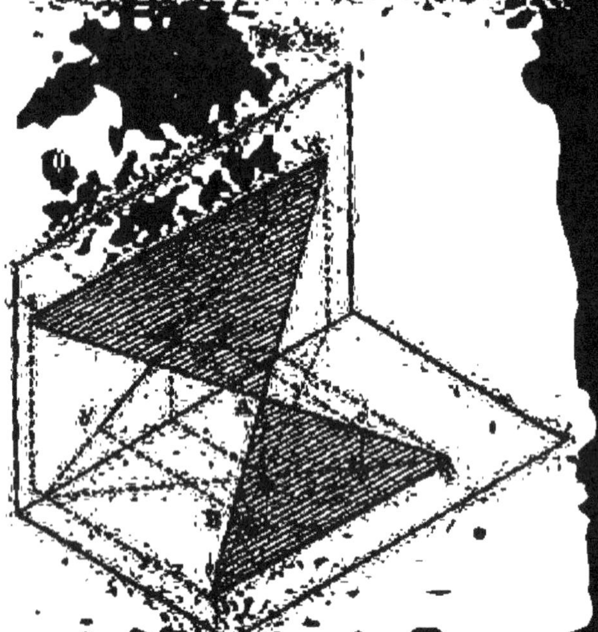

[illegible] is quite evident that such plane or piece of paper will touch the horizontal plane at two known points, [illegible] being where the two lines meet the horizontal plane, [illegible] whole line where the plane meets the horizontal plane will be the line joining the two horizontal traces of the lines.

This line is called the horizontal trace of the plane, and is known by the letters H.T.

It is also quite evident that the plane will meet the vertical plane in two known points, those two points being the vertical traces of the lines. The whole line where the plane meets the vertical plane will be the line joining the two vertical traces. This line is called the vertical trace of the plane, and it is known by the letters V.T.

123. The simplest kind of inclined plane of which the student has to deal is that which is at right angles to the vertical plane and inclined only to the horizontal plane. Such a plane is shown in Fig. 126. It will be observed that H.T., its horizontal trace, is at right angles to the xy, and that V.T., its vertical trace, is really the vertical projection of the whole plane. Whatever lies on the plane, let it be points, lines, or planes, will be shown in V.T.

Fig. 126.

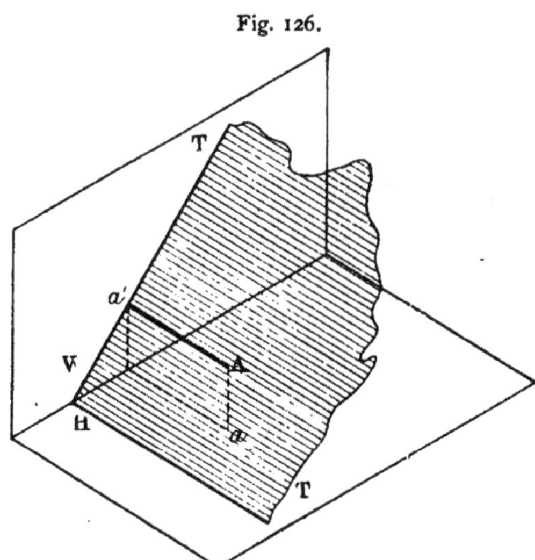

124. The traces of the plane are shown in orthographic projection. V.T. and H.T., Fig. 127, are the traces of the plane shown in Fig 126. The angle which V.T. makes with xy is the inclination of the plane to H.P., its inclination to the vertical plane being 90°.

The vertical projection of any point A contained by the plane will be in the vertical trace of the plane, and will be

Fig. 127.

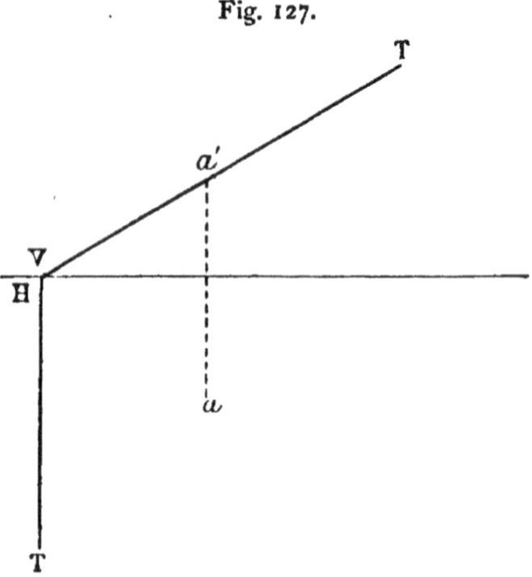

Fig. 128.

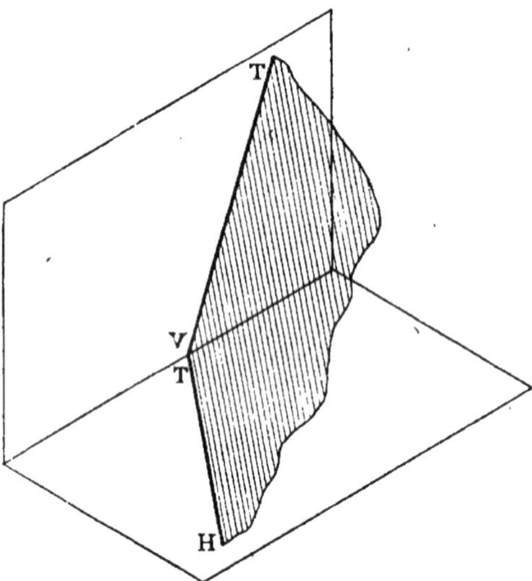

found by drawing a projector from the plan *a*, until it cuts the V.T. The point where the projector cuts V.T. is *a'*, the elevation of the point A. This is quite clear from the picture and orthographic projection figures.

The height of A, is shown by the height of *a′* above *x y*.

Fig. 129.

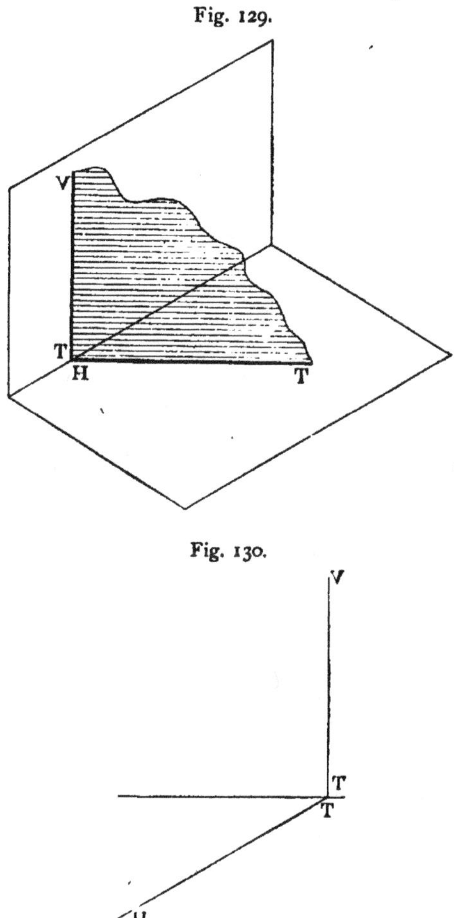

Fig. 130.

125. The traces of planes take a number of different and curious positions. Fig. 128 shows one of these planes with the traces almost opposite each other and in a straight line.

126. Figures 129 and 130 show the picture and orthographic projection of a plane at right angles to H.P. while

inclined to the vertical plane. In this case the inclination of the plane to the vertical plane is shown by the inclination of the H.T. to the vertical plane, and the plane's inclination to H.P. is of course 90°.

A plane may be inclined to both planes of projection, as shown in Fig. 128, in which case neither of its traces will make an angle of 90° to *x y*.

CHAPTER XXIX.

INCLINATION OF INCLINED PLANES.

127. We have seen in Fig. 126 that when the inclined plane is at right angles to the vertical plane, that is, when the horizontal trace H.T. is at right angles to *x y*, the inclination

Fig. 131.

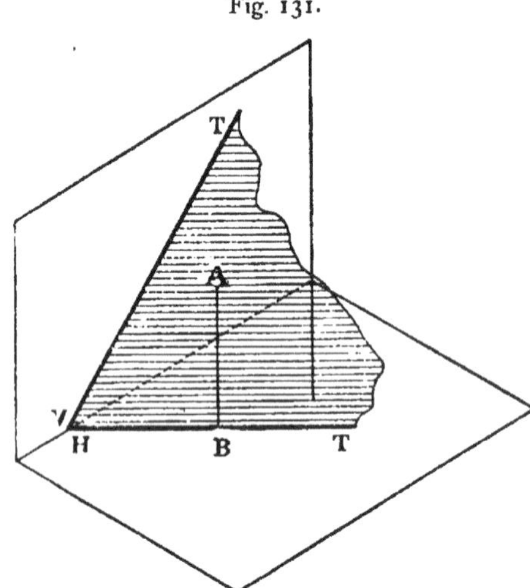

of this plane to the horizontal plane is shown by the angle which V.T. makes with *x y*. This inclination is sometimes called the steepness of the plane.

The inclination of any other plane to the horizontal plane

is often found by determining the angle, which a particular line in that plane makes with H.P. If we take the point A, Fig. 131, we can at pleasure draw any number of straight lines from that point to the horizontal trace H.T. Each of those lines will make a certain definite angle with the H.P. They will all vary in steepness, and consequently the plane itself has all those steepnesses. But when the steepness of a particular plane is spoken of, the angle which one particular line in that plane makes with H.P. is always understood and thought about. That line is always the steepest line in the plane.

128. The steepest line in the plane will be a line such as A B, Fig. 131, going straight up the plane. It is the shortest

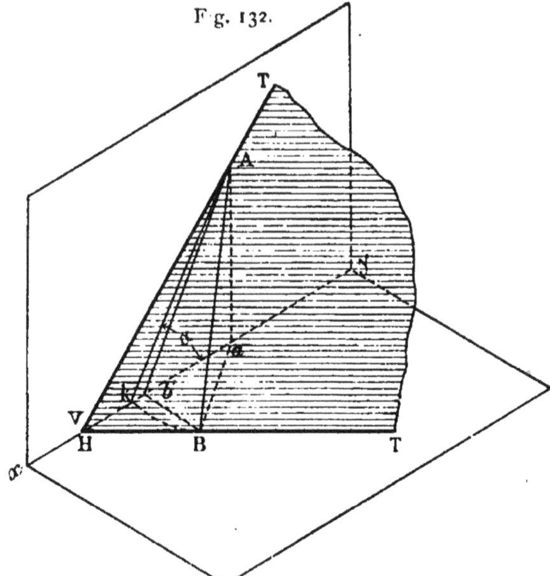

Fig. 132.

distance from the foot of the plane to the point A in the plane. The angle then which the steepest line in the plane makes with the horizontal plane is said to be the inclination of the plane. In the case, Fig. 126, the steepest line is the line V.T., for V.T. is the end view of the plane.

129. The inclination of the plane to H.P. is equal to the

angle which the steepest line in the plane makes with H.P. This straight line is, as shown in Fig. 131, at right angles to the horizontal trace of the plane. So, finding the inclination of such a plane is equivalent to finding the angle made by A B with H.P. This can be done by taking an end view of the plane, or taking a vertical projection of the plane on $x_{,} y_{,}$ parallel to the steepest line and at right angles to H.T. In orthographic projection the plane, as represented by its traces, will look as shown in Fig. 133. The line taken for

Fig. 133.

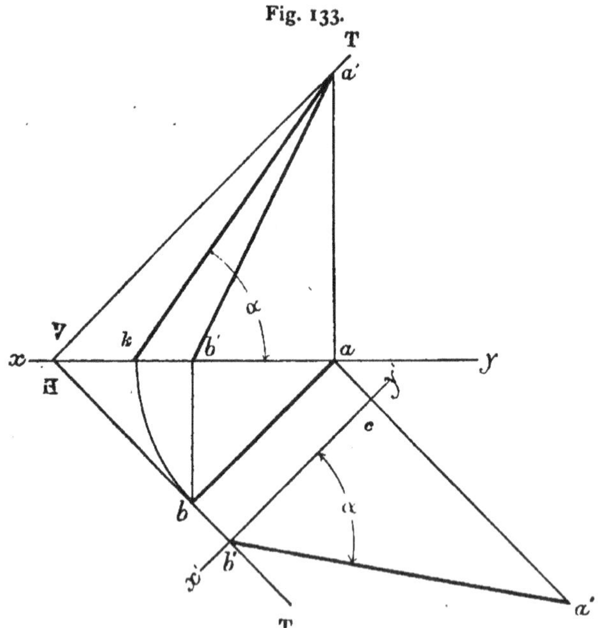

finding the inclination of the plane to H.P. will be *a b*. Shown also in picture, Fig. 132. To get the inclination, take $x' y'$ parallel to *a b*, and show a projection of this line on this new vertical plane. The point *b* is on the ground, so its vertical projection is where $x_{,} y_{,}$ cuts H.T. The point a'' will be at the same height above $x_{,} y_{,}$ as a' is above $x y$. Join b'' a''. Measure the angle a'' b'' $y_{,}$. This is the angle required.

130. Referring to Fig. 132, it will be seen that if the

triangle A B *a* be swung about *a* B as a hinge, and laid on the horizontal plane, the angle shown in plan then will be equal to A B *a*, and therefore to the inclination of the plane. This is just what was done in Fig. 133. The base *c b''* is equal to the base *a* B, and the height *c a''* is equal to the height *a* A. If the base and the perpendicular are the same, the angle which the hypothenuse makes with the base will be the same. So if *a k* in Figs. 132 and 133 be measured equal to *a b*, the angle *a' k a* will be equal to the angle A B *a*, that is, equal to the inclination of the plane. The point *k* is found by swinging *a b* round into *x y* about the centre *a*.

Ex. 166. Show the plan and elevation of a line having the same inclination as a plane and having V.T. making 33° with *xy*, and H.T. making 47°.

Ex. 167. Find the inclination to the H.P. of the plane in the last question.

CHAPTER XXX.

LINES CONTAINED BY INCLINED PLANES.

131. It will be observed that the plan of a line, such as A B, Figs. 134 and 135, contained by a plane and parallel to the horizontal plane, is also parallel to the horizontal trace, the line itself being parallel to the horizontal trace. The first line is also shown in orthographic projection in Fig. 136. In Fig. 135 the plan is produced until it meets *x y*. As the line is horizontal, every point in it will be at the same height from the ground, and so the height of *t*, whose plan is in the *x y*, and elevation necessarily in the vertical trace will, being in the line, have the same height as the line. A vertical line is drawn from *t*, and *t'* gives the height of the line. A horizontal line is drawn through *t'*, and projectors drawn through *a* and *b*, which find *a'* and *b'* in the horizontal line through *t'*.

Ex. 168. V.T. makes 30° with *x y*, H.T. makes 60°, show the plan and elevation of a horizontal line 1 inch long in the plane; the plan being 1 inch distant from the horizontal trace.

Fig. 134.

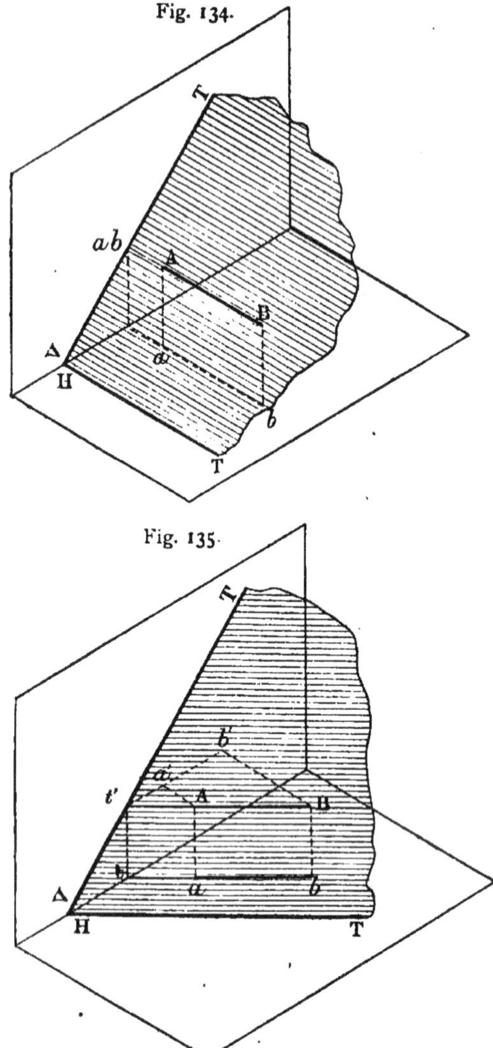

Fig. 135.

Ex. 169. V.T. makes 45° with xy, H.T. makes 30°. Show the plan and elevation of a horizontal line, height 1 inch, and 2 inches long.

132. When the horizontal trace of the plane is at right angles to $x\,y$, that is when the plane is at right angles to V.P., it is very easy finding the elevation of any point which is contained by the plane; but it is not so easy to find the elevation of a point contained by a plane when the horizontal trace is not inclined at an angle of 90°, but at some other angle.

Fig. 136.

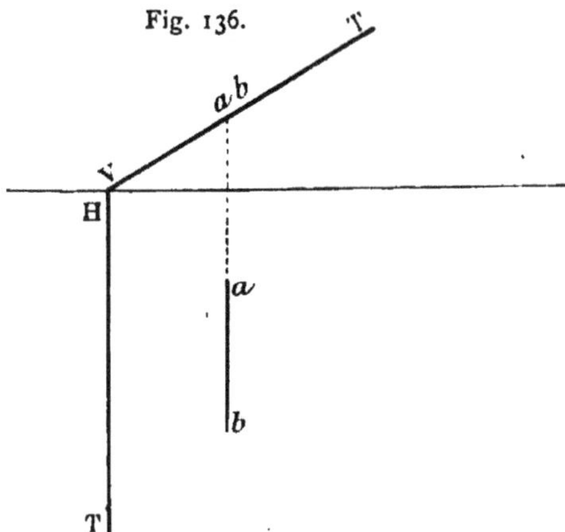

133. For example, take the point A, Fig. 137, whose plan is shown at *a*, and suppose it is required to find the vertical projection of A. The vertical projection of any point lies in the projector drawn from the plan. The only difficulty remaining is to find the exact position of the vertical projection of the point on this line. That is to find how high it is above the $x\,y$.

Now if a horizontal line A *b* be drawn in the plane, every point in that line will be at the same height above the plane as the point A, and therefore *b*, the end of this horizontal line, will be at the same height above the horizontal plane as A. But *b* is in the vertical trace, and the length of the vertical line drawn from *b* to the $x\,y$ will be the height of A. If then a horizontal line be drawn through *b* its point of intersection with the projector through *a*, will be the vertical projection a'.

134. The plan of the point, and the traces of the plane which contains the point, are shown in orthographic projection, Fig. 138. The vertical projection of the point, is found by

drawing a line through *a* parallel to H.T. to represent the plan of a line parallel to H.P. The vertical projection of the point

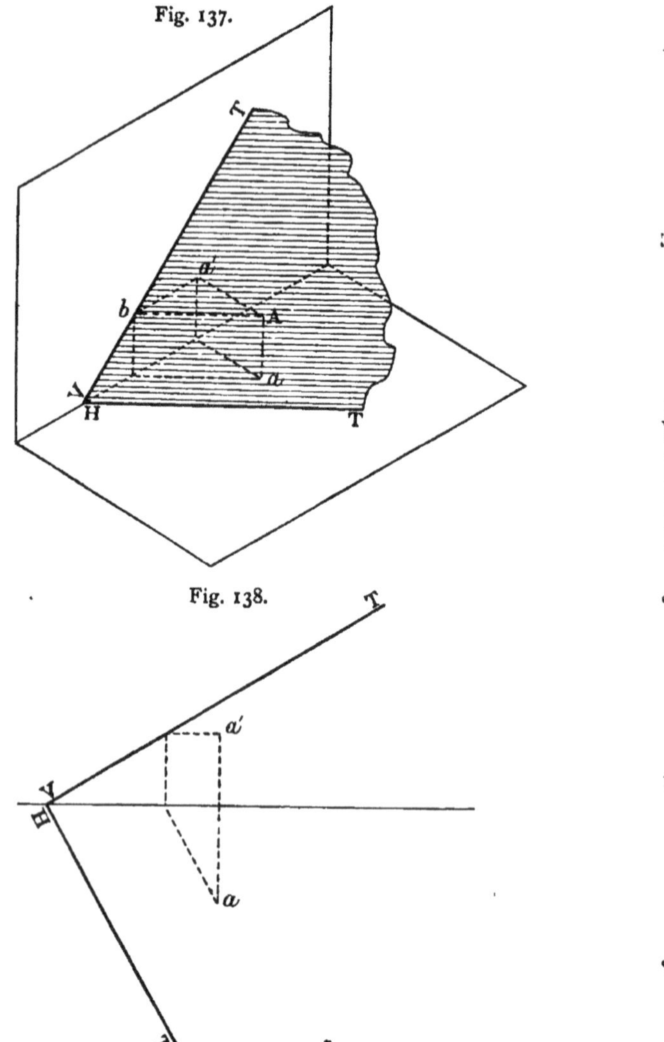

Fig. 137.

Fig. 138.

in this line which meets $x\,y$, is the height, and this height is measured on $a\;a'$ above $x\,y$.

Ex. 170. V.T. makes 43° with $x\,y$, H.T. makes 31°. The

plan of a point is ½ inch from H.T., and 1¼ inch from V.P. Find its vertical projection.

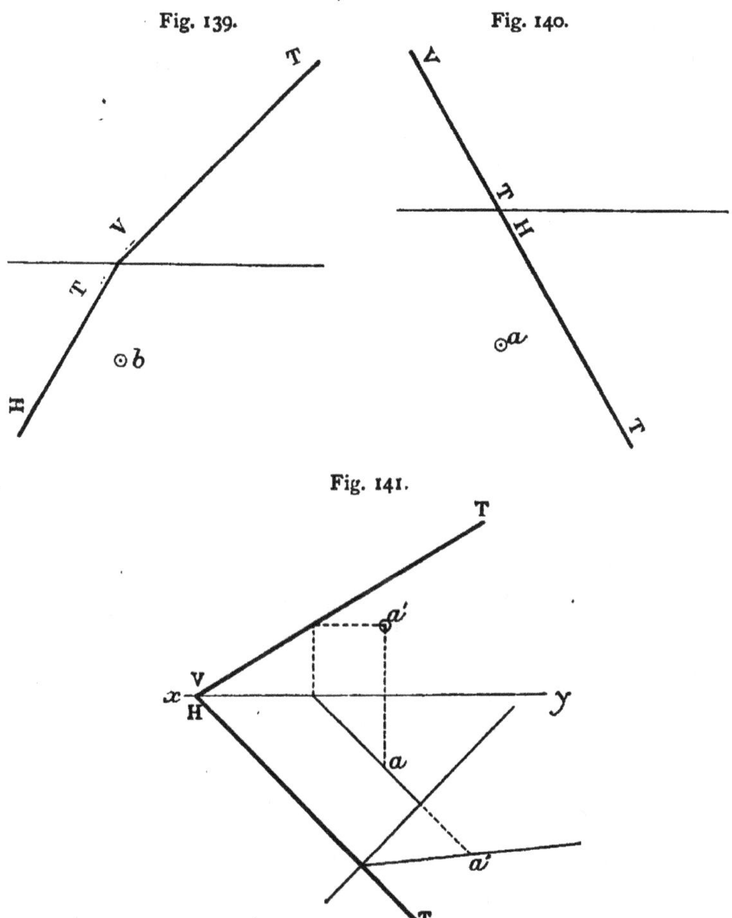

Fig. 139. Fig. 140. Fig. 141.

Ex. 171. In the same plane show a point 1 inch from V.P. and 1¼ inch from H.P.

Ex. 172. In the same plane the elevation of a point is 1½ inches from xy, and 75 inches from V.P. Show its plan.

Ex. 173. Find the elevations of the points whose plans are given, Figs. 139, 140.

135. Sometimes it is necessary to take an end view of a plane whose H.T. is not at 90° to $x\ y$. This is done by drawing a new ground line at right angles to H.T., as shown in Fig. 141, and taking a new vertical projection of a above this ground line. a' will be in the new V.T. The point where the ground line cuts the H.T. is a second point. A line through those two points is the new V.T., and it shows the true inclination of the plane to the H.P.

Ex. 174. Find the inclination of the plane shown in Fig. 139 by the method explained in paragraph 135.

Ex. 175. The V.T. of a plane makes an angle of 35° to $x\ y$, and the H.T. makes an angle of 45°, find the inclination of the plane to H.P. by the above method.

CHAPTER XXXI.

PROJECTION OF LINES AT RIGHT ANGLES TO PLANES.

136. THE plan and elevation of a line which is at right angles to a plane are at right angles to the traces of that plane. This is evident from Fig. 142. If the plan of a point contained by a plane such as b in Fig. 143 be given, and it is required to draw a line from that point at right angles to the plane, then $a\ b$ drawn at right angles to H.T. will be the plan, and $a'\ b'$ drawn from a' at right angles to the V.T. will be an elevation.

Ex. 176. V.T. makes 35° with xy, H.T. 90°. Draw the plan and elevation of a line at right angles to the plane.

137. If the question becomes still more complicated, and it is required to draw the line of a given length, a new elevation is required on which to project an end view of the plane which will contain the perpendicular line to the plane. Draw a new $x\ y$ at right angles to H.T.; Fig. 143. Find b'' the vertical projection of b on the new plane, and from the point d, where H.T. intersects $x_{,}y_{,,}$ draw a line through b''. This line will be the vertical trace in the new plane. From b'' draw a line at right angles to $V_{,}T_{,,}$ and measure off the length $b''\ a''$ required.

Fig. 142.

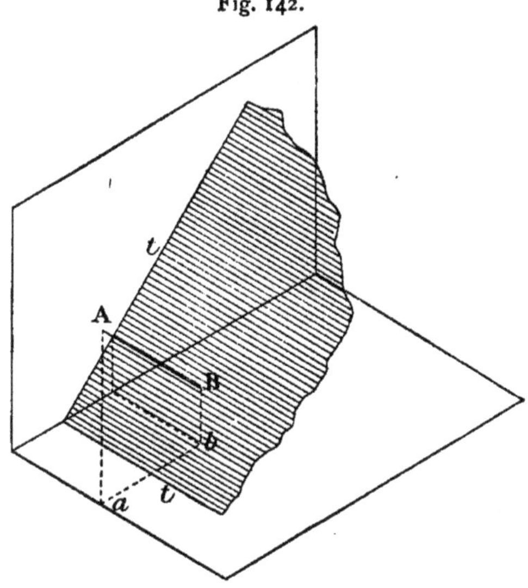

Fig. 143.

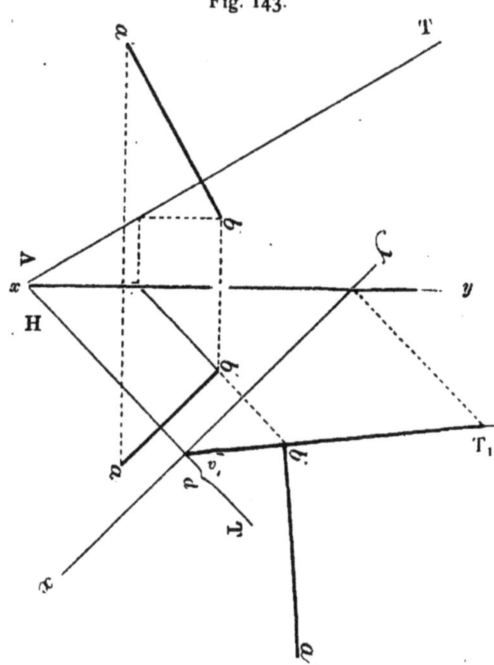

From *a''* draw a projector to the plan of the line. The line *a b* will be the plan. From *a* draw a projector at right angles to *x y*; *a' b'* will be the elevation of the perpendicular to the plane, and it will be of the required length.

Fig. 144.

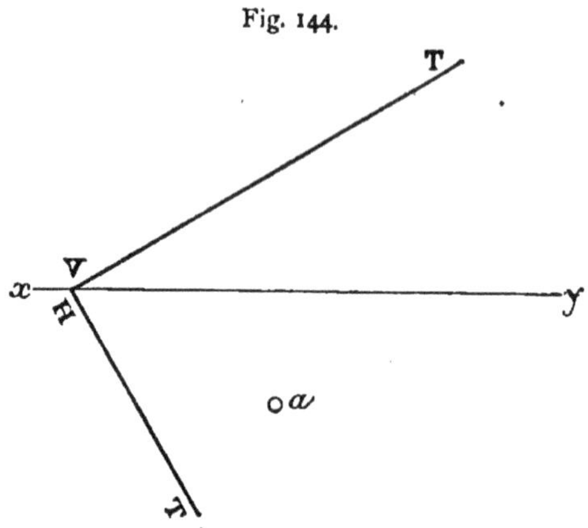

Ex. 177. From *a*, Fig. 144, draw a perpendicular 1½ inch in length.

CHAPTER XXXII.

LINES ON PLANES PARALLEL TO THE VERTICAL PLANE.

138. LINES contained by planes are sometimes parallel to the vertical plane. Fig. 145 shows the picture of such a line. It will be observed that the vertical projection of the line is parallel to V.T., while the plan is parallel to *x y*.

Let *a b*, Fig. 146, be the plan of a line parallel to V.P. contained by the plane whose traces are given. Find the height of *a* by drawing a horizontal line through it. The height of *t* gives it and the intersection of the horizontal line through *t'*, and the projector from *a* gives the elevation *a'*. Through *a'* draw a line parallel to V.T. Draw a projector through *b*. *a' b'* is the vertical projection.

Ex. 178. V.T. makes an angle of 35° with xy, and H.T. makes 70°. Show the elevation of a line in the plane touching H.T. and parallel to V.P.

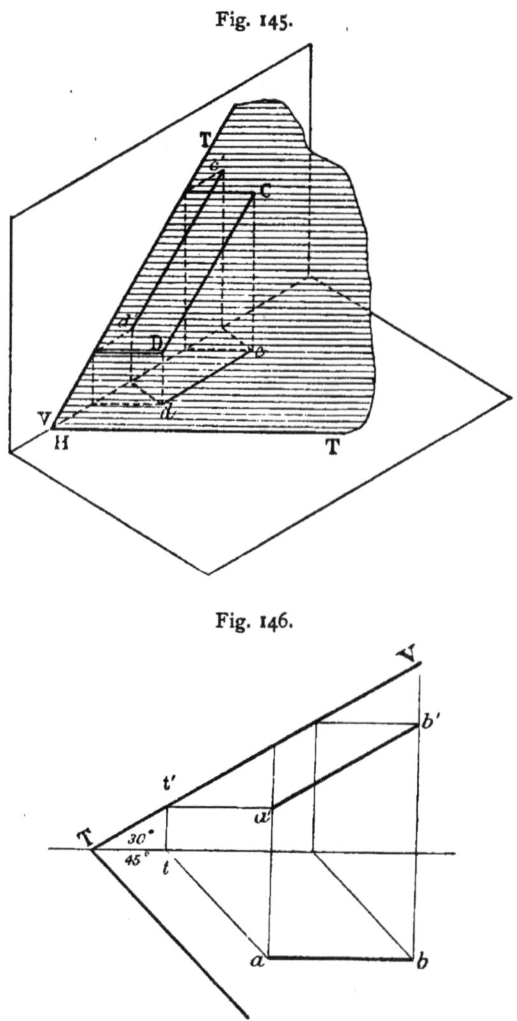

Fig. 145.

Fig. 146.

139. Next, a line may lie in any direction along the plane, and its elevation got by finding the elevations of its ends, as

shown in picture, Fig. 147, and in orthographic projection, Fig. 148.

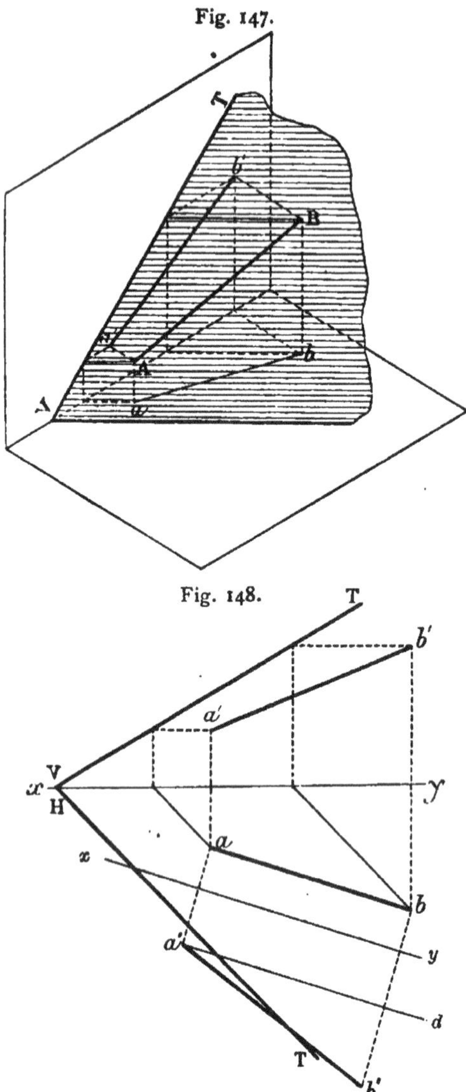

Fig. 147.

Fig. 148.

140. The true length of such a line, or any line in space, of course, may be found by taking a vertical plane parallel to

its plan, of which *xy* is the ground line, and find a projection *a″ b″* on this plane. This projection is shown, Fig. 148. The inclination of such a line to the H.P. is got by drawing a line *a d* parallel to $x_{\prime}y$ and measuring the angle *a* with the protractor.

141. The projections of any line in a plane may be looked at as the lines joining the plans and elevations of any two points in the plane at different distances from H.P. and different distances from V.P. If the two points representing the plans be joined, the line drawn will be in the plane. Its plan will be the line joining the two plans, and its elevation the line joining the elevations of the points. The elevation of any line in a plane can therefore be found by joining the elevations of the end points of the line.

Ex. 179. Take any V.T. and H.T., and show any line in the plane by its plan. Find the elevation. Also find its true length.

CHAPTER XXXIII.

PLANES LYING ON INCLINED PLANES.

142. THIN surfaces also may lie on inclined planes, and their plans and elevations found, as shown in Fig. 149. Here we have a rectangle lying on the plane with two sides parallel to the horizontal plane. The plans and elevations of A B and C D are found just as if they were separate lines, and then in the elevation *c′ d′* joined to each other, which completes the elevation *a′ b′ c′ d′* of the square.

143. Fig. 150 shows the method for finding the elevation of the same rectangle when the plan is given in orthographic projection. The height of *a b* is found by finding the height the point above *xy* in the line *a b*, and in the same way the height of the line *c d* is found. Projectors from *a*, *b*, *c*, and *d* determine the points *a′*, *b′*, *c′*, and *d′*. The joining of these points completes the elevation.

in length, is measured along the vertical trace, and projectors drawn from its ends. As the side A B is horizontal, its full length will be seen when looked at from above. So from any point *a* in the projector from *a'*, measure a distance, *a b*, $\frac{7}{8}$ inch in length, to represent one side of the square. From *a*

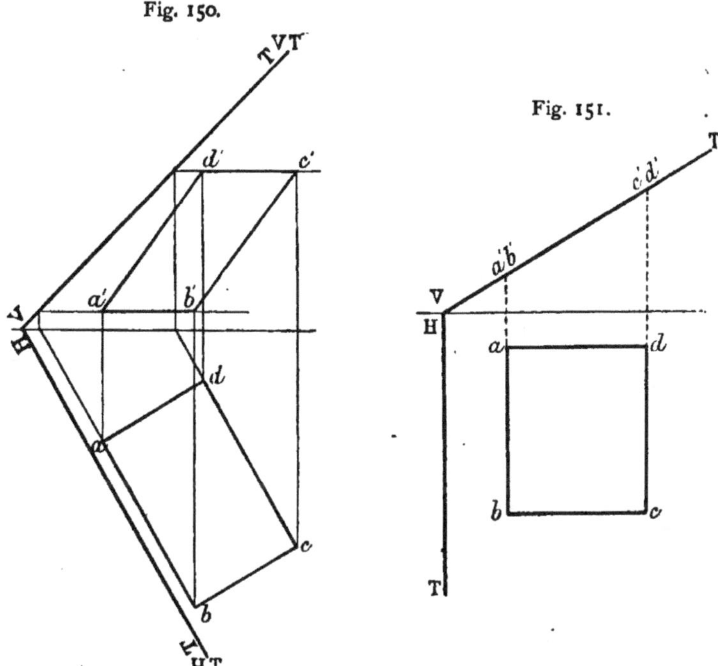

Fig. 150.

Fig. 151.

draw *a d* parallel to *x y*, intersecting the projector from *c'* in *d*. In the same way draw *b c*. The rectangle *a b c d* is the plan. The line *a' b' c' d'* is the elevation.

Ex. 179 A. V.T. makes 45° with *x y*, H.T. 90° draw the plan and elevation of a square lying on the plane with one diagonal horizontal: side of square $1\frac{1}{2}$ inch.

146. When, however, the H.T. is not at right angles to *x y* another elevation must be taken which will give the same condition of things as the last easy case. Take an $x_1 y_1$ at right angles to H.T., Fig. 152, so as to get an elevation which will be

an end view of the plane, and such that the V.T. will contain everything in the plane, and of course the square. To do this, take any point *a* as the plan of a point in the plane, and find its elevation as shown in paragraph 135 on the new x, y.

Fig. 152.

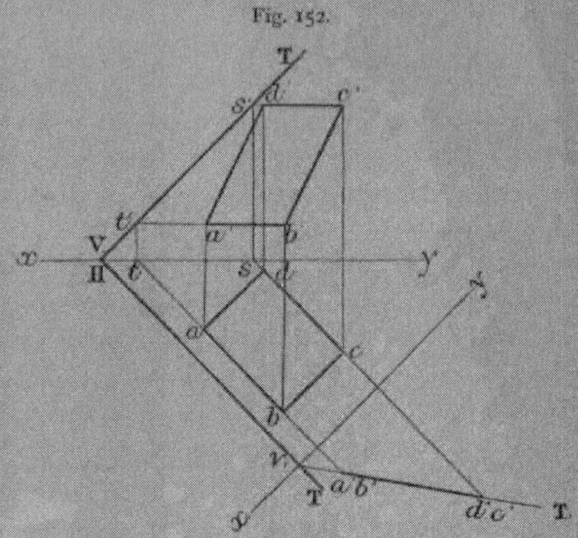

This will be one point in V_1T_1. The other is where $x_1 y_1$ cuts H.T. V_1T_1 bears the same relation to H.T. as V.T. did to H.T. in Fig. 134, so the square can be constructed and its plan found as shown in paragraph 134.

Having found the plan, each point may be projected up into the original vertical plane of projection, as shown in Fig. 150.

Ex. 180. V.T. makes 35° with $x y$, H.T. 45°; draw the plan and elevation of an equilateral triangle lying on the plane with one side horizontal: side of triangle 2 inches.

Ex. 181. Same traces draw the plan and elevation of a rectangle lying on the plane, with one diagonal making the greatest possible angle with H.P: sides of rectangle, 2½ inches and 1¾ inches.

CHAPTER XXXIV.

INCLINED PLANES LAID FLAT ON THE GROUND.

147. SUPPOSE next a plane figure, such as a triangle, is given as lying on a plane whose traces are given, and it is required to find its plan and elevation. To do this it is found convenient often to lay the plane flat out on the ground first, and while there to construct on it the figure. Next, raise plane

Fig. 153.

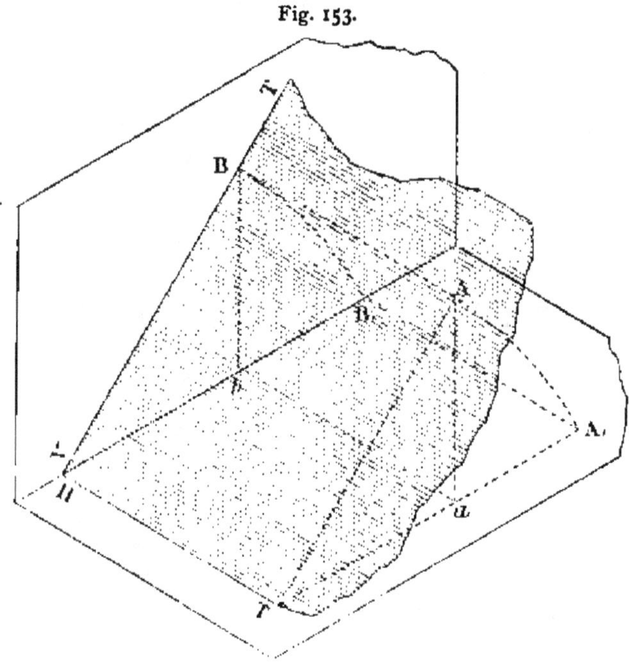

and figure together into its former position, and so get the plan and elevation. Take first the easiest case of planes, that which has the H.T. at right angles to $x y$, Fig. 153. Now, if the plane be laid flat out on the ground it will swing about H.T. as a hinge, and such a point as A in the plane will swing round H.T.

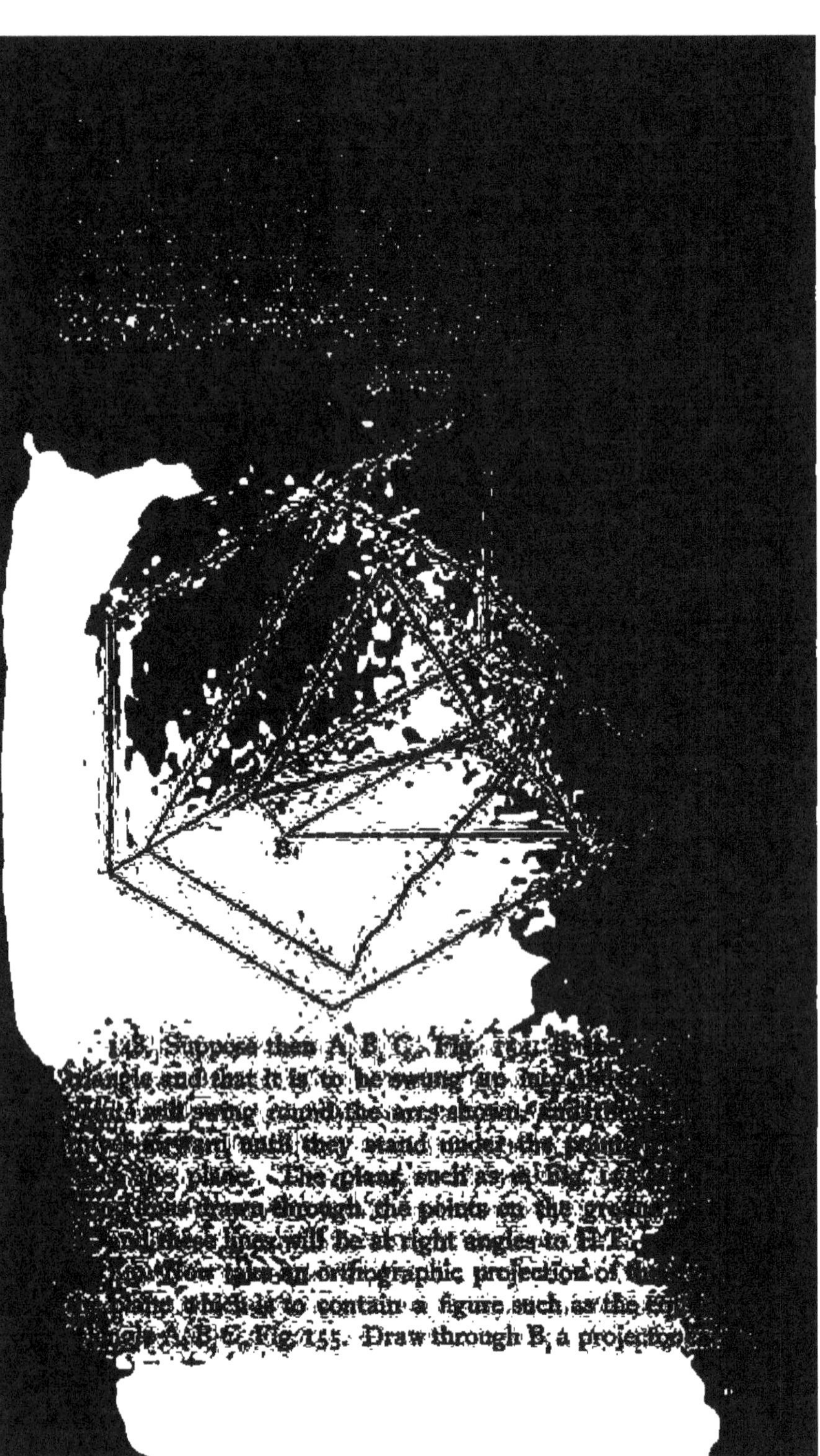

148. Suppose then A, B, C, Fig. 154, [illegible] triangle and that it is to be swung up [illegible] [illegible] will swing round the arcs shown [illegible] [illegible] forward until they stand under the point[illegible] [illegible] the plane. The plans, such as in Fig. 1[illegible] [illegible] lines drawn through the points on the groun[illegible] and these lines will be at right angles to E F.

[illegible] Now take an orthographic projection of the [illegible] plane which is to contain a figure such as the eq[illegible] [illegible] A, B, C, Fig. 155. Draw through B, a projection[illegible] *x y*. About H as centre and distance equal to the distance of projector through B′, describe an arc cutting the V.T. in *b*′. This point *b*′ will be the vertical projection of the point B when it reaches the plane. The plan will travel forward in a line drawn through B, at right angles to its hinge H.T. It

Fig. 155.

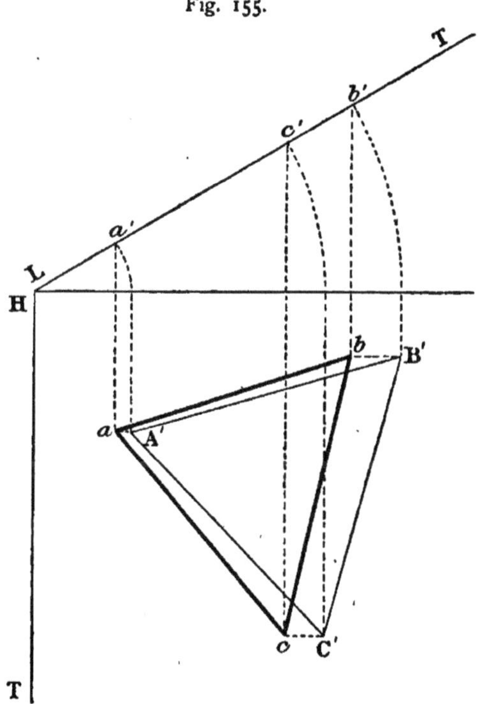

must also lie in the projector from *b*′. It will therefore be at *b* where these two lines intersect; *a* and *c* are found in the same way, and *abc* is the plan of the triangle, and *a*′ *c*′ *b*′ the elevation.

150. When the H.T. is not at right angles to *x y*, a new *x y* is drawn at right angles to H.T., and a new V.T. is taken, so as to get the same condition of things as the above.

Ex. 182. V.T. makes 33°, H.T. 55°. The plan of a figure lying on the plane is a square 1 inch side, and one side is parallel to H.T. Find its true shape.

vertical trace of the plane. **From *a''* measure a distance to represent the side of the base of the pyramid. From *d''* a projector *d' d*. This projector will contain**

Fig. 157.

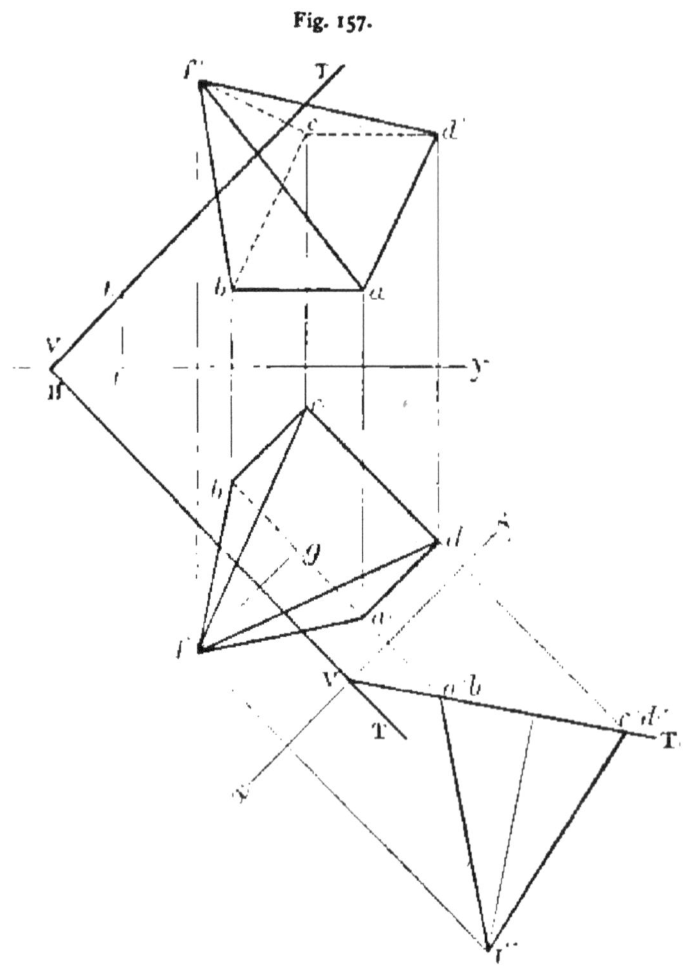

plans of the points. Draw from *a* and *b*, lines at right angles to H.T. These two lines will also contain the plans of *c* and *d*. The plans will be where these last two lines intersect the projector from $c'' d''$. The points c and d are the plans of the remaining corners of the square.

Next bisect $a'' c''$ and draw from the middle of $a'' c''$ the thin line to f'' at right angles to V.T. Make it 1¼ inch in length, equal to the length of the axis. Join $a'' f''$ and $c'' f''$.

Find next the centre of gravity of the plan of the base of the pyramid by joining $b\ d$ and $a\ c$ with their construction lines. These need only be in pencil. The plan of the apex f will lie somewhere in a line drawn from this point e, or from g the middle point of $a\ b$ at right angles to H.T. A projector from f'' will find the plan in $e\ f$. Join f and $a\ b\ c\ d$, and complete the plan of pyramid.

Projectors drawn from the plans of the corners of the pyramid, to the original $x\ y$ will contain the elevations of these corners on the original vertical plane. These vertical projections are easily found, if it be remembered that their heights above $x\ y$ are exactly equal to their heights above $x_1\ y_1$.

Ex. 190. Draw the plan and elevation of a cube which rests on an inclined plane with traces V.T. 30° to $x\ y$ and H.T. 90°: four edges of cube are parallel to H.T: edge of cube 1½ inch.

Ex. 191. Draw the plan and elevation of a tetrahedron, lying on same plane with one side of base parallel to H.T: edge of tetrahedron 1½ inch.

Ex. 192. Draw the plan and elevation of a square based pyramid lying on a plane with two sides of base inclined at 45° to V.P., the lower being ¾ inch high; traces of plane V.T. 30° and H.T. 45°; side of base 1¼ inch; length of axis 2½ inches.

Ex. 193. Draw plan and elevation of the tetrahedron described in Ex. 191 lying on the inclined plane, Ex. 192, with one side of base making greatest possible angle with H.P. Also draw plan and elevation of same solid, when one face is on the plane, and one edge is parallel to V.P.

CHAPTER XXXVI.

LINES IN PLANES INCLINED TO THE H.P.

154. A LINE is sometimes given as being contained in a plane, and at the same time as making a given angle with H.P. In finding the projections of such a line recourse is had to an ingenious device. The device is this. A point is taken in the plane from which to draw the line, and this point is taken as the apex of a cone whose slant sides have exactly the

Fig. 158.

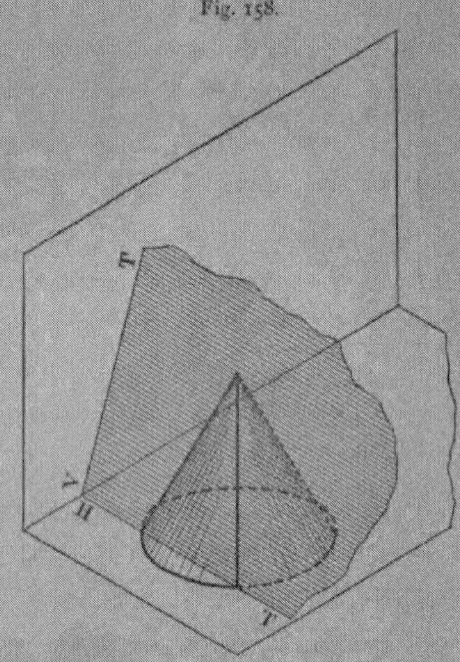

same inclination as the line has to the H.P. Now the reasoning is of this kind. All lines drawn from the apex of the cone to the base of the cone will make the same angle with the ground, and this angle will be equal to the given angle. The base of the cone cuts the H.T. in two places, and lines drawn from the apex of the cone, to the points of section of base of cone and H.T. will be contained by the surface of the cone, as well as by the plane itself. But the inclination of all lines in the cone have the given inclination. Therefore, the lines from apex to points of section have given inclination and are contained by the plane. This is clearly shown in Fig. 158. In Fig. 159 the line is shown in orthographic projection.

155. Take *a* as the plan of the point from which the line has to be drawn. Find *a'* and take A as the apex of a cone

Fig. 159.

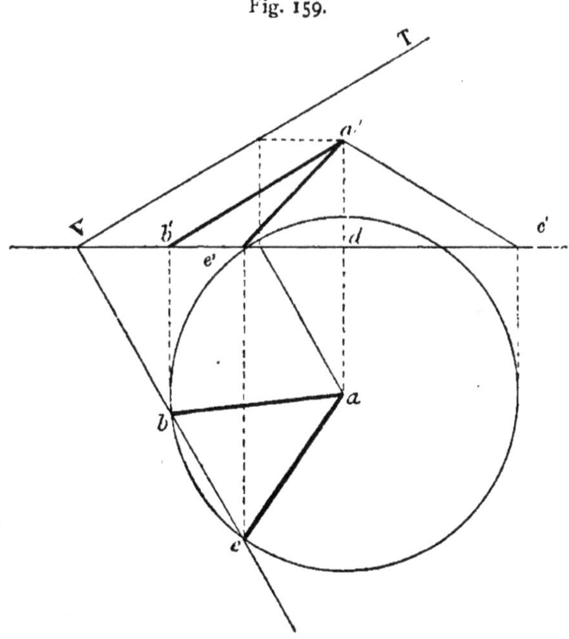

having the same inclination as the required line. Draw the elevation of the cone, with *b a'* making same angle, as the angle which the line has to make with H.P. Draw a circle about *a* to represent the plan of cone, and join *a* with the points *e* and *b*, the intersections of circle with H.T. Find *a' b'*, the elevation of the A B line. The line a' e', a e is another line in the plane having the same inclination.

156. Again, suppose a b, Fig. 159, is a line in the plane, a part of this line may be supposed to be the side of a square

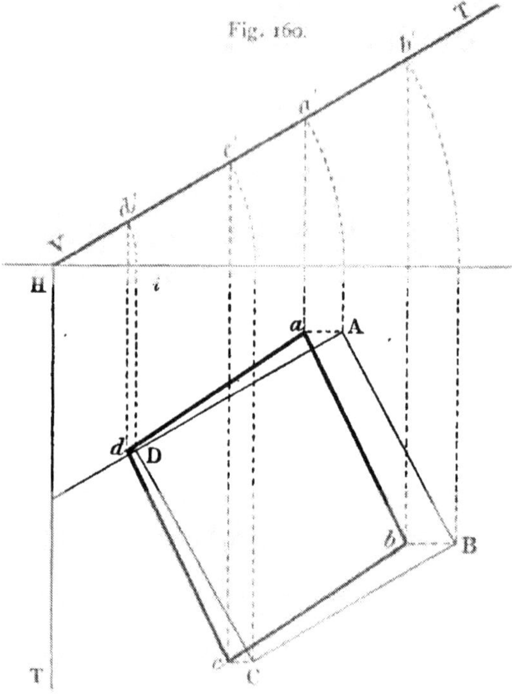

having this inclination, and the problem would then resolve itself into one in which a square has one side inclined at a given angle to the horizontal plane, and with its plane inclined also at a given angle to the horizontal plane.

157. To find the plan, first lay the line down on the ground construct on A D, Fig. 160, the figure required, such as are in figure. As the square is lifted into its place, the corners will travel forward in lines at right angles same inclin...y will be found in the lines A a, D d, B b, and C c. reasoning is is to find the elevation of the square. It will of the cone the point a' will be one. Draw a projector from with the grou

D, and about H as centre and radius equal to distance of projector describe an arc cutting V.T. d' is the elevation of d. In the same way, find b' and c', and from each draw projectors cutting the horizontal lines drawn through A B C D. The points of intersection, a, b, c, and d, of those lines will be the plans required. A B C D might, in the same way, be taken as the plan of a cube which has an edge and face making certain angles with the horizontal plane.

Ex. 194. A square has one side making 30° to H.P., its plane makes 45°. The nearest corner to H.P. is ½ inch from it. Show plan and elevation.

Ex. 195. A cube has one edge making 20° to H.P. and one face making 30° to H.P. Show plan and elevation.

Ex. 196. A pyramid side 1¼" has one side of square base making 30° to H.P., plane of base 45° to H.P. The length of axis is 2½ inches. Show plan and elevation.

158. If two lines, $a\,b$, $a\,c$, Fig. 161, whose projections are given, meet in space, the plane containing them can be found by finding the traces of the lines. The H.T. of the plane will go through the horizontal traces of the lines, and the V.T. of the plane is found thus. Through a draw a line $a\,t$ parallel to H.T. and from the point where it cuts $x\,y$ draw a projector. Through a' draw a line $a'\,t'$ parallel to $x\,y$. The point of intersection t' is a point in the V.T. The point T where H.T. cuts $x\,y$ is another. The line V.T. is therefore the vertical trace.

Ex. 197. V.T. makes 59° with $x\,y$, H.T. makes 75°. A point B is 2¼ inches from V.P., and 1¼ inch from H.P. Show plan and elevation of a cone with apex B, and having same inclination as plane.

Ex. 198. V.T. makes 40°, H.T. 60°. C is a point in the plane 2¾ inches from V.T., and 1½ inch high. Show plan and elevation of a cone with apex C, and with slant side having same inclination to V.P. as plane, Fig. 159.

Ex. 199. V.T. makes 35° to $x\,y$, H.T. makes 55°. A point D in the plane is 2¾ inches from V.P., and 2 inches from H.P. Show plan and elevation of a cone with apex D, and with slant side touching the plane.

Ex. 200. H.T. makes 35°. Find the V.T. of a plane making 60° with H.P.

Ex. 201. V.T. makes 73°. Find H.T. of a plane making 33° to H.P.

Fig. 161.

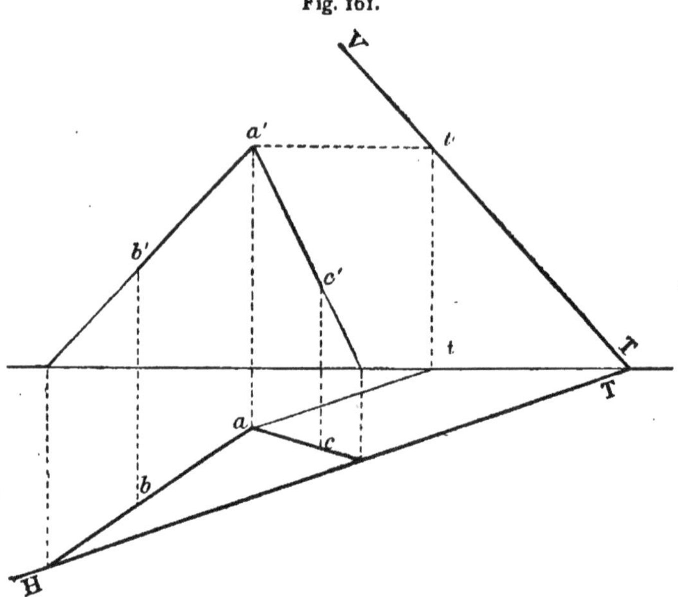

Ex. 202. V.T. makes 35°. Find the H.T. of a plane inclined at 60° to H.P.

Ex. 203. H.T. makes 75° to xy. Find the V.T. of a plane inclined 32° to V.P.

The limits of the inclination of the line are of course the inclination of the plane, for the line cannot be steeper than the plane; else the base of cone would fail to be within H.T., and could not cut it. We can have all lines between that and a horizontal line; that is from 0° to the inclination of the plane.

Ex. 204. V.T. 35°, H.T. 60°. Draw the plan and elevation of a line in the plane making an angle of 30° with H.P.

Ex. 205. V.T. makes 25° to xy, H.T. 75°. Show plan and elevation of a line in the plane making an angle of 30° with H.P.

Ex. 206. V.T. makes 30°, H.T. makes 70°. Show plan and elevation of a line in the plane making an angle of 30° with H.P.

Ex. 207. Same traces, draw the plan and elevation of a line in the plane making angle of 25° with H.P., the highest point being 1 inch high.

Ex. 208. Same traces and same line; but with line 1¼ inches in length.

CHAPTER XXXVII.

THE TRUE ANGLE BETWEEN TWO LINES LYING ON PLANES.

159. SUPPOSE next that the plans and elevations of two lines A B and A C are given, and that it is required to find the angle between them.

160. The true angle C A B between the lines C A and B A will not be shown by the angle *b a c*, Fig. 162, made by the plans of the lines. To find the true angle between them it is necessary to lay the lines down on the horizontal plane.

This is done as shown in Fig. 163. First the horizontal traces of the lines are found as shown in Fig. 162, and the horizontal trace of the plane which contains the lines. These lines and plane containing them are laid down on the ground as shown in Fig. 163. That is the points *a b c*, where the ends of the lines meet the ground, are found, as has been explained above, and then the angle contained *ba* and *c a* is measured. This is the true angle.

Ex. 209. B C is at right angles to *x y* and in H.P. A is 1 inch high, and the plans of C A and B A contain an angle of 60°. Find the true angle between the lines.

If the plane containing the lines has its H.T. not at right angles to *xy*, we can take a vertical plane at right angles to *xy*, and then get the required lines under the same conditions as before.

161. So if the projections of three points A B C, Fig. 164, are given, the traces of the plane containing them are found by finding the traces of the lines joining them, *a b* and *a c*, as shown, Fig. 164.

Fig. 162.

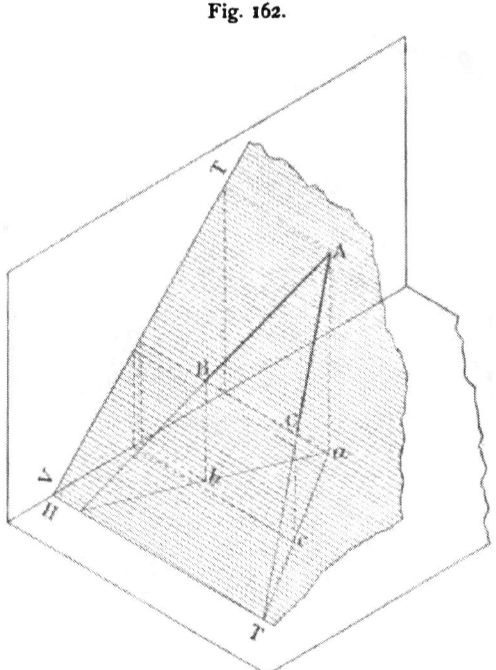

The true length of a line in a plane could be obtained by taking a vertical plane parallel to *a b* the plan of A B, and projecting the line *a b* on to that plane. The projection thus obtained would show its true length.

But there is another way of getting the true length of a line, and that is by laying down flat on the horizontal plane the inclined plane containing that line. For example, the line *a* B, Fig. 163, shows the true length of the line A B.

Ex. 210. V.T. makes 35° with *xy*, H.T. 90°. A line whose plan is 2¾ inches is in the plane, and its inclination to H.P. is 25° Find its true length.

Fig. 163.

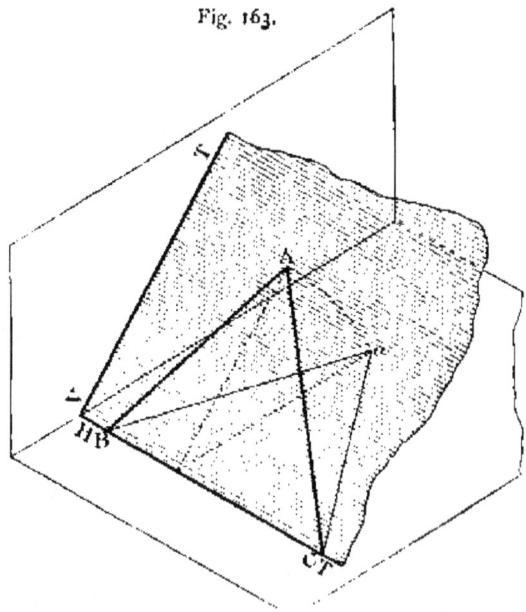

Fig. 164.

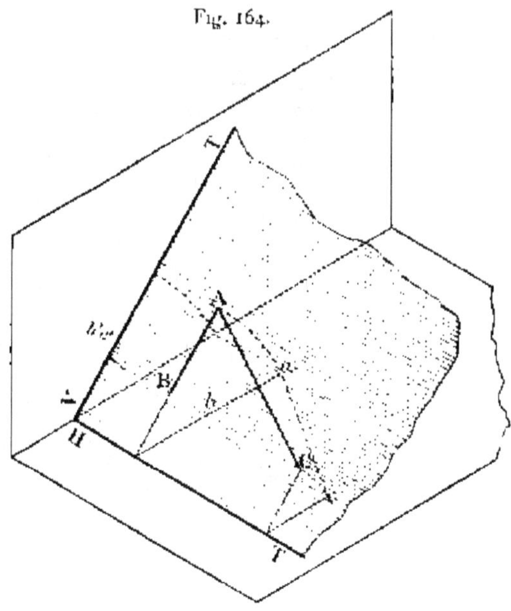

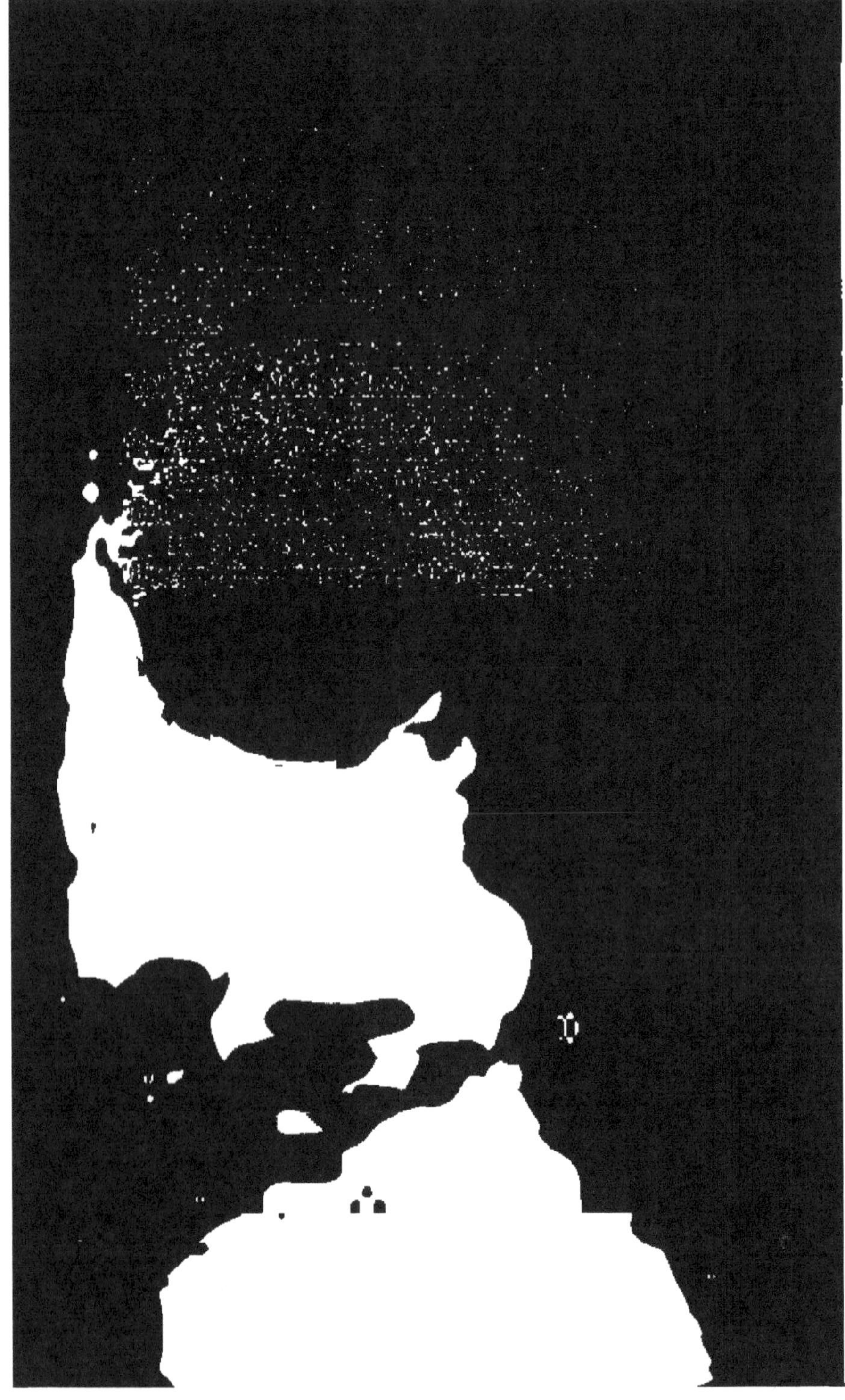

SECTION VI.

TANGENT PLANES.

CHAPTER XXXVIII.

PLANES TANGENT TO A CONE.

162. WHEN a plane rests against or touches a cylindrical, or spherical surface, it is said to be tangent to that surface.

The three sketches, Figs. 165, 166, and 167, show three examples of tangent planes. The lines *a b* in figures are the lines of contact, and in each case the perpendicular to the surface of the solid where the plane touches, is at right angles to the plane. In the case of a plane being tangent to a cone

Fig. 165.

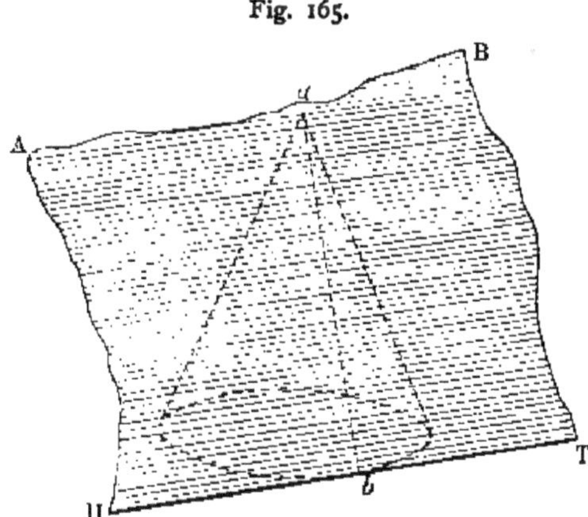

the horizontal trace of the plane, one of the factors to be found, will be tangent to the base of the cone.

These planes which lie against the solids of revolution, the cone, the cylinder and the sphere above, are just like stiff sheets of cardboard. The subject can be very easily illustrated by the use of wooden models of a cone, a sphere, and a cylinder, and a piece of white cardboard.

Fig. 166.

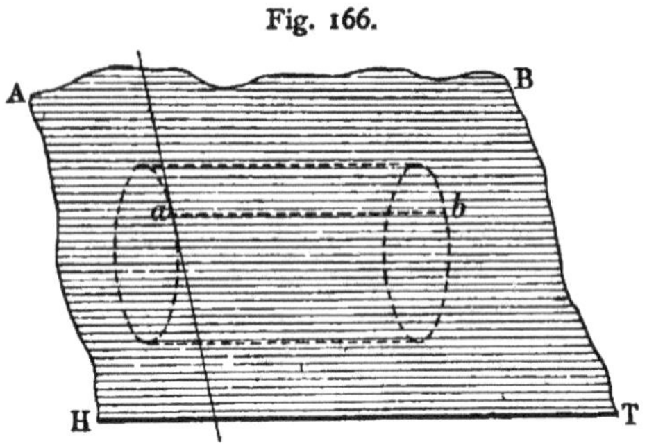

Fig. 167.

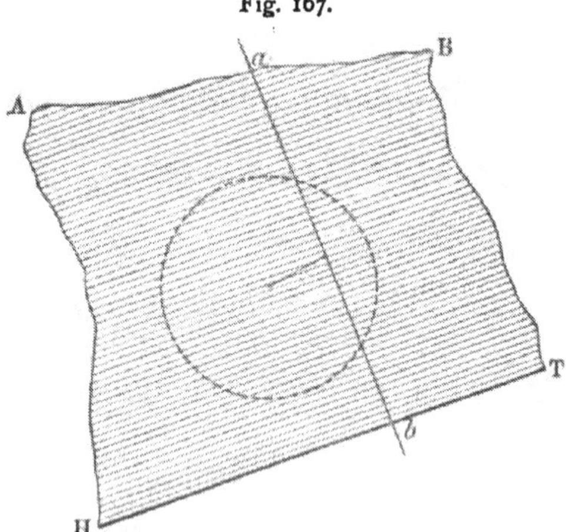

163. The simplest case is when the tangent plane touches a cone, and at the same time is at right angles to the vertical plane. Fig. 168, shows a picture of a cone standing on the horizontal plane, with a shaded inclined plane resting against it. In this case, it is seen that H.T. is at right angles to the $x\,y$, and that the plane touches a generating line, which is parallel to the vertical plane. The apex of the cone which has a tangent plane resting against it will of course always be

contained by the plane; but in this particular case, the vertical trace which contains all the vertical projection of the plane, contains also the vertical projection of the apex.

Fig. 168.

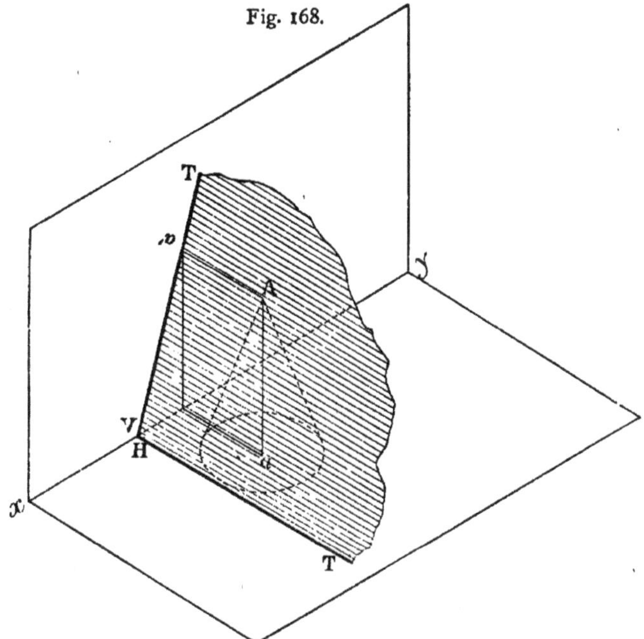

164. This problem would present itself to the student in the following form:—The plan and elevation of a cone are given, and it is required to draw the traces of a plane touching the cone along a generating line parallel to the vertical plane.

Suppose then, that the circle shown in picture, Fig. 168, and in orthographic projection, Fig. 169, represents the plan of the base of the cone. Let *b* represent the plan of the apex and *b* the elevation.

We want the traces of the plane. First then we see by the picture that the H.T. will be at right angles to *x y*. So draw a line tangent to the circle, and at right angles to *x y*. The V.T. always begins where the H.T. cuts *x y*. So T is a point in the vertical trace. The vertical trace contains the vertical projection of the apex of the cone, so *b'* is a second point in the vertical trace. Draw V.T. through *b'* and T. V.T. is the vertical trace of the tangent plane required.

Fig. 169.

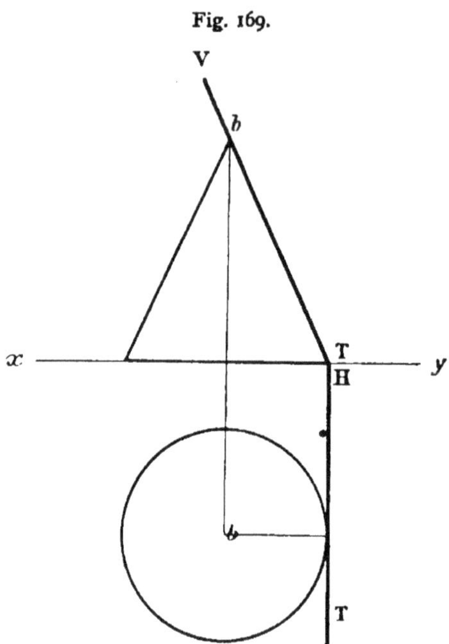

165. Suppose next the plan of a generating line *a b* is given in the cone, which is not parallel to V.P. Here the horizontal trace of the plane which contains *a b* will be at right angles to it, and tangent to the base of the cone at the point *b*.

So draw H.T., Fig. 171, tangent to the circle which repre sents the base at the point B and find *e*, the point where H.T. cuts *x y*. Next, draw a horizontal line A *c* through A the apex of the cone, cutting the V.P. in *c*. The point *c'*, the vertical projection of *c*, will be one point in the vertical trace; V is another. So V.T. is the trace required.

166. The orthographic projection of the plane and cone are shown in Fig. 171. The construction is this. Let *a b* be

Fig. 170.

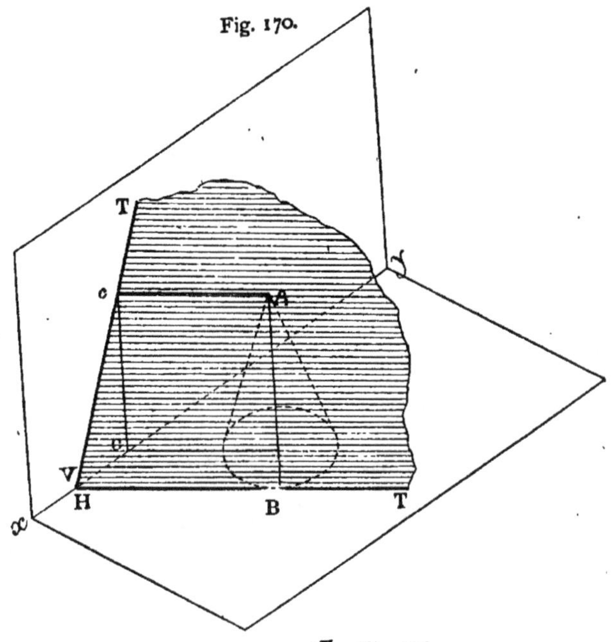

Fig. 171.

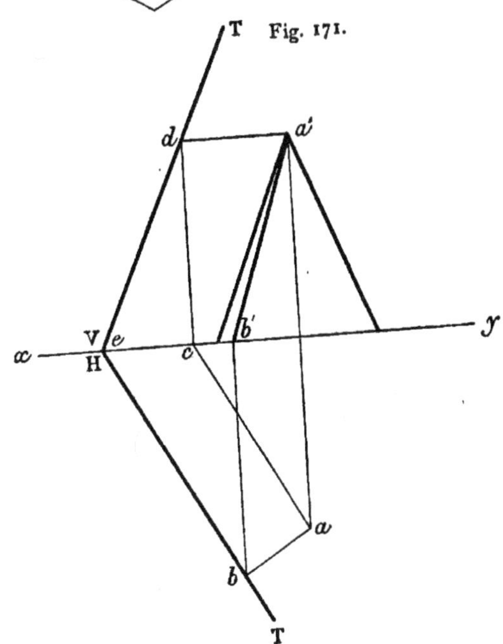

the plan and $a' b'$ be the elevation of the generating line in the cone along which the plane lies. Draw H.T. at right angles to the plan of the line $a\ b$, find e where it cuts $x\ y$. Draw $a\ c$, the plan of a horizontal line through the plan of the apex. The height of this line is equal to the height of the apex. So draw a horizontal line through a' until it cuts the projector $c\ d$. d is a point in the vertical trace. Through e and d draw a line $e\ d$—this line is the vertical trace of the plane.

CHAPTER XXXIX.

INCLINED PLANES TANGENT TO THE CYLINDER.

167. TAKE next the case of a cylinder A B, Fig. 172, and suppose that a tangent plane is to be drawn and its traces found when it touches the cylinder along the line $c\ d$. First draw $x_, y_,$ at right angles to the axis of the cylinder, and show a vertical projection of the cylinder on the new vertical plane shown to the right. The projection will be a circle, and it will contain the point $c\ d$. Draw a tangent to the circle at this point. This tangent will be the end view of a plane tangent to the cylinder. H.T. drawn from the point where the V.T. in this plane meets $x_, y_{,,}$ and at right angles to the $x_, y_,$ will be the horizontal trace of the plane. Produce $d\ c$ to i, and draw a line $h\ i$ in the original V.P. This line is the vertical trace of the tangent plane.

168. The orthographic projection of the traces of the plane to be found, and the method of finding it, will be easily understood after studying the above figure. Let $a\ b$, Fig. 173, be the line of the cylinder on which the plane is to rest. Take a vertical projection of the cylinder on $x' y'$ at right angles to the plan of the axis. Draw $V_, T_,$ through $a'' b''$ tangent to the circle at that point, and from the point where the line meets $x_, y_,$. Draw H.T. parallel to $a\ b$, and produce $a\ b$ until it meets $x\ y$. The point e will have the same height as $a'' b''$ or $a' b'$.

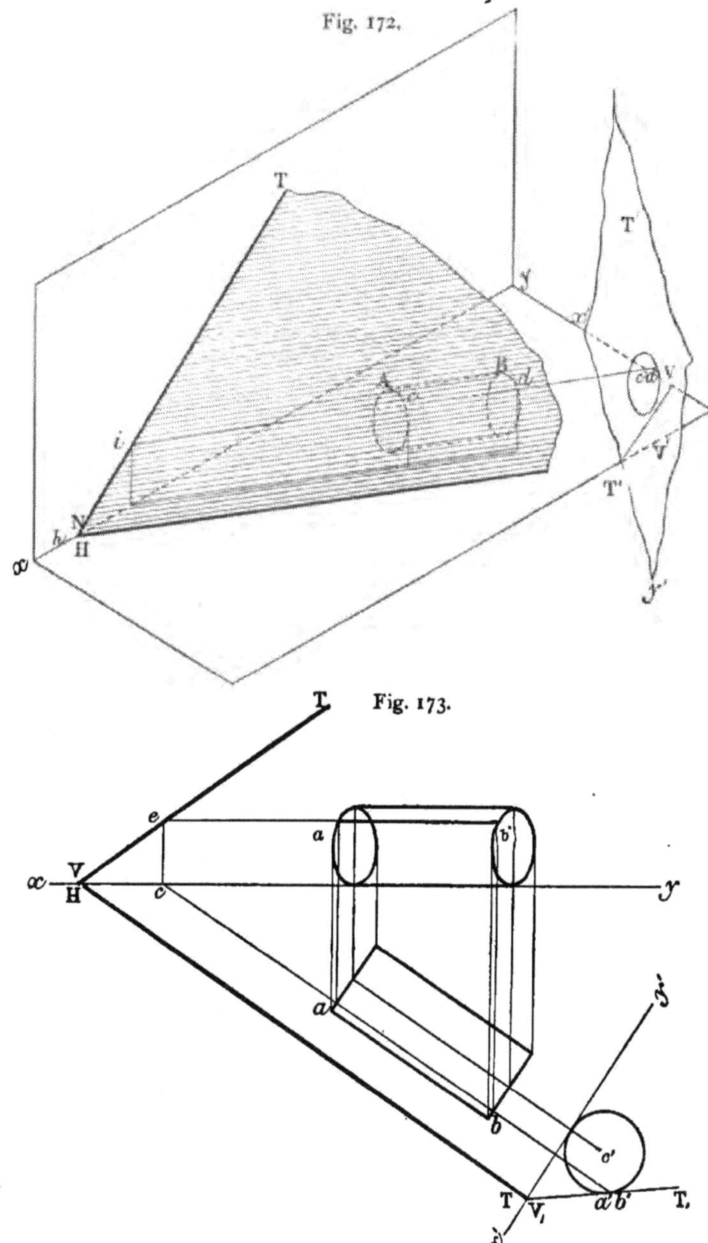

Fig. 172.

Fig. 173.

Through H *e'* draw a line. This line is the vertical trace of the required plane.

Ex. 216. Show traces of plane touching cylinder, 2 inches diameter along line *a b*, Fig. 174.

Fig. 174.

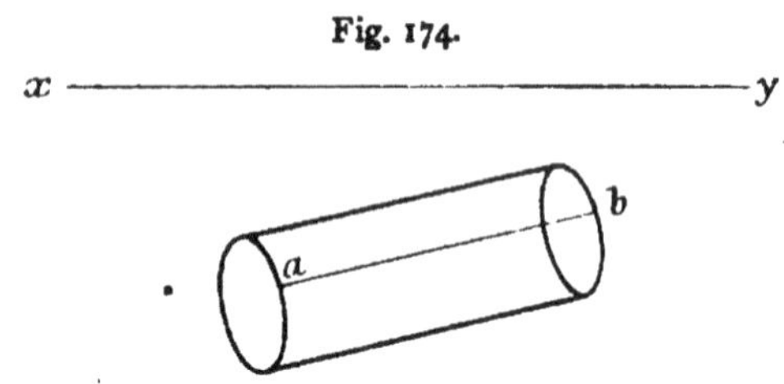

Show plane touching sphere at point *a*, 2 inches high, plan in line making 30° to *x y*; diameter of sphere 3 inches.

CHAPTER XL.

TANGENT PLANES TO TWO CONES.

169. TAKE next two cones having the same vertical angle, and suppose the traces of a common tangent plane to both cones is required.

170. The plane will lie against both cones, and at the ground must of necessity touch the bases of the cones. But the ground line where the plane touches the two circles, is the horizontal trace of the plane. Therefore, a line drawn tangent to the circles which represent the bases of the cones, will be the horizontal trace of the plane. This is clearly shown in the picture, Fig. 175. The line H.T. is the horizontal trace, and H is a point in the vertical trace.

If a horizontal line be drawn along the plane passing through the apex of either cone as shown, it will meet the vertical plane in a point which will give another point in the vertical trace. The line V.T. is shown in the picture, passing through this point, and through H the point where H.T. cuts *x y*.

Fig. 175.

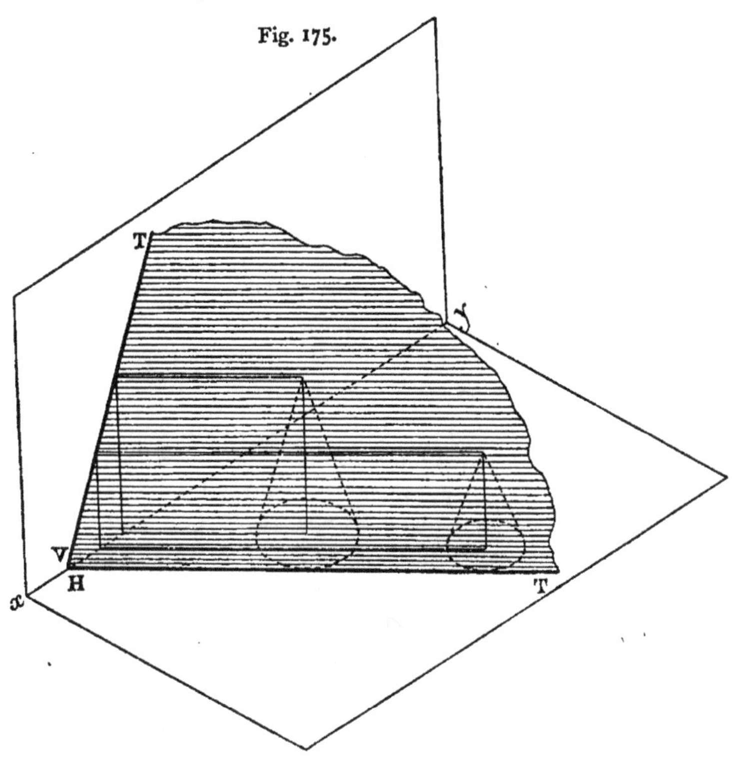

Fig. 176.

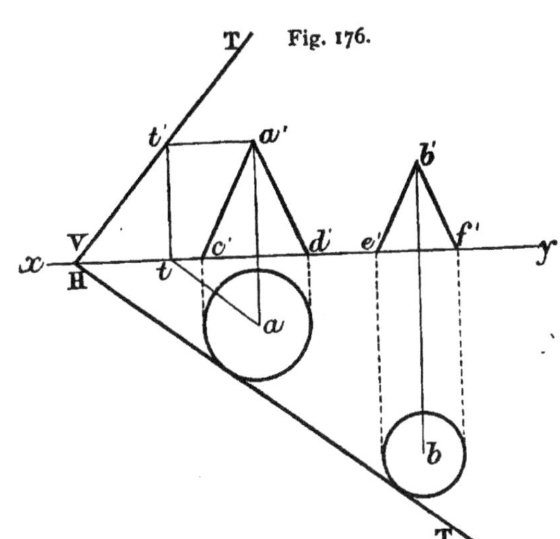

171. Let the circles in Fig. 176 be the plans, and *c' a' d'* and *e' b' f'* be the elevations of two cones with equal vertical angles. As has been explained above, H.T. drawn tangent to the two circles will be the horizontal trace. H, the point where the horizontal trace cuts *x y*, will be one point in the vertical trace. To find another point, draw a horizontal line *a t* through *a* the apex of the larger cone. The point *t* is the plan of the point where this line meets the vertical plane. The height of *t* will be *t'* equal to the height of *a'*. So the second point in V.T. is found, and V.T. drawn through H *t'* is the vertical trace of the plane required.

172. When a common tangent plane of given inclination to two spheres is required, it will be found convenient to envelop both spheres with cones whose slant sides have the given inclination. The tangent plane to the two cones will touch both spheres and have the given inclination.

Let the circles, Fig. 177, represent the plans and elevations of two spheres of different radii, and suppose the inclination of the common tangent plane is to be 70° to H.P. Begin with the elevations, and draw two lines touching each cone; each line being inclined to *x y* at an angle of 70°. Draw two circles to represent the bases of the cones. It is quite clear that any plane which touches either cone will touch the enveloped sphere, because the sphere touches the cone all round. As the cone has an inclination of 70°, the plane which lies against it must also have, of necessity, an inclination of 70°. The tangent plane has to touch both spheres, and consequently both cones, so its H.T. will be tangent to the two circles which are the plans of the cones.

Draw then the H.T. of the required plane tangent to the two plans of the bases. Draw a horizontal line through the apex *c* and so find the point *e'*, where this horizontal line meets the vertical plane. A line through *f*, the point where H.T. meets *xy*, and passing through *e'*, is the V.T. of the required plane.

Ex. 217. The centre of a sphere 1 inch diameter is ½ inch in front of V.P., and the centre of another sphere ¾ inch diameter is 1 inch in front of H.P., both stand on the ground. Find the traces of a plane tangent to both spheres and inclined at 60° to the H.P.

Fig. 177.

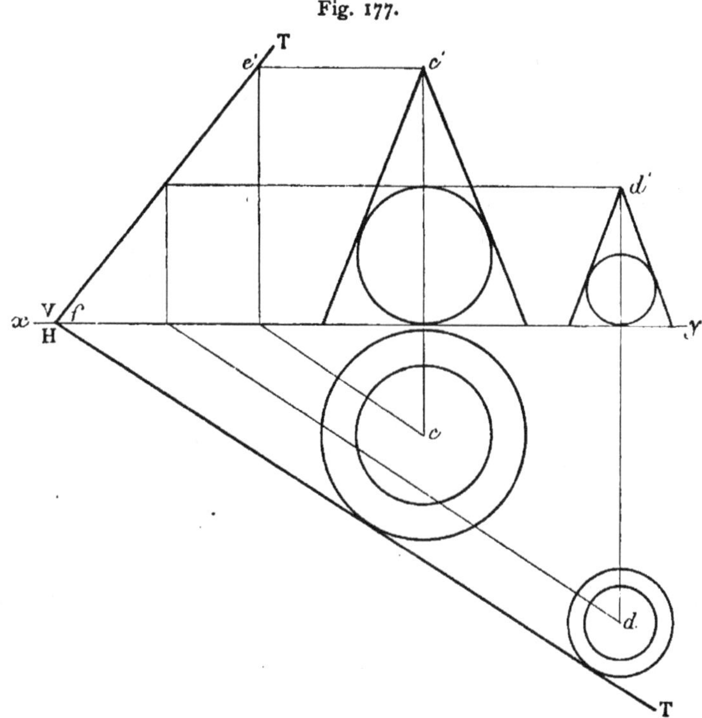

Ex. 218. Two spheres, 2 inches and 1½ inch diameter, with centres 3 inches apart, the centre of larger 1¼ inch from V.P. The centre of the other 2 inches from *x y*. Show plane inclined at 60° touching them.

173. If it be next required that the plane, must contain a given point as well as be a common tangent to two spheres, the problem becomes slightly more complicated, and requires more work in the construction, but does not require any more mental effort. In such a case the enveloping cones are again used, and both are taken with a common apex. The cones have their axes slanting, and their bases are ellipses. The

H.T. is the tangent to the bases. A horizontal line is drawn through *a* meeting the V.P. The V.T. is a line passing through this point and that where H.T. meets *xy*.

Fig. 178.

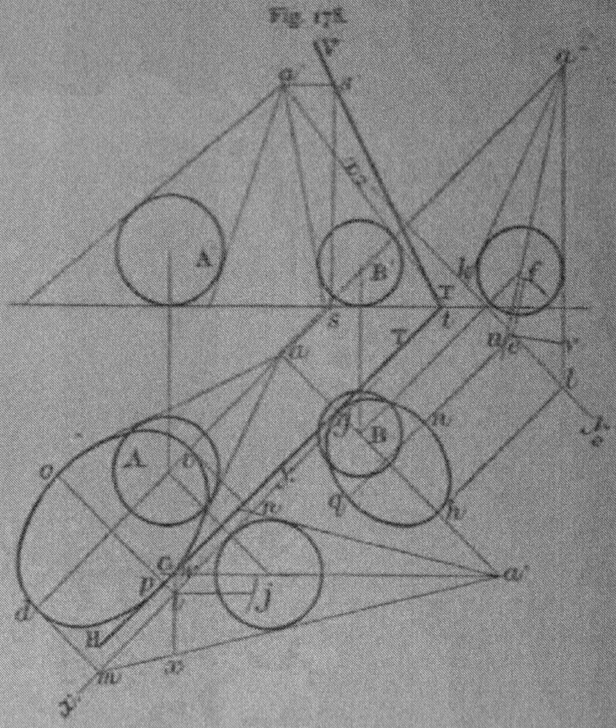

174. Suppose A and B, Fig. 178, are the two spheres, and *a a'* the projections of the point which is to be contained by the plane.

Show a vertical projection of A and the point *a* on $x_1 y_1$ a plane parallel to the axis of the cone with *a* as apex and enveloping A. Do the same with B on $x_2 y_2$. *c d* is the major axis of the first cone, *g h* the major axis of the second. The minor axes of the two cones are found in the following way:—

Bisect *k l* in *e* and draw $a''' u$ bisecting angle of cone. Draw *u v* through *e* at right angles to $a''' u$. And about *u* as centre and *u v* as radius describe an arc. Draw *e f* parallel to $a''' u$.

The line *ef* is half the minor axis of the smaller ellipse. Bisect *mn* in *i*. Draw *a″ w* bisecting angle of cone. Draw *w x* through *i* at right angles to *w a″*. About *w* with radius *w x* describe arc. Draw *ij* parallel to axis of cone. The line *ij* is the minor axis of the larger ellipse. Construct the ellipses.

The horizontal trace of the inclined plane which contains the point A and touches the enveloping cones, and consequently the spheres will be tangent to the bases of the cones. So draw H.T. tangent to the ellipses.

Draw *a s* parallel to H.T. The point *s* will be the same height as *a*. Draw a projector from *s* and through *a′* a horizontal line. The point *s′* is a point in the V.T. The V.T. will be the line through *s′* and *t* the point where H.T. meets *x y*.

CHAPTER XLI.

TANGENT PLANE TO CONTAIN POINT AND TOUCH CONE.

175. THE last case is when a tangent plane is to be found which contains a given point and is tangent to a cone.

Suppose A, Fig. 179, is the given point, and it is required to find a plane containing A and tangent to the cone in figure.

If the plane touches the cone it must contain the apex B.

A plane which contains B and A will contain the line passing through B A. Also B A produced will meet the ground at some point in the horizontal trace of the plane. The horizontal trace will then pass through T, and be tangent to the base of the cone.

The point where T B meets the vertical plane will also be a point in the V.T. Or a horizontal line drawn through A or B to the vertical plane will find a point in the vertical trace. H of course is another point.

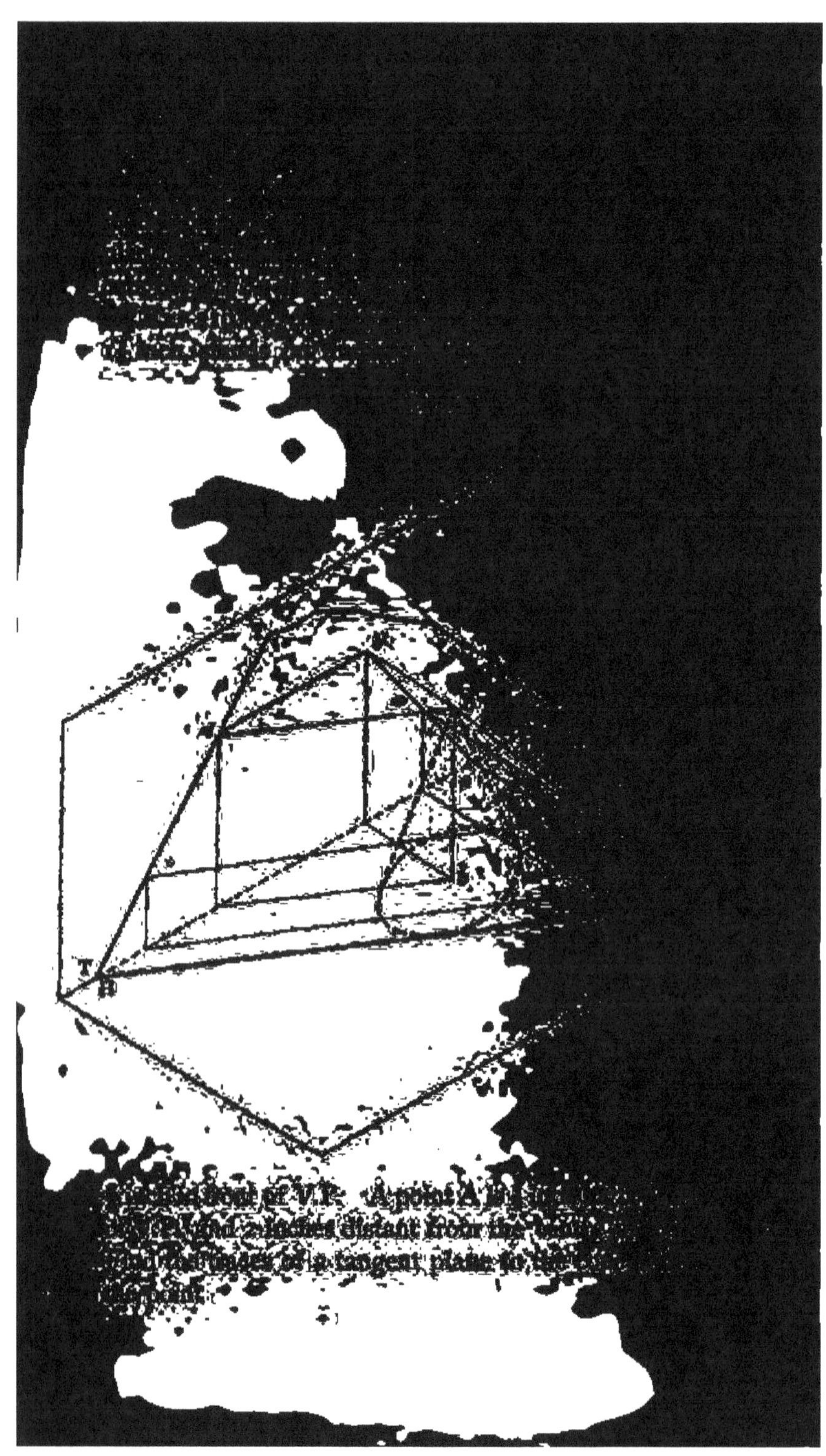

[illegible] foot of V.P. A point A is [illegible] V.P. and 2 inches distant from the [illegible] the traces of a tangent plane to the [illegible] the point.

Ex. 220. A plane contains a point B $1\frac{1}{2}$ inch high and 1 inch from V.P., and touches a cone 3 inches high, base

Fig. 180.

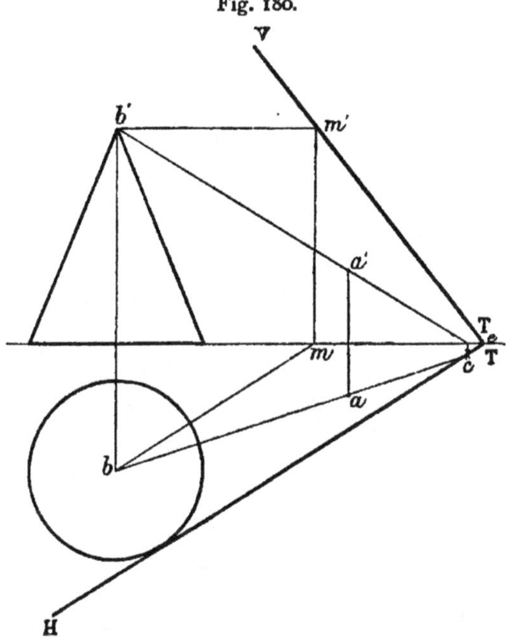

2 inches diameter. Centre of base is $1\frac{1}{2}$ inch from V.P., and 2 inches from plan of point B. Find traces of plane.

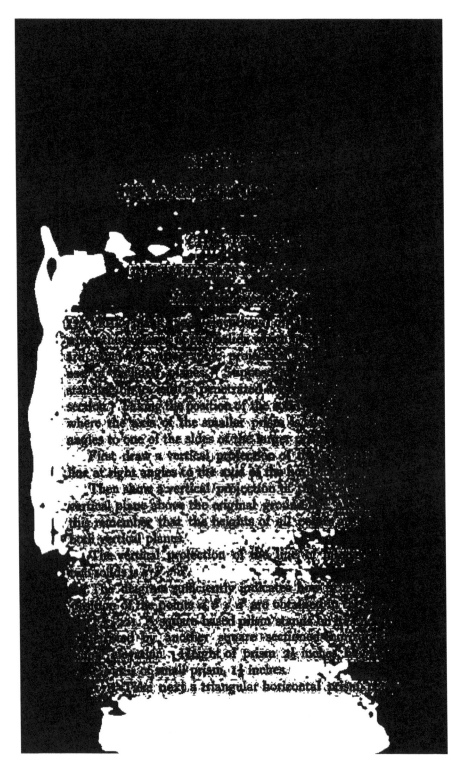

a square-based pyramid. First take the long edges of the triangular prism parallel to V.P., as shown in Fig. 183.

Fig. 181.

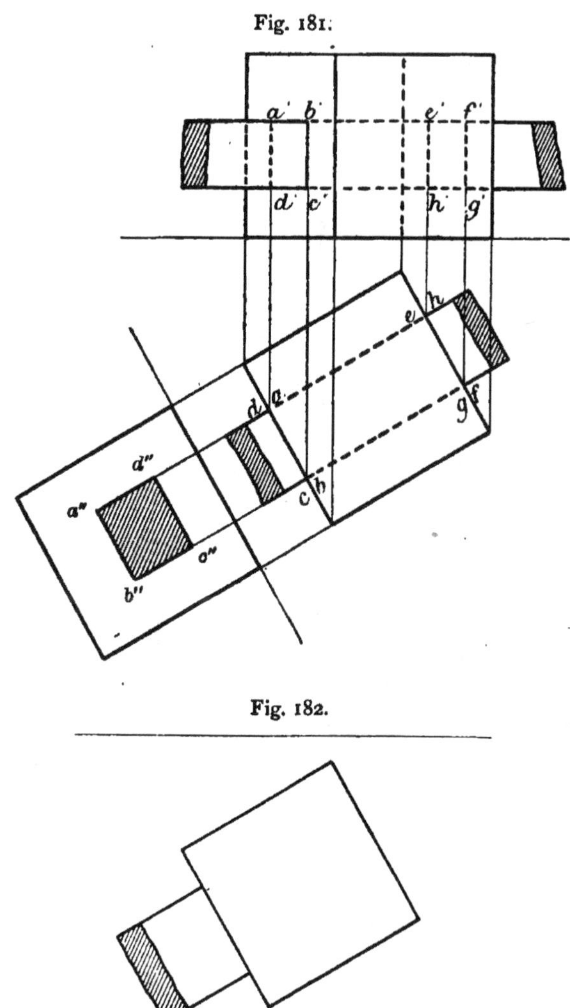

Fig. 182.

Take a vertical projection of the two prisms on a plane at right angles to the axis of the triangular prism.

Draw a line through $a'' f''$, cutting the vertical projection of the larger pyramid in the point *i*". Find plan of I and join *i a*. The elevation of *f*", the edge of the prism, is in *a*" *i*, and therefore its plan will be in *i a*. From *f*" draw a projector to *i a*. *f* is the point required.

Fig. 183.

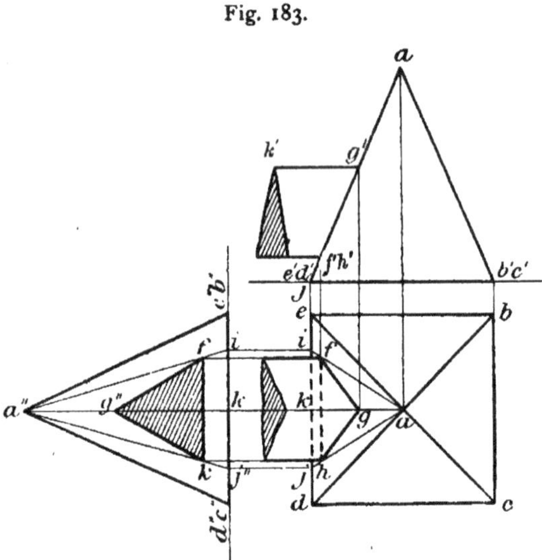

In the same way find *h* and join *f h* with a dotted line. Draw a vertical projection on the original vertical plane, draw a projector from *f*, and measure a height *f'*, equal to *f*". Draw a horizontal line *m g'* at a height equal to *g*". A projector from *g'* finds *g* in *a g*". Join *f g* and *g h*. *f g h* is the figure required.

179. Of course there is an easier method for working this particular problem. It is not necessary in this particular case to draw an auxiliary elevation. The line *k' g'*, can be drawn to represent the vertex of the prism at the given height, while another line can be drawn to represent the base. From *g'*, the point where the vertex of prism meets the elevation, a projector can be drawn. The point where this projector meets *k g*, the plan of vertex, is one point in the intersection. By drawing -jectors from the intersecting points of the lower edges of

the prism, the points *f* and *h* are found. This last method is only applicable in particularly easy cases of interpenetration.

180. Next take the case of a triangular prism penetrating a pyramid in the way shown in sketch. This being one of the more difficult problems in penetration, it will be best to confine the attention to the line where the two solids intersect on the right hand side of the pyramid.

First draw a vertical projection of the pyramid on a ground line at right angles to the axis of the triangular prism. Draw through *e''* and *g''*, a line meeting the base in the point *f''*.

Fig. 184.

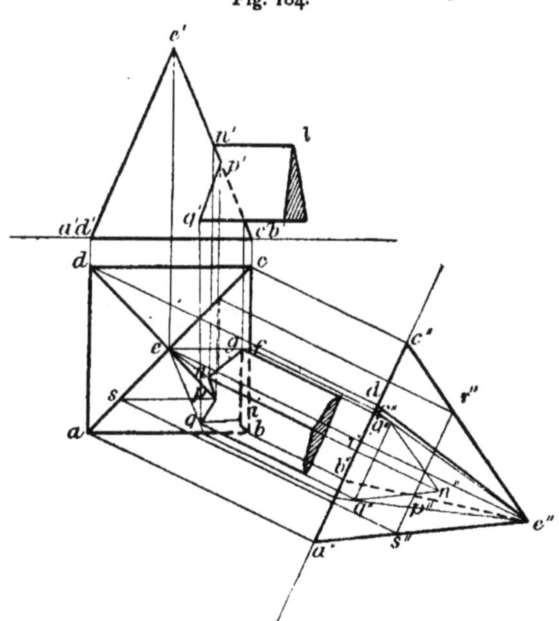

From *f''* draw a projector cutting the plan of the base in *f*. Join *e f*. Draw a projector from *g''*, cutting *e f* in *g*. *g* is one point in the intersection.

Next draw a line through *e''* and *n''*, and draw a projector from the point where this line cuts the base. Join the point where this projector cuts the base and *e*. The point where *n'' n* meets this line is the point required. As this projector and the ridge of the triangular prism are very nearly parallel, it is difficult to find the exact point where they meet, so the following construction is found better in such cases.

Draw any horizontal line in V.P., making n' equal to the height of n''. Let it cut $e'c'$ in n'. Draw a projector from n'' and find where it cuts the plan of the ridge of prism. This point n of the intersection of the ridge and the projector is the point required.

Then draw $g\ o$ parallel to $c\ b$, to represent the horizontal base of prism. From o draw $o\ q$ parallel to $a\ b$, to represent the other part of base. The point q is another extreme point of intersection, and it is found thus. Draw $e''\ q''$ and find its plan $e\ q$. The line $e\ q$ terminates $o\ q$.

Fig. 185. Fig. 186.

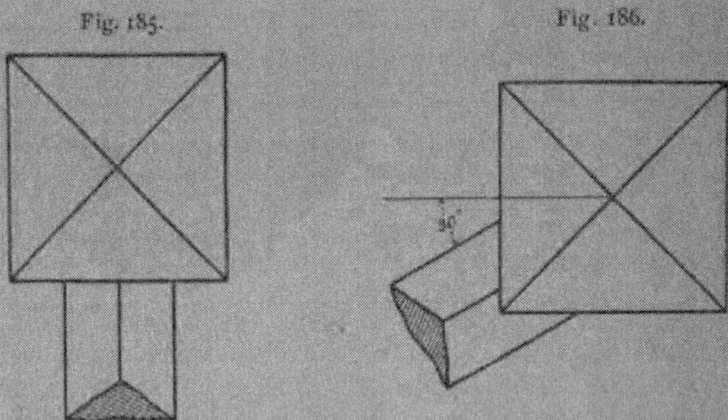

Lastly, find where the prism cuts $e\ b$. Draw through p'', the point where $e''\ b''$, the elevation of $e\ b$, cuts the prism, a horizontal line $p''\ s''$. From s'' draw a projector to s. Through s draw a horizontal line $s\ p$. The point p is that required.

Ex. 222. Prick this Fig. 185 on to your paper, and show the curve of interpenetration. Length of axis of pyramid 2 inches, and the edges of the prism which is equilateral in section are horizontal; the lower being $\frac{1}{2}''$ high.

Ex. 223. Show the curve of interpenetration of the solids, Fig. 186, dimensions same as in last exercise.

CHAPTER XLIII.

INTERPENETRATION OF CYLINDRICAL SURFACES.

181 TWO CYLINDERS:—The most convenient method of finding the intersection of solids for this kind of interpenetra-

Fig. 187.

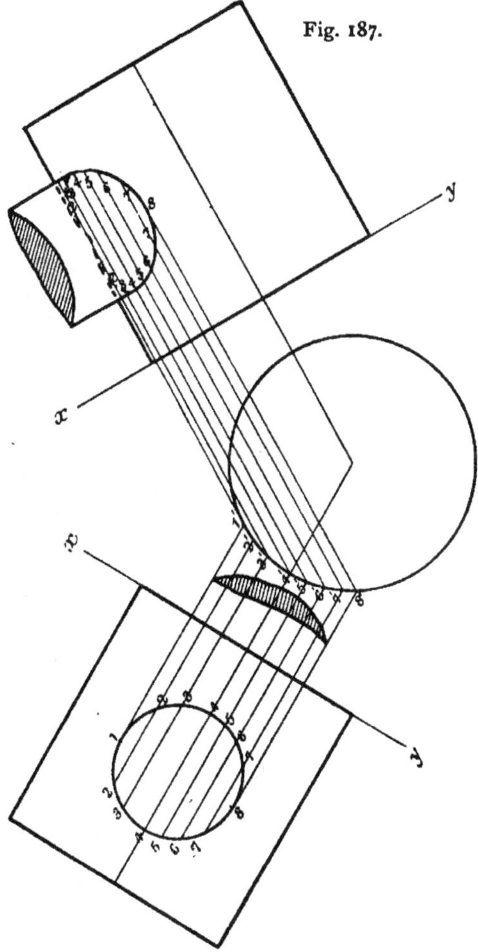

tion is to take a vertical projection at right angles to the axis of small cylinder, and divide the small circle in this projection

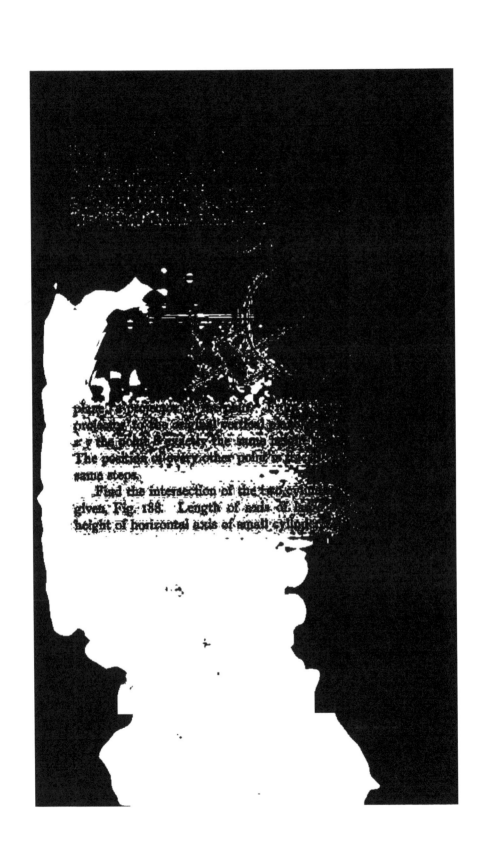

[illegible] $x\,y$ the point [illegible] same steps.

Find the intersection of the two [illegible] given, Fig. 188. Length of axis of [illegible] height of horizontal axis of small cylinder [illegible]

SECTION VIII.

SHADOWS.

CHAPTER XLIV.

SHADOWS CAST BY RECTANGULAR SOLIDS.

182. PARALLEL rays of light falling on a vertical plate, represented in plan and elevation by *a b c d* and *a′ b′ c′ d′*, and

Fig. 189.

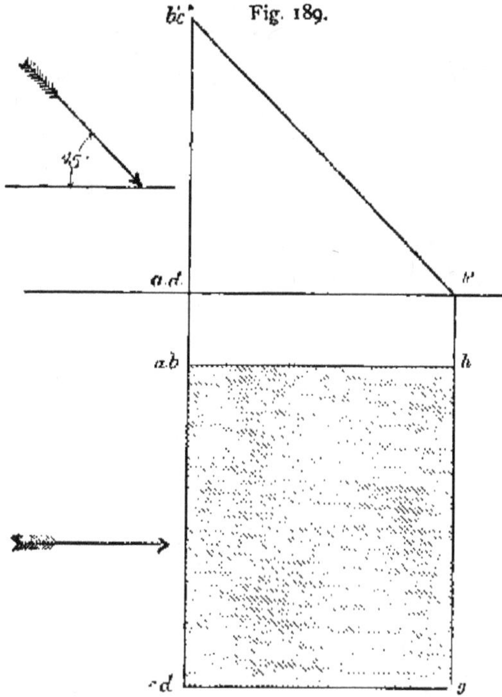

coming in the direction of the arrow in diagram, will darken the surface sectioned which lies behind the plate. The surface [illegible] All the [illegible] darkness [illegible] It is [illegible] light [illegible] shadow [illegible]

[illegible] its height [illegible] of the shadow.

A cube behind the plate would [illegible] effect in obstructing the light and [illegible] Therefore if we could fill in the boundary [illegible] rays leave the solid, this plate would [illegible] shadow as the solid.

Ex. 224. Show the shadow cast by [illegible] having two sides parallel to V.P. [illegible] at 45° to H.P. and parallel to V.P.

Ex. 224. Show the shadow cast by a [illegible] Side of base 1½ inch, height of pyramid [illegible] the base is parallel to V.P. Light [illegible] the last question.

Ex. 226. Show shadow cast by [illegible] [illegible] with one diagonal [illegible]

[illegible]

Ex. 227. Pyramid of third question stand[illegible] [illegible] Light same as before.

CHAPTER XLV.

SHADOWS CAST BY SOLIDS OF REVOLUTION.

184. LET the rays of light fall on a sphere. One side of that sphere will be lit up and the other side darkened, and on the ground the sphere will cast a curved shadow.

The furthest point to which the shadow will reach, will be the horizontal trace of the ray of light *a' c'*. As this *a' c'* is just

Fig. 190.

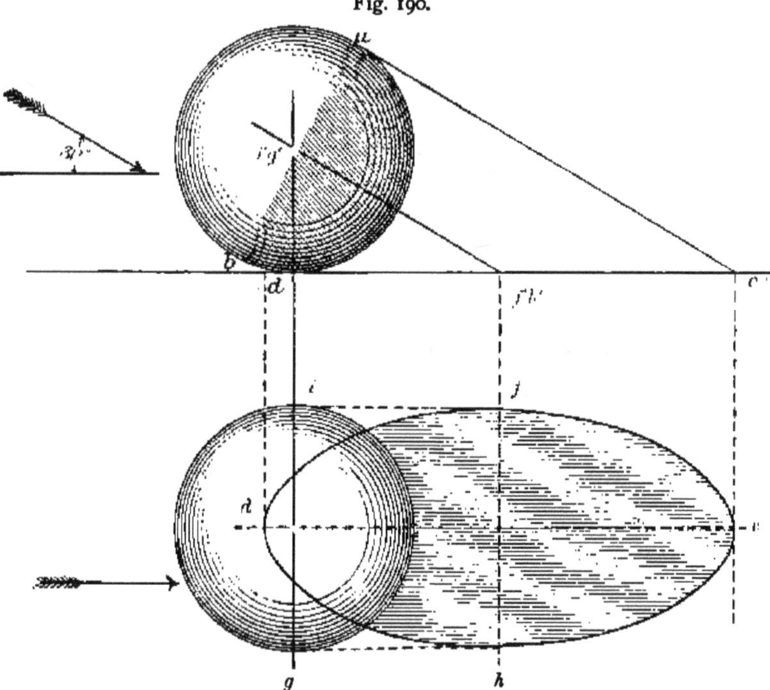

over the top, its plan will be in the middle of the plan of the sphere. So *c* where *dc* and the projector from *c'* intersect will be one limit of the shadow. The point *d* is found in the same way. The extreme width of the shadow will be the distance between the lines *i f* and *g h*. That is the extreme width is equal to the diameter of the sphere. And the line where the extreme width is will coincide with the horizontal trace of *e f* and *g h*. Evidently the effect of the sphere is to shut off a cylinder of rays of light; that cylinder having a diameter equal to the diameter of the sphere, and the direction of its axis parallel to *i f*. The shadow will coincide with the section of this cylinder made by the ground. The section is an ellipse, and the major and minor axis of this ellipse we have found to be *d c* and *f h* respectively. With these axes construct an ellipse, and the shadow is obtained.

Fig. 191.

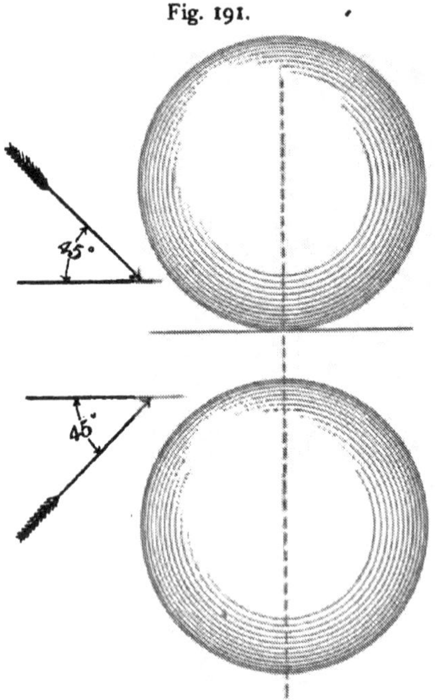

Ex. 228. Show shadow cast by a sphere—position as in Fig. 191, and lines of light falling as shown by arrows. Do not mind the shadow going into the vertical plane and over the *x y*.

185. If light falls on a cone parallel to the horizontal plane then all the surface behind the base is theoretically in shadow, because the ray of light just over the apex meets the ground

in infinity, and limiting lines drawn from it tangent to the base will be parallel lines. The other extreme way in which light can fall on the surface of a cone is when it comes vertically down. In this case there is no shadow. When the

Fig. 192.

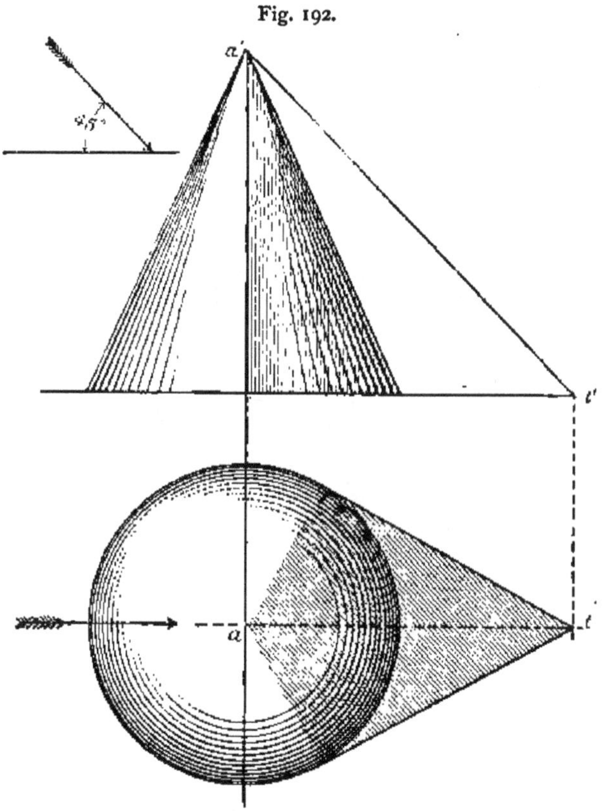

rays fall on the cone in a slanting direction, as shown in Fig. 192, the ray of light over the apex reaches the ground at such a point as *t*, and the shadow has for its boundaries the two tangents drawn from that point to the base.

CHAPTER XLVI.

SHADOWS ON THE VERTICAL PLANE.

186. SOMETIMES the light falls in such a way and the object is in such a position as to throw part of the shadow of the object on the vertical plane. This happens to the shadow of

Fig. 193.

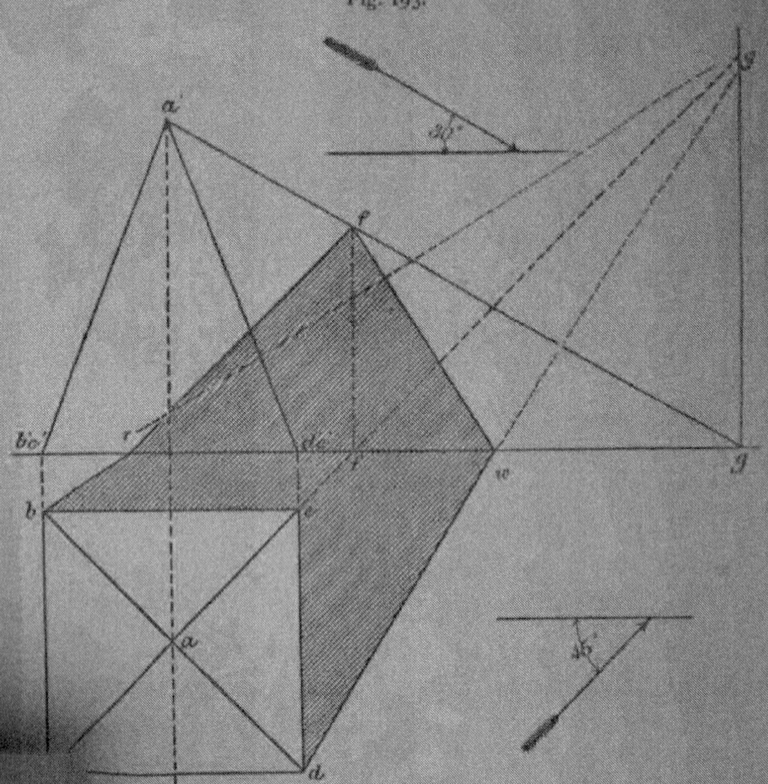

[illegible]amid such as that shown in Fig. 193, which is situated near [illegible]e V.P. and the rays of light having a small angle to the [illegible]zontal plane.

A pyramid will cast a shadow as shown in the diagram, Fig. 193, when the light falls on it in the direction of the arrow.

In the part of the shadow on the horizontal plane we must suppose the whole paper to be the H.P. and then find the horizontal trace of the ray of light going through the apex. To do this draw through *a'* a line parallel to the arrow in the vertical plane. This line meets *xy* in *g'*. So *g'* gives the vertical projection of the point where the light striking the apex comes to the H.P. The line *a g* is the plan of the same ray, and *g* is therefore the extreme limit of shadow. Now

Fig. 194.

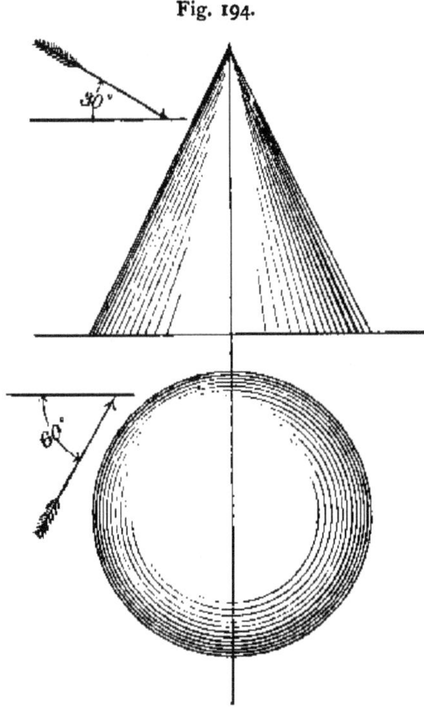

the extreme width of the shadow will be the distance between *b* and *d*. So join *b g* and *d g*. Were all the paper on H.P., and were there no V.P., the shadow would be *b g d*. But the highest ray of light is intercepted at a point of which *f* is the plan, hence *f'*, the vertical projection of *f*, is the limit of shadow on the vertical plan. The line *b g*, the boundary line of the shadow on the horizontal plane, meets *x y* in *r*. The shadow in the vertical plane will begin at the point where the shadow on the H.P. ends, so *r* will be the lower limit of the shadow in the vertical plane. The point *w*, where *d g* meets *x y*, will be another lower limit. Join *f r* and *f w*. The shaded part *r f w* is the shadow in the vertical plane, and *b r w d* the shadow in the horizontal plane.

Ex. 229. Show the shadow cast by a cone, position as in Fig. 194. The direction of the rays of light is shown by the arrows.

Ex. 230. Turn back to exercise 228, and try to find the part of the shadow of the sphere in the vertical plane.

CHAPTER XLVII.

SHADING WITH COLOURS.

187. IN mechanical drawing light is taken as falling over the left shoulder, or more precisely in the direction of the diagonal of a cube with two faces parallel to the V.P., as in Fig. 195. This conventional direction is the one supposed when shading any figure in mechanical drawing.

188. A cylinder lying with its 'axis parallel to V.P. has the darkest shadow lines at *c*, *b*, the colour is shaded away towards the centre and towards the bottom generatrix; the other side of the cylinder has also a slight part shaded. The darkest part being at the outside generatrix when shading with colour. The line *o a* is at 45° to the horizontal.

189. Two sable brushes are used for shading—one thin and fine, the other fairly broad. The small brush is dipped into colour of a darker shade than that used for a flat tint.

and then the large sable, wetted with water, is run along parallel to the colour newly laid on, and with its point just in the colour.

This causes the colour to run down towards the thick part of the brush, and by this means a fine shade is obtained—beginning at the middle, where it is scarcely distinguishable from the colour of the paper.

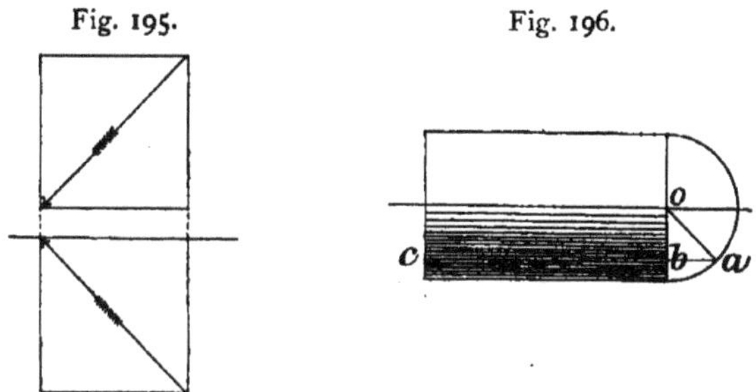

Fig. 195. Fig. 196.

190. Another method of shading is to get a dark shade by repeating flat tints.

From the middle of the generatrix at *o* would by this method be washed over with a thin flat tint. At a little distance from the edge of this first another wash is given it, and so on, deepening the shade of repeated washes until the line *c b* is reached.

Shading not only gives a more finished appearance to a drawing, but also assists to indicate what an object really is. For example, in the cylinder, Fig. 196, no elevation is necessary to aid us in understanding the figure to be a cylinder—without shading we might have felt doubtful as to whether a prism or a cylinder was meant.

191. The different metals are represented by characteristic colours. Some metals, such as wrought iron, cast iron, and brass are always distinguished by the colours: Prussian blue, Payne's grey, or Neutral, and Gamboge. Others, such as lead and steel, depend on tints, and are not uniformly represented.

The following are the colours used for all Government drawings :—

Metal.	Colour.
Cast iron	Payne's grey.
Wrought iron	Prussian blue.
Steel	Prussian blue and crimson lake.
Brass	Gamboge. Section, dark.
Copper	Gamboge and crimson lake.
Brick	Light red.
Wood	Burnt sienna.
Earth	Burnt umber.

Ex. 231. Take a sheet of geometrical drawing paper, and divide it into nine equal parts as shown in Fig. 197, mix a very thin wash ; a great amount of water and as little colour as

Fig. 197.

1	2	3
4	5	6
7	8	9

possible, and colour each of the divisions with it. When dry begin at number two, and colour all the higher numbered spaces. When dry begin at number three, and colour all the higher numbered spaces, and so on until each space had has as many washes as its number denotes.

SECTION IX.

ISOMETRIC PROJECTION.

CHAPTER XLVIII.

RECTANGULAR SOLIDS.

192. PROFESSOR STOKES, of Cambridge, introduced a system of projection of solids which gave all the information that was required about the solid, and obviated the necessity of making two projections of it, as is done when an orthographic projection of a solid is made. Not very much has come of the idea, but carpenters and builders often use it for explaining their meaning to workmen. The principle of this isometric projection is best explained by showing a simple object in isometric projection, with an explanation of the manner in which it is done.

193. When a rectangular block *a b c d*, Fig. 198, is tipped up into such a position that the vertical projection of a fixed

Fig. 198.

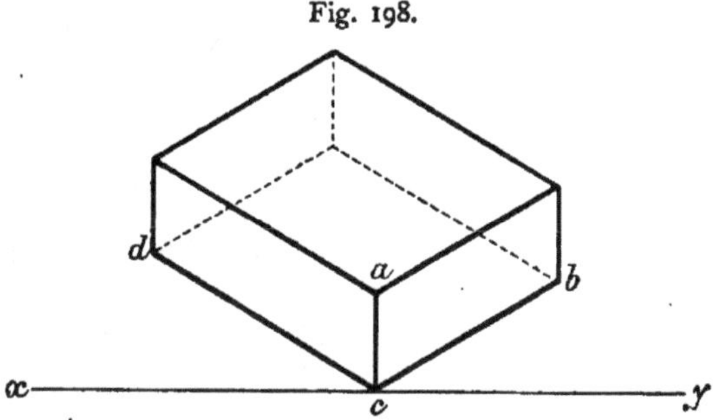

length measured equally along *c a*, *c b*, and *c d* will have the same length in the vertical plane, the solid is said to be in isometric projection. When this has been done the angles *x c d* and *y c b* will measure 30°.

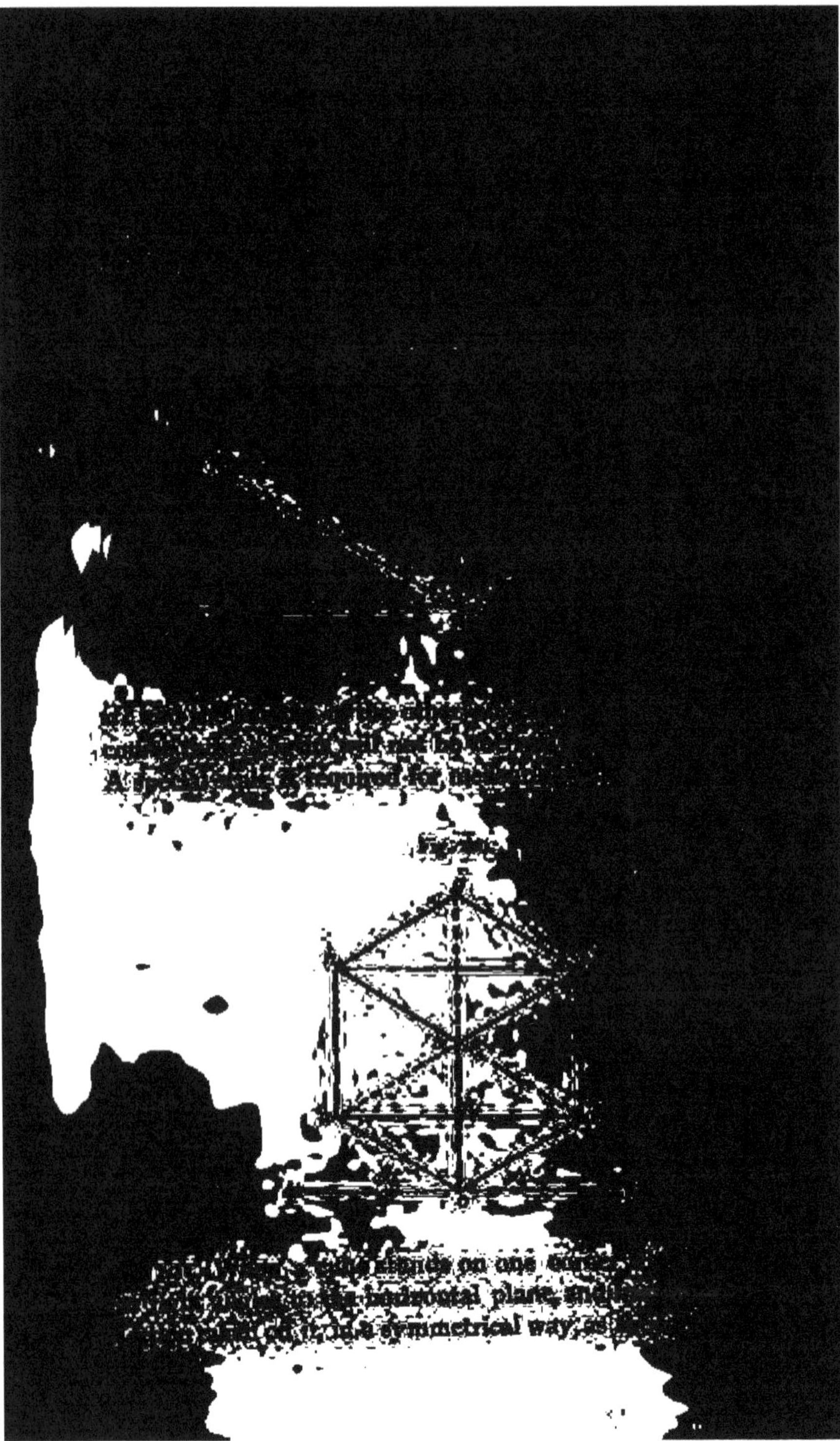

that vertical projection is an isometrical projection of the cube. Each edge of the solid is of the same length.

196. The length of *a d*, Fig. 200, the vertical projection of the diagonal of the face *a b d c*, is shown in real length, however, and this enables one to find the numerical relation between

Fig. 201.

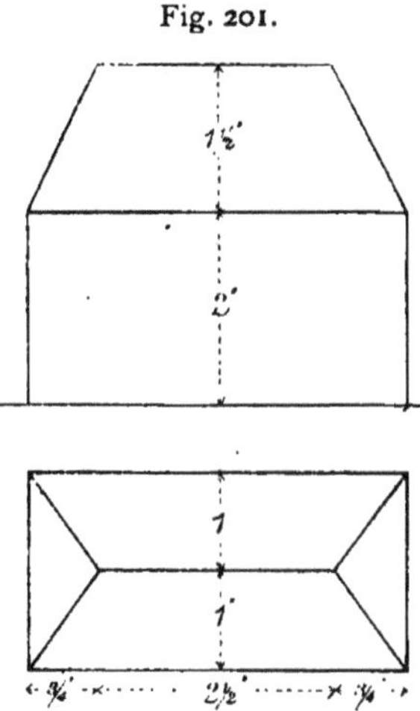

an isometric projection of an edge of a solid and its real length.

The diagonal of any square such as *a b c d* is to the side as $\sqrt{2} : 1$.

That is:

$$\frac{\text{Real length of } c\,d}{\text{Real length of } a\,d} = \frac{1}{\sqrt{2}} \qquad (1)$$

But *c d k* being an angle of 30° in a right-angled triangle *c k d*,

$$\frac{\text{The length of } c\,d \text{ as shown}}{k\,d} = \frac{2}{\sqrt{3}}$$

$$\therefore \quad \frac{c\,d}{2\,k\,d} = \frac{c\,d}{a\,d} = \frac{1}{\sqrt{3}} \qquad (2)$$

Dividing equation 1 by 2 we have

$$\frac{\frac{\text{Real length of } c\,d}{a\,d}}{\frac{\text{Proj. length of } c\,d}{a\,d}} = \frac{\frac{1}{\sqrt{2}}}{\frac{1}{\sqrt{3}}} = \frac{\sqrt{3}}{\sqrt{2}}$$

$$\therefore \frac{\text{Real length of } c\,d}{\text{Isometric length of } c\,d} = \frac{\sqrt{3}}{\sqrt{2}}$$

Fig. 202.

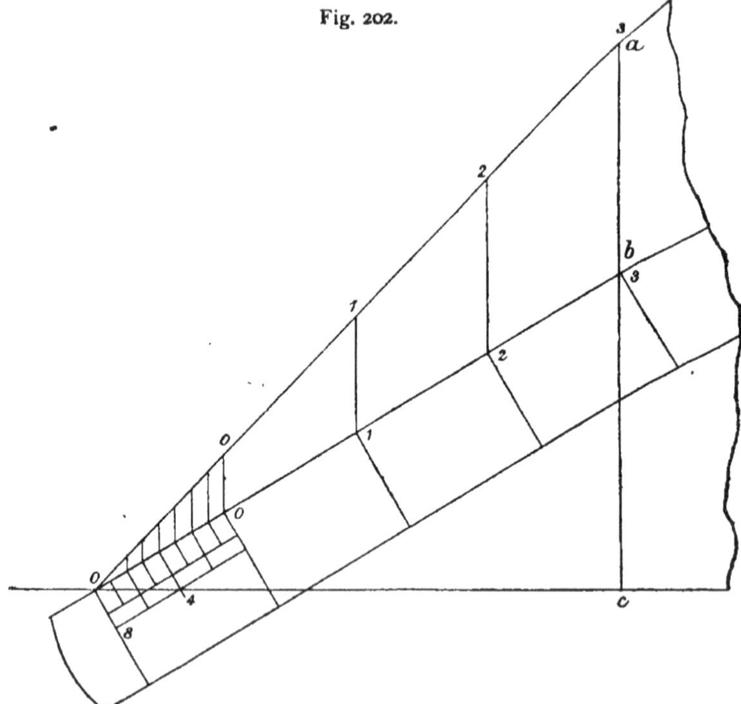

Now take any horizontal line $o\,c$, Fig. 202, and draw $o\,b$ and $o\,a$ inclined respectively at angles of 30° and 45° to $o\,c$.

Then

$$\frac{oa}{oc} = \frac{\sqrt{2}}{1} \qquad (1)$$

$$\frac{ob}{oc} = \frac{2}{\sqrt{3}} \qquad (2)$$

Dividing the one equation by the other we have

$$\frac{oa}{ob} = \frac{\sqrt{3}}{2} \times \frac{\sqrt{2}}{1} = \frac{\sqrt{3}}{\sqrt{2}}$$

And $o\,a$ bears the same ratio to $o\,b$ as the real length of a line bears to its isometric projection.

197. All that is to be done for the purpose of making an isometric scale is to draw two lines $o\,a$ at 45° and $o\,b$ at 30°, and set off real inches along $o\,a$, from the divisions draw vertical lines, and construct a scale with the divisions obtained by the intersections of these vertical lines with $o\,b$.

CHAPTER XLIX.

PROJECTION OF CIRCLES.

198. SUPPOSE next that it is required to draw a prism with a cylindrical hole bored through it in the direction of the axis; the axis of the hole coinciding with the axis of the prism in Fig. 203.

Fig. 203.

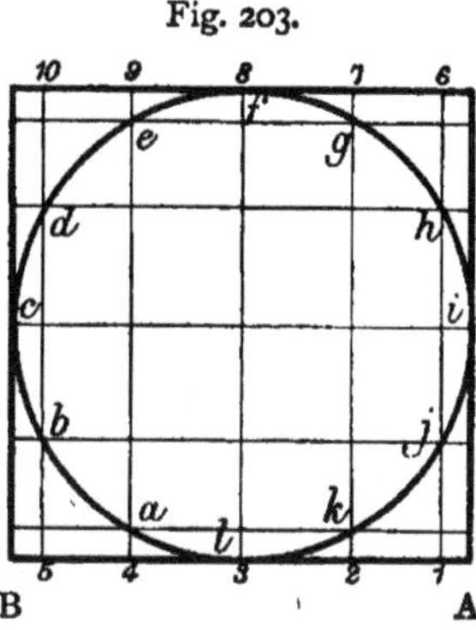

Draw a rectangle equal to the end of the prism and describe in it a circle. Divide A B into six parts in something of the same proportion as shown in sketch, and make A 1 equal to B 5, 1 2 to 5 4. Next draw vertical lines from 1, 2, 3, 4, and 5, and horizontal lines through the points when the vertical lines cut the circle.

Find next the length of A 1 in isometric scale, and lay it along A 1, Fig. 204. Lay off next 1 *j* and 6 *h* from bottom and top respectively; *j* and *h* are points in the curve; *i* in the middle of A D is another. Lay of 7 *g* and 2 *k*, and the

Fig. 204.

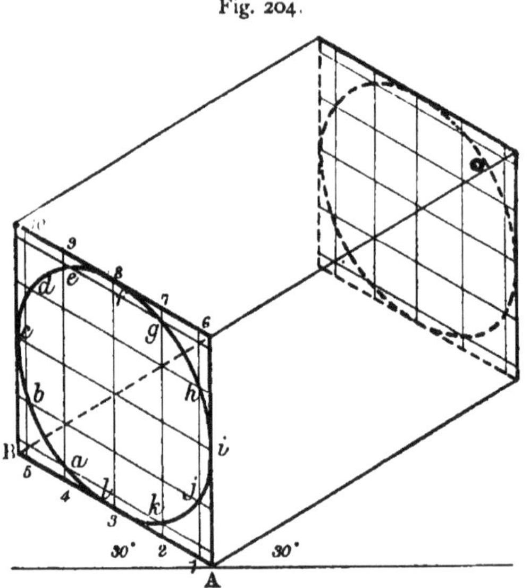

other points in the same way. The curve in the end of the solid, Fig. 204, is an ellipse.

Ex. 232. Draw in isometric projection a prism 3″ × 4″ × 3″ with a cylindrical hole 2 inches diameter bored in it. The axis of the prism and cylinder coinciding.

Ex. 233. Draw in isometric projection a prism 1″ × 2″ × 2″, with a hole 2 inches diameter bored through it. The axis of going through to the opposite vertical ridges.

99. Suppose next a solid like that shown in sketch, Fig. to be shown in isometric projection.

Draw A D and A B, Fig. 206; the isometric projection of A D and A B, Fig. 205; and complete the parallelogram A B C D. Bisect B A and draw through the point of bi-section G H parallel to A D. Draw E G and F H, the isometric

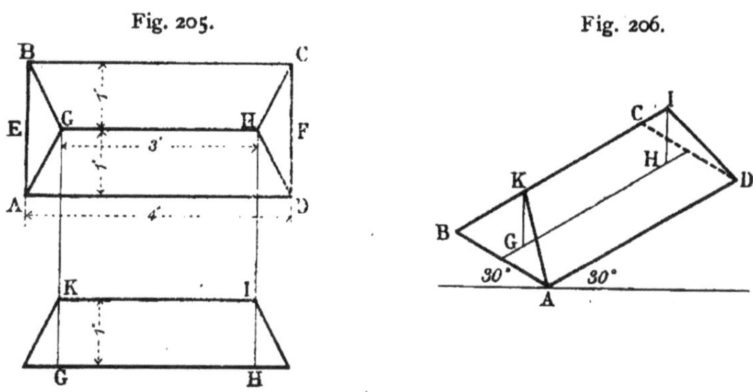

Fig. 205. Fig. 206.

projections of G E and H F, Fig. 205, and from G and H draw perpendicular lines 1 inch high in isometric scale. Join K B, K A, I D, I C and join K I. Fig. 206 is the isometric projection of the solid in Fig. 205.

Ex. 234. Show in isometric projection a pyramid with square base 2 inches sides and axes 3 inches in length.

Ex. 235. Show in isometric projection a cross 4 inches high, section of base 1 inch square, arm section 1 inch square and 2½ inches long.

Show in isometric projection the solid represented in orthographic projection in sketch in Fig. 201.

SECTION X.

PERSPECTIVE PROJECTION.

CHAPTER L.

PERSPECTIVE PROJECTION OF LINES.

200. If *a b*, Fig. 207, be the plan of a horizontal line 1 inch high, and S the plan of the point from which a person looks on the line *a b*, the lines *a* S and *b* S will be the lines in which the light comes from the ends *a* and *b* to the eye. A glass plane interposed between the line *a b* and S will be cut by the lines *a* S and *b* S in points which have plans *c* and *d*; and a line in the glass plane having a plan *c d* and equal in length to *c d*, will convey the same idea to the mind as the true object would. In showing the shape as seen in the glass plane, the glass plane is turned about the line *p p*, and of course the height at which the line stands, of which *c d* is the plan, above the line *p p* is measured up from *p p*. To get this height an elevation is taken on a vertical plane at right angles to the glass plane. The ground line of this plane is shown, and *a' b'* the elevation of the line A B, S' the elevation of S, and *c' d'* the point in the elevation of the glass plane where the lines of light *a'* S and *b'* S cut that elevation, gives the height of C D. Turning the glass plane down about the centre *p*, the elevation *c' d'* comes to *g*.

If now *p p* be considered, the ground line, that is the original *x y*, the height of *g* shows the height of the picture of the line. Draw then from *g* a line parallel to *p p*. This line will contain the picture when the picture plane has been turned back into the vertical plane. From *c* and *d*, draw projectors. The points *e* and *f*, where the projectors intersect the line through *g*, is the perspective of the line A B.

201. Take next a line A B, Fig. 208, at right angles to the picture plane, and let *a b* be the plan, and S the sight point. As before take a vertical projection of the whole affair on a vertical plane at right angles to the picture plane. The line *a' b'*

Fig. 207.

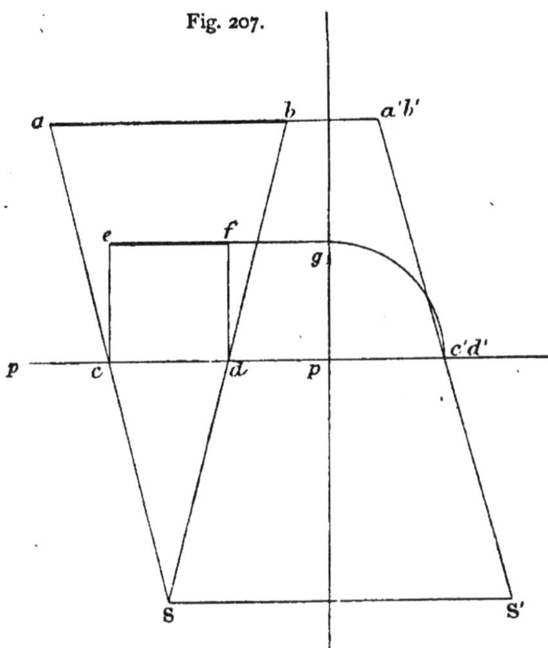

is the vertical projection of A B; S' is the vertical projection of sight point, and the intersections of the lines *c'* S' and *d'* S' are the vertical projections of the points where the lines of light cut the picture plane. As before turn these points about *p*, so as to get the height of the pictures of the ends of the lines when the picture plane is laid back into the V.P.

The student will observe without explanation that the projection *c d* of the line *a b* will be the shape of the line in the glass plane which will produce the same effect on the eye as the line *a b*. The glass plane is called the picture plane.

Ex. 236. A line A B parallel to *p p* and H.P., 2 inches long, is 2½ inches behind the picture plane and 1 inch above the H.P. Show how it will appear in the picture plane from a point S 3 inches in front of the picture plane and 4 inches high, and opposite the middle of the line.

Ex. 237. A horizontal line A B 1¾ inches long is at right angles to the picture plane and 1 inch high. Its nearest point

Fig. 208.

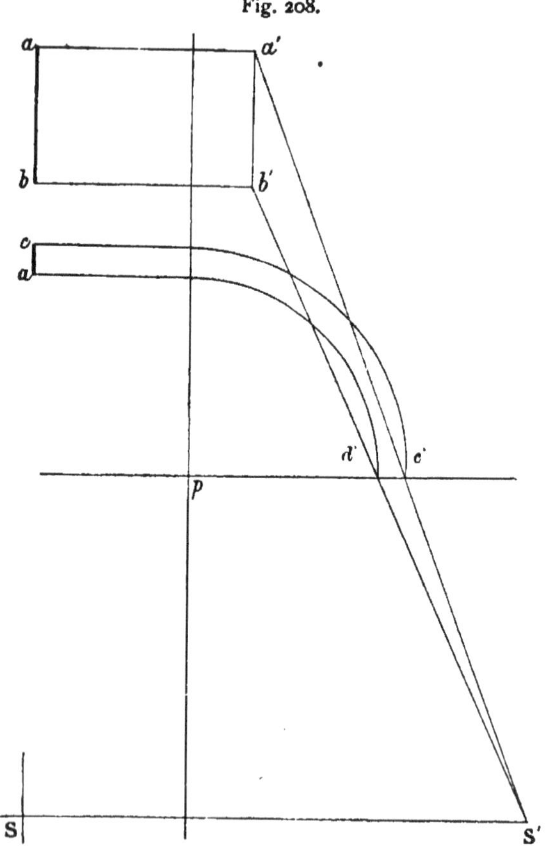

is ½ inch in front of *p p*. Show how it would look in the picture plane from a sight point 3 inches in front of *p p* and 4 inches high, and in a line with A B.

Ex. 238. Suppose A B in question 236 to be the lower side of a square. Show how it would look in the picture plane from a point of sight in the same situation.

Ex. 239. Suppose A B question 237 to be the lower side of a square. Show how it would look in the picture plane from the same point of view as taken in question 237.

Ex. 240. Square 1½ inch side is horizontal and 1 inch high, it has two sides parallel to *p p*, nearest 2 inches behind. Supposing this square to be the lower face of a cube, show how the cube would look in the picture plane. S point 3 inches in front of *p p* and 4 inches high.

Ex. 241. A square-based pyramid 3 inches high stands on the H.P., two sides of base are parallel to *p p*, nearest 1½ inches behind, length of side of base 1½ inch. S 3 inches in front of *p p* and 3 inches high. Show its perspective.

CHAPTER LI.

PERSPECTIVE OF CIRCLES.

202. THE perspective of a circle is found by finding the perspective of points in it. For example, suppose we are given a horizontal circle as shown, Fig. 209, with S in the middle line of circle.

Take any points 2 3 *b*, 4 *a* 5 6 in the plan, and draw converging lines from them to S. Where these converging lines cut the other side of the circle mark points 1 *d o c* 7. Now take a vertical projection of the circle, and project up the points in the plan. From the elevations of those points, draw converging lines to S′, and so find the points where the lines of light cut the edge view of the picture plane. Take any *x y* as shown. This is taken low down to avoid confusing the perspective with the plan of the circle. From the plans of the points where the converging lines of light cut *p p*, draw projectors on the middle projector, measure up a distance *o*′ equal to *p o*″. On the projector corresponding to *d* measure up a distance *p d*″, and so on. The figure *o*, *d*, 1, 2, 3, *b*, 4, *a*, 5, 6, 7, *c*, is the perspective projection of the horizontal circle.

Ex. 242. Taking point of sight 4 inches high, 3 inches in front of picture plane.

Show perspective of a circle horizontal, 2 inches diameter, 1 inch above H.P., 2 inches distant from *p p*.

Fig. 209.

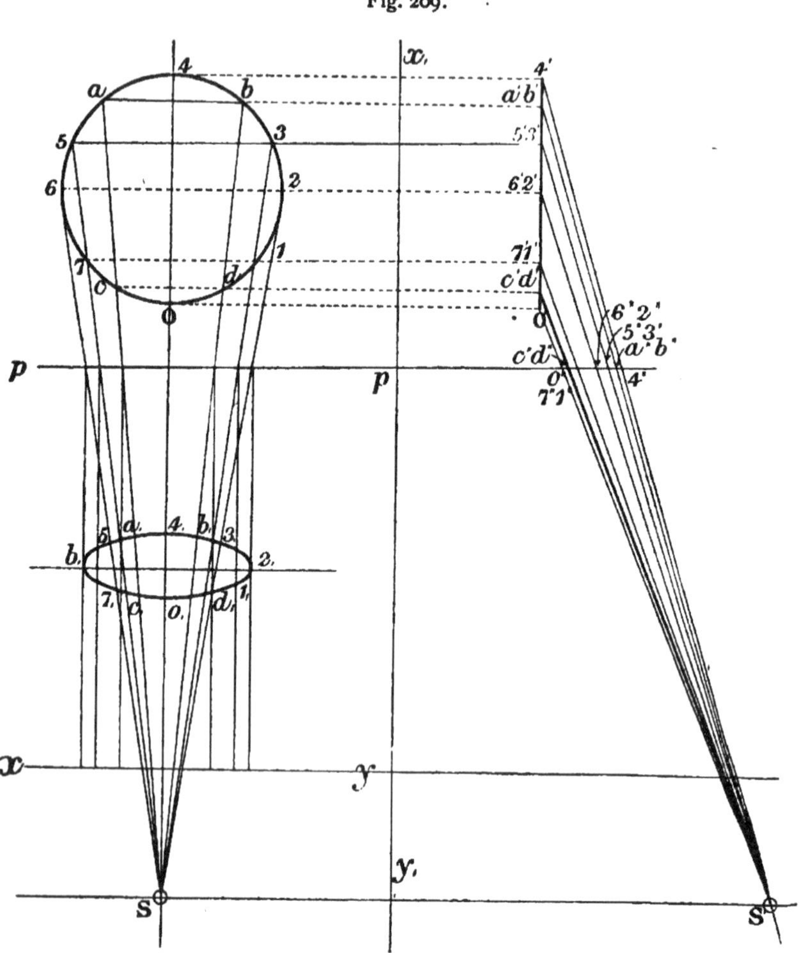

Ex. 243. Show perspective of a cone 3 inches high with circle of last question for base, and same sight point.

Ex. 244. Show perspective of a circle standing on H.P. parallel to *pp*, and 2½ inches behind it; same sight point.

Ex. 245. Show perspective of a cylinder standing on H.P. axis, at right angles to *pp*; 3 inches long, nearest end, 1 inch distant from *pp*.

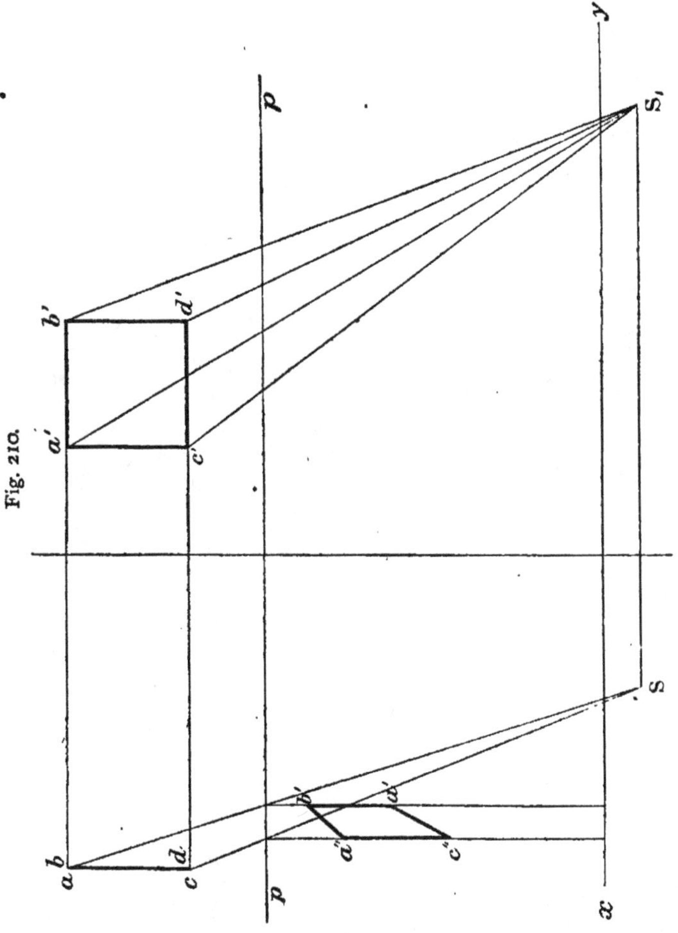

203. We have as yet only taken cases where the point of sight is in the centre of figure. We will now take cases where the point of sight is on one side of the object; *a b c d*, *a' b' c' d*

CHAPTER [illegible]

PERSPECTIVE BY [illegible]

206. When the lines or planes [illegible] picture plane, they can be projected [illegible] there is a much simpler method [illegible] use of a projection on a vertical [illegible] picture plane.

The line $a\,b$ lying on H.P. [illegible] plane in [illegible]. Project the [illegible] parallel to $a\,b$ to cut [illegible] and measure up from [illegible] height of the [illegible] points where [illegible] picture plane. Drawing [illegible] get the points c and d [illegible] perspective. The line *c d* is the perspective projection of A B.

Ex. 247. Draw the perspective of a line *a b* 2 inches long lying on H.P. inclined at 60° to *p p*, and nearest point 1 inch behind the picture plane. S 3 inches in front and 2½ inches high.

Fig. 211.

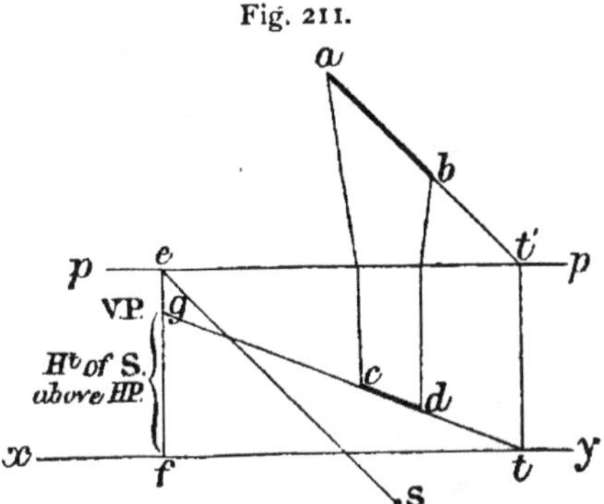

Ex. 248. A line C D 2¼ inches long makes 45° with *p p*, is on the H.P. One point touches *p p*. Same sight point as in Ex. 247.

206. Take next the square *a b c d*, Fig. 212. The lines *a d* and *b c* produced will have traces *t t'*; S *g* drawn parallel to *a d* gives us the point *g*, from which drop the perpendicular *g l*. The line *l m* made equal in height to S gives us V.P. Joining this with *e* and *f*, and dropping projectors from the points where the converging lines to S meet *p p*, we get the points *a' b' c' d'*, the points cut by the projectors. These joined give us the square in perspective.

Ex. 249. A square of 1½ inch side is on the H.P., with two sides making an angle of 45° with *p p*; S 3½ inches high and 4 inches in front of *p p*.; nearest corner 1 inch behind *p p*.

Ex. 250. S as in 249. A square 2 inches side with two sides making 55° with *p p*, and nearest corner 1½ inch behind *p p*. Show perspective.

207. If a line should be above the horizontal plane its height is measured up the projector *fe*, Fig. 213, drawn from

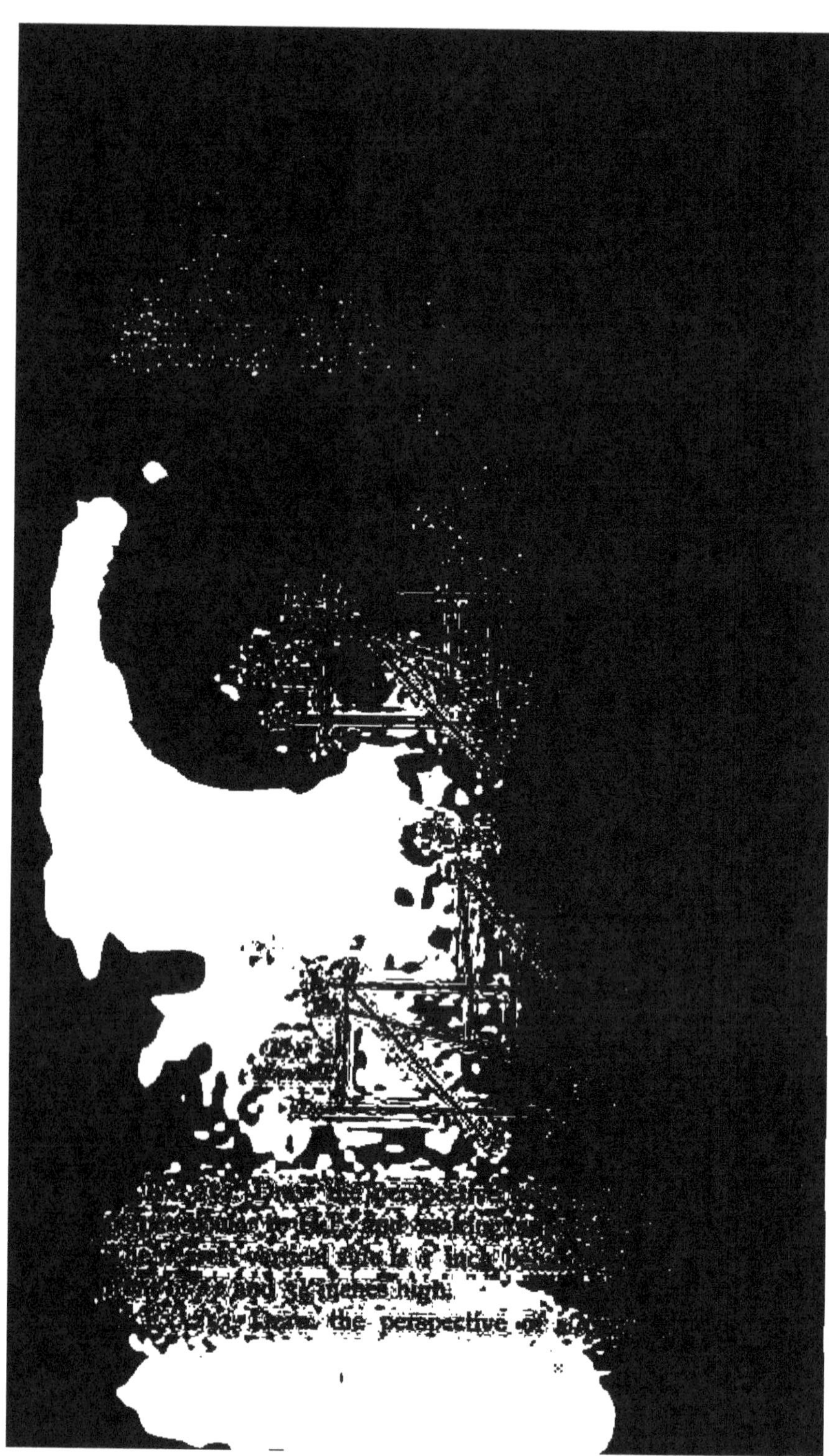

[illegible] Draw the perspective [illegible] each vertical side is 2 inches [illegible] and six inches high.

[illegible] Draw the perspective of [illegible]

standing on H.P., with two faces making an angle of 45° to *p p*; the nearest edge is 1½ inch from *pp*; S is 3 inches high and 4 inches in front of *p p*.

Ex. 254. Draw the perspective of your instrument box with lid open and two sides making an angle of 55° to *p p*; nearest corner 1 inch behind *p p*; S in last case.

SECTION XI.

GRAPHICAL STATICS.

CHAPTER LIII.

REPRESENTATION OF THE RESULTANT OF FORCES.

208. A FORCE is that which, acting on a body, produces, or tends to produce motion. A force may be represented on paper by a line with an arrow-head; the length of the line represents the magnitude of the force, it is also drawn parallel to the line in which the body moves, or tends to move, and it thereby represents the direction of the force; while the parts towards which the body moves or tends to move is pointed to by the arrow-head. This latter is called the sense of the force.

209. Forces may act in any direction, and the lines which represent them may lie on the paper in any direction. In speaking of them, it is found convenient to refer all their directions to one horizontal line like O X, Fig. 214.

The line O P, Fig. 215, with the arrow pointing towards the point O, represents a force of 3 lb. acting towards O at an angle of 45° to the horizontal.

The line O Q, Fig. 216, represents a force of 4 lb. acting at 120° to the horizontal.

210. It can be shown by experiment and proved mathematically that the diagonal O R, Fig. 217, of the parallelogram O Q R P will represent the resultant of two forces represented by the lines O P and O Q. It must always be remembered that it is the diagonal drawn from the point on which the forces act.

Ex. 255. Find the resultant of two forces: one of 7 lb.,

making 30° with the horizontal, the other of 5 lb., making 90°.

Ex. 256. Find the resultant of two forces: one of 9 lb., making 25° with the horizontal, the other of 6 lb., making 108°.

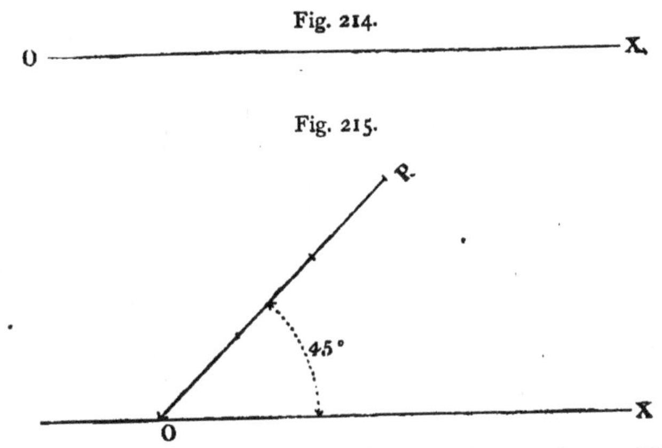

Fig. 214.

Fig. 215.

211. If the force which would keep the two in equilibrium is to be found, we find the resultant, but reverse the arrow; for the equilibriant we know neutralises the resultant, and it can only do so when exactly equal and opposite.

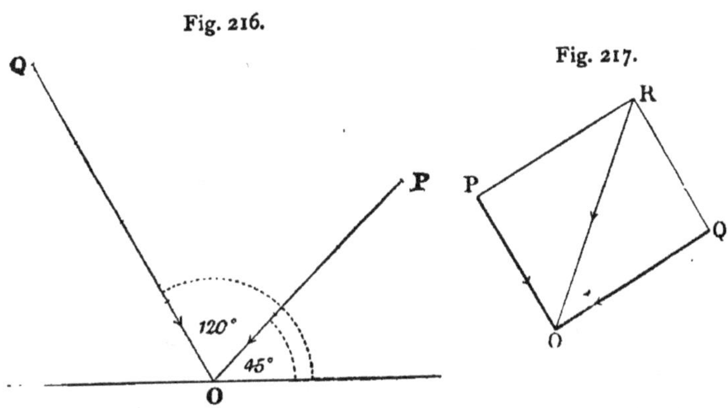

Fig. 216.

Fig. 217.

212. Not only can the resultant of two forces be found, but we can by the same means find the resultant of any number of forces.

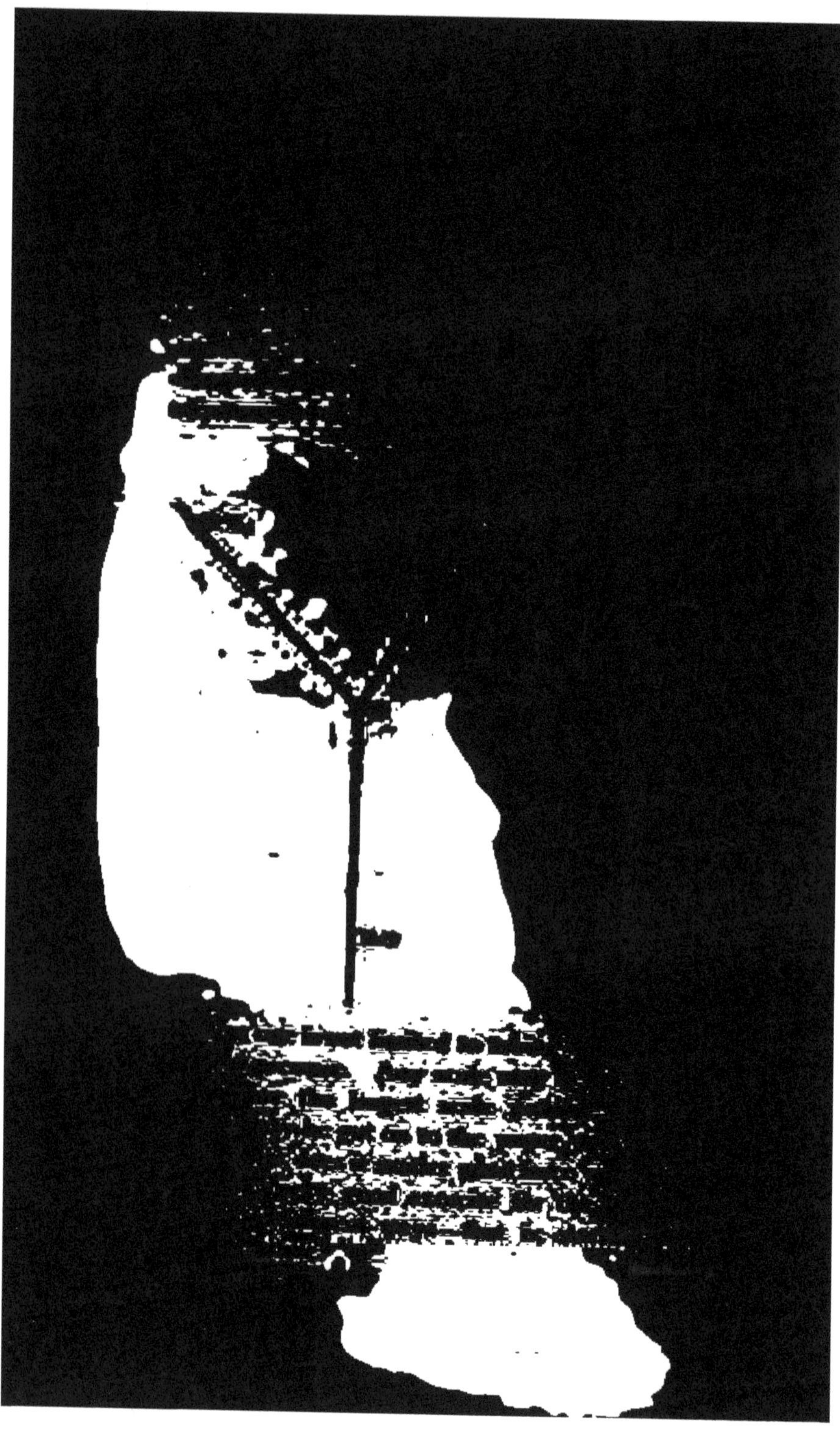

CHAPTER LIV.

RESULTANT OF ANY NUMBER OF FORCES ACTING IN A PLANE.

213. FORCES are not given always as acting on a point: sometimes they act on different points, and do not meet if produced.

The resultant of forces not acting on a point can be found in the following way:—Suppose three forces, P, Q, and T, act as shown.

Take any point, A, Fig. 220, draw a line A B parallel to P, and containing as many units of length as P contains units of force, that is four units. From B draw B C parallel to Q, five units in length, and from C draw C D, six units in length. Join A D. The length of A D represents the magnitude of the resultant. The magnitude of the force is found and a line parallel to the direction of the real force, but not the line in which it acts. To find a point in the line of the force another construction is required, but before we begin to make that other construction it will be better, perhaps, to explain another way of naming forces and spaces.

214. Instead of calling a force simply by one letter, it is found convenient to put a letter on each side of the force, that is, name the space between two forces by means of a letter. The space between P and Q, Fig. 220, is here called B, and between Q and T, C. The force P is called A B; Q, B C; and T is called C D.

215. Take any point *o*, and draw radiating lines from *o* to A B C and D.

From any point *g* in A B draw a line *g h* in the space B parallel to the line *o* B, and from *h* draw the line *h k* in the space C parallel to *o* C; *l k* parallel to *o* D, and *g l* parallel to *o* A. Through C draw *l m* parallel to A D. *l m* or D A shows the direction in which the equilibriant acts, and the arrow

polygon of forces becomes a straight line. Let four forces act on the line *a b* as shown in Fig. 221. Take any point A, Fig. 222, and draw a line representing the force A B. From B draw a line representing the force B C, and so on. A B, B C, C D, D E, represent the four forces acting on the line.

As before, take any point *o*, and draw lines to the extremities of the forces in the force polygon, which is here represented by a straight line. In A B take any point *l*, draw *l m*, *m n*, *n p*, *p q*, and *l q* parallel to *o* B, *o* C, *o* D, *o* E, and *o* A. Through *q* draw a line parallel to A E. The length A E in the force polygon represents the magnitude of the resultant, and *q* is a point through which it acts. The arrow shows its sense.

Ex. 259. Find the resultant of the forces acting as shown, Fig. 223.

Fig. 223.

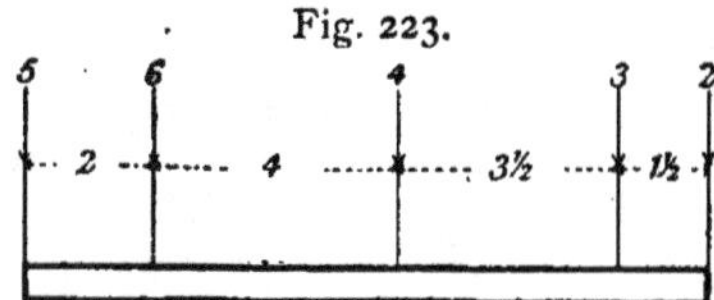

Ex. 260. Find the force necessary to keep the Fig. 224 forces in equilibrium.

Fig. 224.

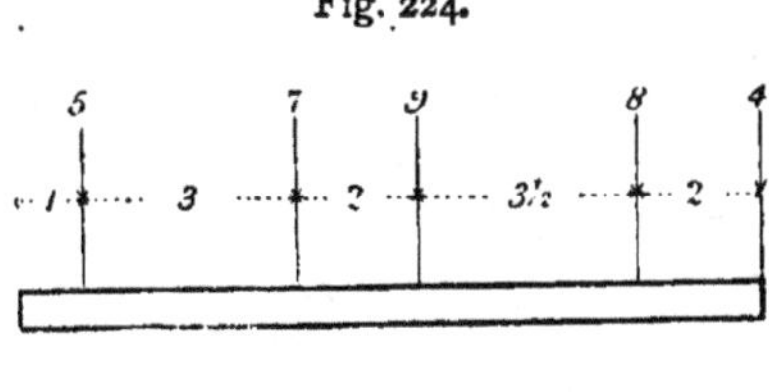

CHAPTER LV.

MOMENTS OF FORCES.

217. IF a beam *a g* acted on by forces 6 and 7 in the position shown be supported at its ends, the forces acting at the ends may be found by taking the moments about each end. Now, the moment of a force about any point, or its importance due

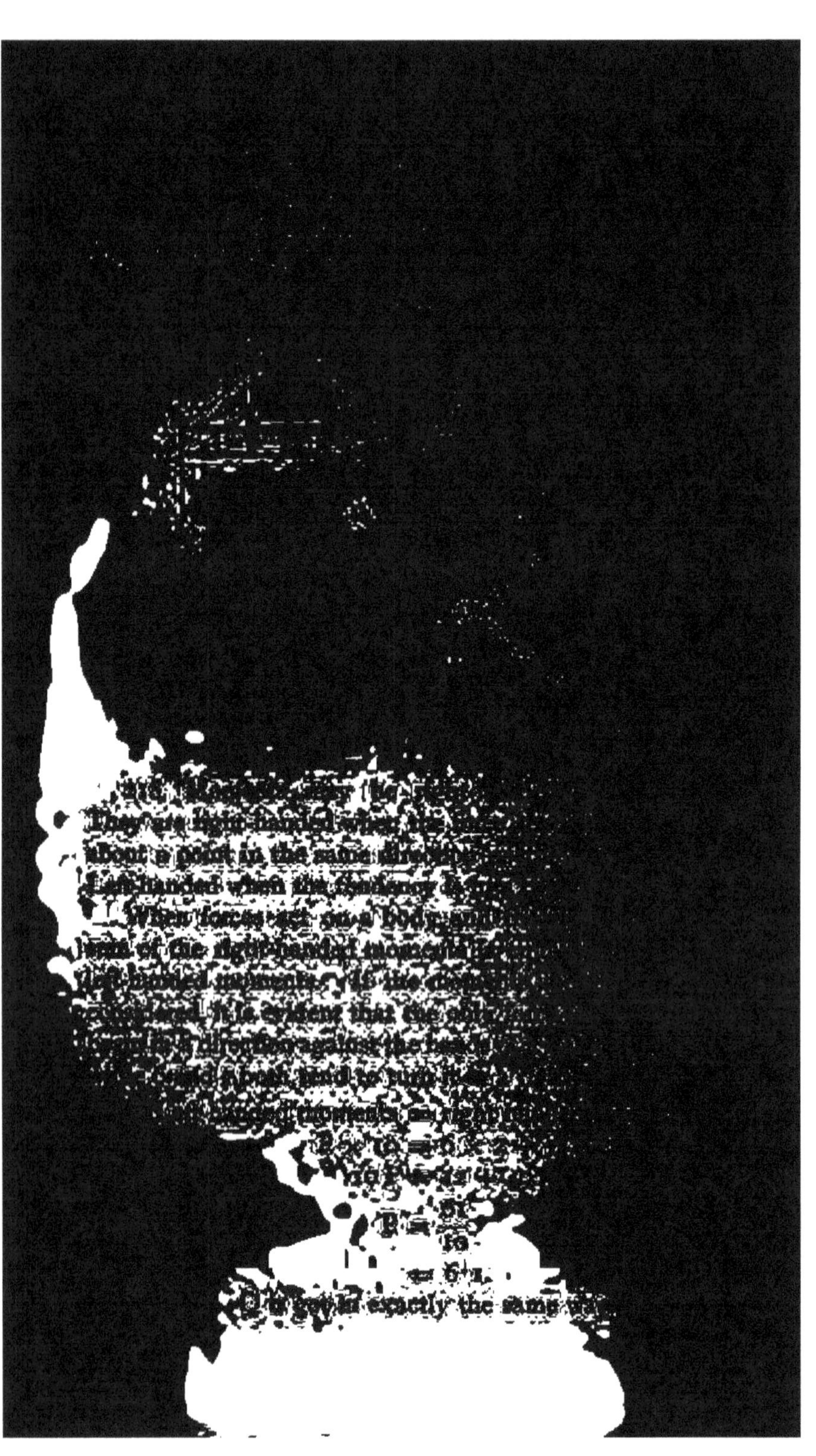

They are right-handed when the ... about a point in the same direction ... Left-handed when the tendency is ...

When forces act on a body ... sum of the right-handed moments ... left-handed moments ... the ... It is evident that the ... direction against the ... tend to turn ...

... moments ... right ...

$= 6 \cdot 1.$

... in exactly the same way

Taking moments about B :—

$$\text{Left-handed} = \text{right-handed}.$$
$$7 \times 3 + 6 \times 8 = Q \times 10.$$
$$21 + 48 = 10\,Q.$$
$$\frac{69}{10} = Q.$$
$$6{\cdot}9 = Q.$$

219. But we can also get these forces by graphical statics.

Let A B and B C, Fig. 225, represent the forces 6 and 7, using the same notation as before. Take any point *o* and draw *o* A, *o* B, and *o* C.

From any point *h* in Q draw *h e* parallel to *o* A, *e f* parallel to *o* B, and *f g* parallel to *o* C. Join *g h* and complete the polygon *h e f g*. The line *g h* through the space D will give the direction in which the line is to be drawn which is to divide A C into two parts representing Q and P. Draw *o* D parallel to *h g*, magnitudes of C D and D A are therefore obtained.

Ex. 261. Find the forces P and Q, Fig. 226.

Ex. 262. Find the forces R and S, Fig. 226.

Fig. 226.

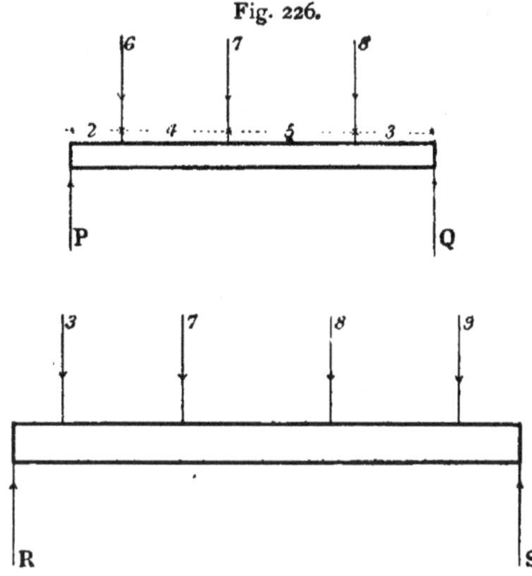

CHAPTER LVI.

FRAMES HINGED AT ONE END.

220. WHEN a body is given as supported by a hinge at one end and by a vertical force at the other, like that in Fig. 227, we proceed to solve it, that is to find the supporting forces, in the following way:

Fig. 227.

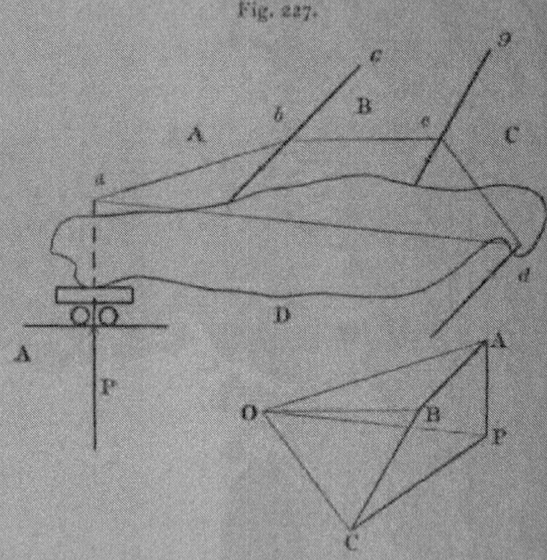

Draw the lines A B and B C to represent the forces 6 and 9. These are the only two of which we know the direction and magnitude. Of D A the direction, because of its being on a truck, is known, but not the magnitude. Neither direction nor magnitude of C D has been given, but only a point in its line, namely, the point *d*. Take any point O as pole, and draw O A, O B, and O C, and starting from the point *d*, draw lines *d c*, *c b*, and *b a*, parallel to C O, B O, and A O. The line *d a* of the link polygon gives the direction of the line which has to be drawn from O to find the point D in the stress diagram. Join *d* and *a*, and draw O P parallel to *d a*.

C P gives the magnitude of the force through *d*, and it is parallel to C P D.

Ex. 263. In the body in Fig. 228 find P and the force acting through *a*.

Fig. 228.

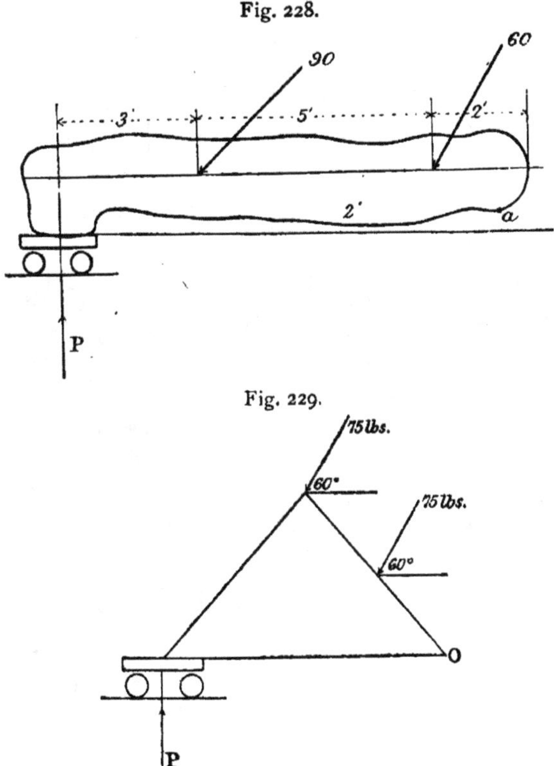

Fig. 229.

Ex. 264. Find the magnitude of P and the force acting through the hinge O.

The forces producing strains in linked structures can also be found by means of the stress diagram and linked polygon.

221. Suppose we have three linked pieces *a b*, *b c*, *c a*, supported at *a* and *c* and having a force of 12 lbs. acting at the

have but to trace out the triangle to satisfy ourselves that the forces are represented and that the diagram is complete.

The force on *ab* is represented by D B, that on *b c* is represented by D C, and that on *ac* by the line D A. The length of these, on the same scale as used for drawing the line B C will give the amount of strain on the parts. The figures representing the strains are written on the figure, as shown.

Fig. 230 is inked in with Indian ink. The lines B C, D B, D A, and D C, which represent the stress diagram, are in red.

CHAPTER LVII.

ROOF PRINCIPAL.

222. MORE complicated structures can be treated in the same way.

The distributed load along the roof principal *a b*, Fig. 231, may be supposed to be concentrated at the points *a*, *d* and *b*. That between *a* and *d* will cause a load of 30 at *a* and 30 at *d*. The load between *d* and *b* will cause a load of 30 at *d* and 30 at *b*, so that, due to the distributed load along the principal we will have really 30 at *a*, 60 at *d*, and 30 at *b*.

In considering the other side of the roof in the same way we will see that, due to the distributed load, 30 come on *b*, 60 on *e*, and 30 on *c*.

The upward pressure of each wall on the roof will be 90.

Set off A B on the stress diagram, Fig. 231A, to represent the force A B acting on the frame, and B C to represent the force acting on the part *a d*, and C A to represent the tension to which *f f* is subjected. The triangle A B C represents therefore the forces acting on the point *f*. In the same way the forces acting on the point *d* are represented by the polygon B D E C B. Next the forces acting on *f* by the polygon

E F A C E, and so on. Observe that the forces at each point are represented by a closed polygon.

Fig. 231.

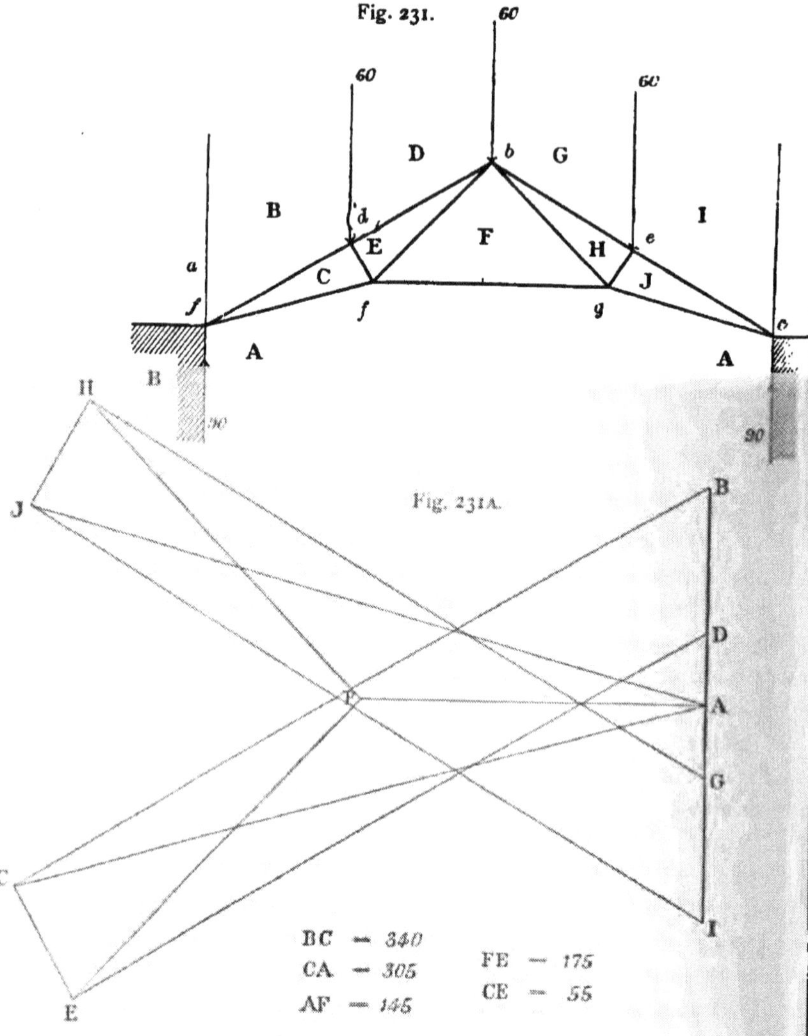

Fig. 231A.

The forces acting along D E, E F, F H, H G, and G D on the point *b*, are represented by the lines D G, D E, E F, and a line drawn from G, Fig. 231*a*, parallel to G H, Fig. 231, will meet a line drawn from F parallel to F H, and so determine the remaining forces G H and F H. The forces acting on *e* are G I, I J, J H, and H G, Fig. 231, and these are found by making G I, 60, and drawing I J, Fig. 231*a*, parallel to I J Fig. 231, and drawing from H a line H J parallel to H J Fig. 231, and intersecting I J in the point J. Next the forces acting along the lines H J, J A, A F, and F H, Fig. 231, on the point *g*, are found by beginning with H J, which is already found, and joining J A, A F, which is found, and F H, which also is found. The last point is *c*, and the forces acting on it are the forces acting along J I, I A and A J, and they are represented by lines already found in determining the forces acting on other joints. They are I J, J A and A I, Fig. 231A.

Ex. 264*a*. Find the strains on all the parts of a roof similar in shape to that in Fig. 231. The strut C E is in the middle of the length. Each rafter has to support 10 feet of roof length. The weight on each square foot is 40 pounds. Take distance from one support to the other 30 feet.

223. Next let allowance be made for the wind, then the amount which must be supported by each end of the members *a d* and *d b* is found, and the resultant of this force and the vertical load is taken at the points *d* and *b*. If Q, which is horizontal, is half the wind pressure for every ten feet of roof, and P its effective component, that is, the component at right angles to the roof (for the component of Q parallel to the roof and at right angles to P will have no effect on the roof), the resultant of P and the vertical load gives the force with which we have to deal in obtaining the effect on the parts.

Ex. 265. Taking *a c*, Fig. 231, to be 25 feet, the angle of *b a* 30° to the horizon, and *d a f* 15°, find the strains, first when the wind comes from the left, and second when it comes from the right. The roof in both cases being jointed at *f* and free to move at the other corner *c*.

224. The forces acting on the members of girders produced by loads, acting vertically on them, can be very easily determined by these graphical methods. In working out such

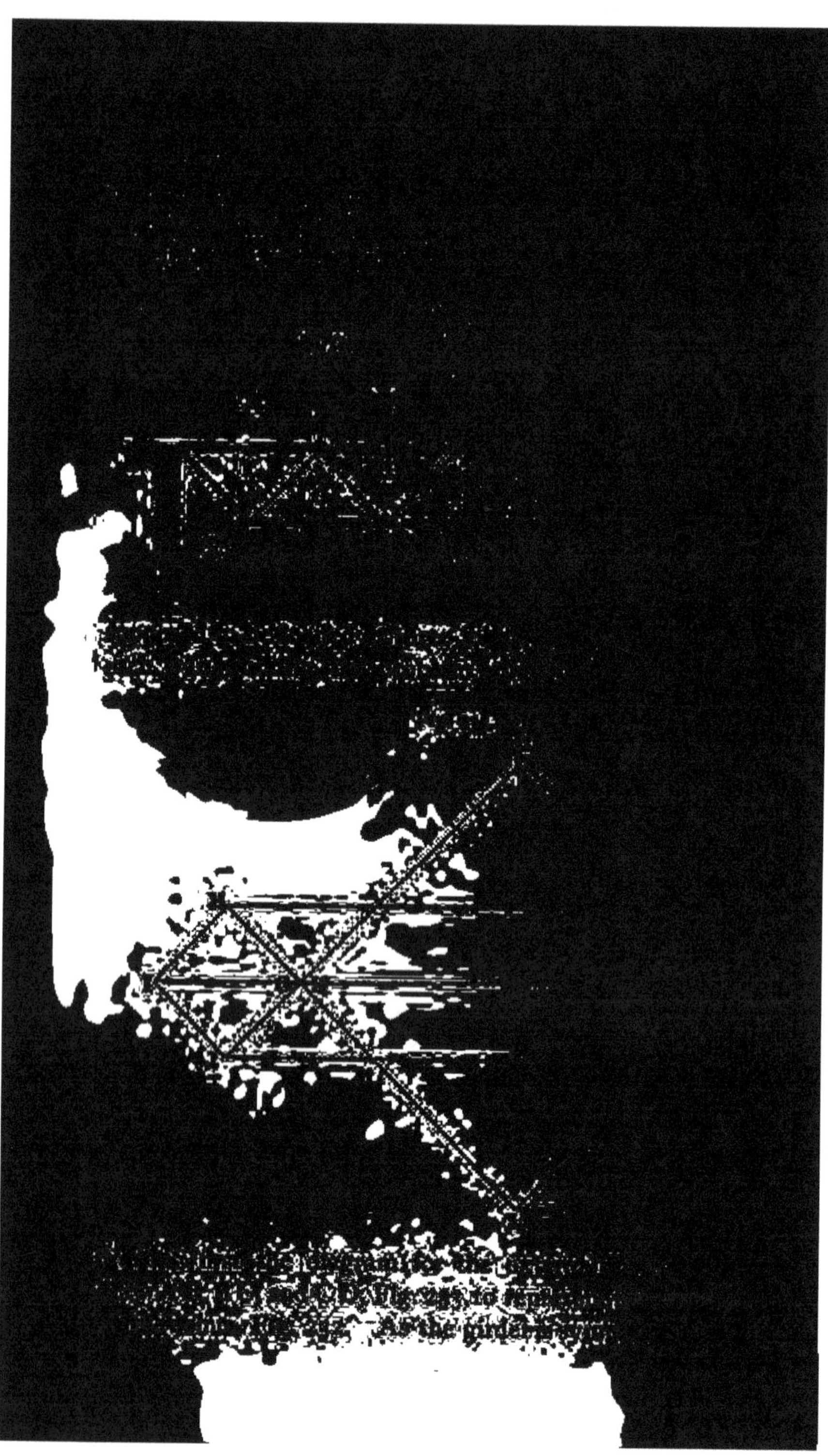

porting forces D E and A E will be equal, and each half the total load. These will be represented by D E and E A, Fig. 233. Next letter the bays of the girder F, G, H, I, J, K and L. Begin with joint at left end. The forces acting on it are, A F, F E, and E A. From A, Fig. 233, draw A F parallel to A F, Fig. 232, and from E draw E F parallel to F E, Fig. 232, the lines A F and F E will represent the forces acting on A F and F E, Fig. 232. Next take the joint acted on by F E. From F, Fig. 233, draw F G parallel to F G, Fig. 232, and from E draw E G, Fig. 233, parallel to E G, Fig. 232. Next take joint A B H G F. From B, Fig. 233, draw B H parallel to B H, Fig. 232, and from G, Fig. 233, draw G H parallel to G H, Fig. 232, A B H G F, is the polygon for this joint. Take next joint G H I E, Fig. 232. Draw H I, Fig. 233, parallel to H I, Fig. 232, E I parallel to E I, Fig. 232. Next joint B C J I H. Draw C J, and then I J. Next joint I J K E. Draw J K. Next joint C D L K J. Draw D L then K L. Next joint K L E. Join L E. This completes the solution. The lines must be next carefully measured, and the results tabulated thus

D L = A F = 595	B H = C J = 1385
L E = F E = 850	G H = J K = 285
K L = F G = 1182	H I = I J = 285
K E = G E = 850	= I E = 1585

Ex. 266. A chain consists of 26 six-foot links, and is attached at the ends to the joints A and B. Show the form

Fig. 234.

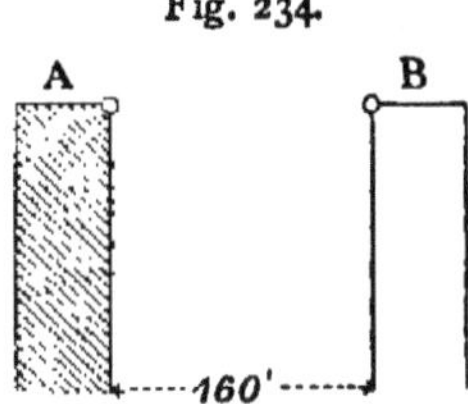

which the chain will take when the fall in the middle is as nearly as possible 15 feet.

CHAPTER LVIII.

BENDING MOMENT DIAGRAMS.

BY means of the linked polygon we can also find the bending moment at any section of a beam.

Let P, Fig. 235, be a force acting on the middle of the beam $e f$. Then the external forces will be represented by the line B C.

From A draw a perpendicular to B C and measure 10 units to the left, on the same scale as taken for measuring the length of the beam. From any point m in the line of the force A B draw a line parallel to o A, $m n$ to o B, and n P to o C.

225. We have seen already that the bending moment of a force about a point is equal to the force into the perpendicular distance of that force from that point. The moment at the section $g h$ will therefore be $\frac{P}{2} \times e h$.

Now,

$$\frac{k l}{m l} = \frac{A B}{O A} = \frac{\frac{P}{2}}{O A} = \frac{\frac{P}{2}}{10},$$

$$k l \times 10 = \frac{P}{2} \times m l,$$

$$= \frac{P}{2} \times e h,$$

$$= \text{moment of force at section } g h.$$

Hence $k l$ measured on the scale of forces and multiplied by 10 gives the bending moment.

226. As we did not fix on any particular section at which to take the bending moment, the above reasoning would have been true for any section, and the bending moment would have been represented by the line drawn directly below the

section in the polygon *m n* P, always, of course, remembering that one unit on this scale will represent 10 units of B.M.

The scale of bending moments is thus seen to be made up of the scale of lengths and scale of forces; for *o* A is measured on the scale of lengths. The scale of bending

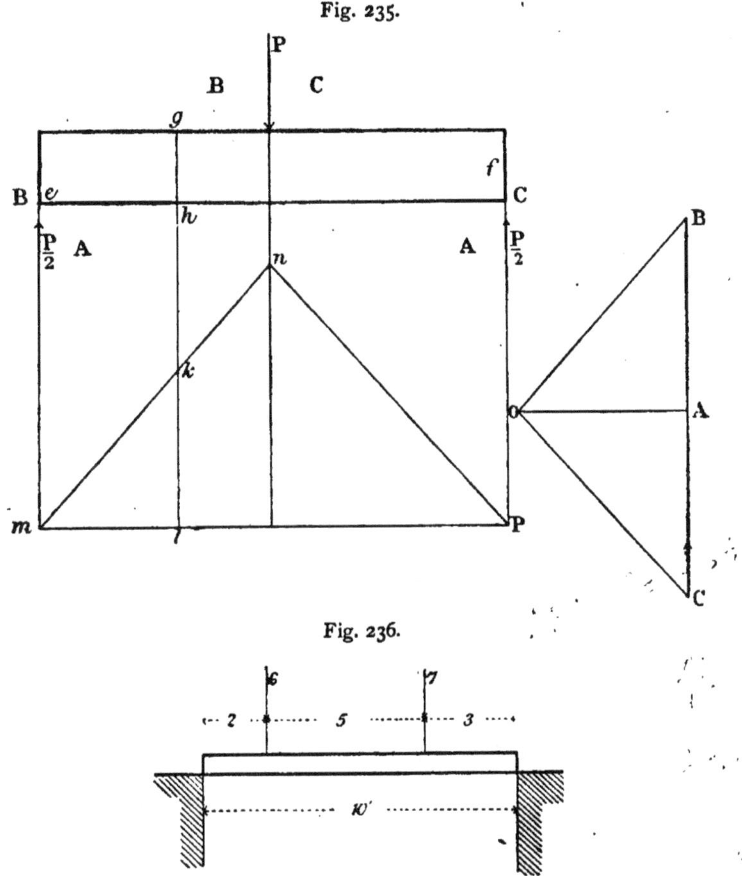

Fig. 235.

Fig. 236.

moments is always the scale of forces multiplied by *o* A units, or the length of the perpendicular from the line of forces to the pole *o*. For example, if the scale of forces was 10 lbs. to the inch, the scale of lengths 12 feet to the inch, and *o* A measured to units on this last scale, then the scale of bending moments would be 10 × 8 = 80 foot-lbs. per inch.

Ex. 267. Find the diagram representing the bending moment at any section of the beam, Fig. 236.

Find the diagram of bending moments for this beam Fig. 237, and write down the scales of length forces and bending moments. Write also down the B.M. at a section 5·25 feet from end A, and 9·9 from end A, Fig. 237.

Fig. 237.

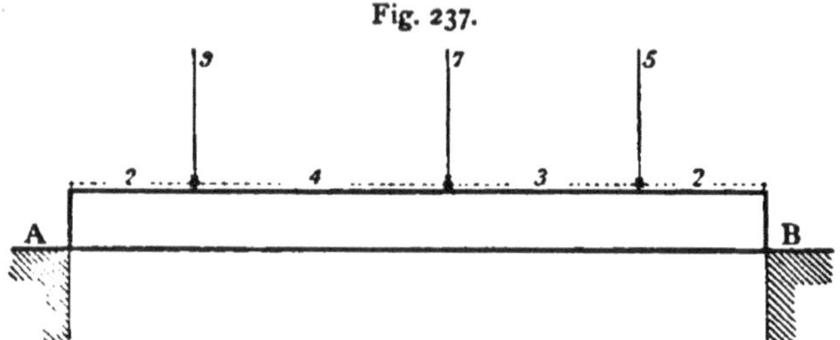

Ex. 268. A beam 35 feet long has a distributed load of 40 tons, find the diagram of bending moments.

CHAPTER LIX.

SHEARING STRESS DIAGRAMS.

227. At any section *a b* of the beam, Fig. 238, subjected to a load like P, the part of the beam to the right of *ab* has a tendency to go upwards, due to the pressure $\frac{P}{2}$, and the left-hand side a tendency to go downwards, due to the pressure P. For the sake of simplicity, we do not take the weight of the beam into consideration.

Now, since the part on the right of the section *a b* tries to go up from the part on the left, there will be strain on the material at that section.

228. This kind of strain is called shear strain. At any section on the right-hand side of the force P the tendency of

the part on the right of that section is to go up. We may represent this shearing force by a line *c d*; as the force from the middle of the beam to its end is uniform, it may be represented by any line in the rectangle *e f g h*.

Fig. 238.

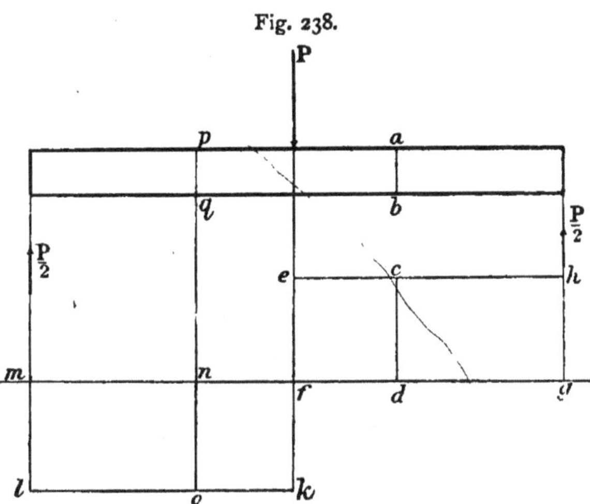

When we come from the right to P, we have on any section on the left of P a force P acting downwards and giving the beam a tendency to go downwards at that section, and a force $\frac{P}{2}$ acting upwards and tending to push the beam upwards against the force P. Still, of course, neglecting the weight of the beam. On the whole, therefore, the beam due to those two forces will have a tendency to go downwards, and that, due to a force $P - \frac{P}{2} = \frac{P}{2}$. The shearing force is therefore $\frac{P}{2}$, but as due to this force the beam on the right-hand side of the section tries to go downwards, we will settle on calling it a minus shearing strain; and being minus, we must draw a line on the lower side of *m g* to represent it. The line *n o* would represent this force at the section *p q*. And the force being uniform to the left of P, it may be represented by any line in the rectangle *m l k f* below the section taken.

Ex. 269. Show the curve of shearing strain due to the load on the beam, Fig. 239.

Ex. 270. Show the curve of bending moment for these two loads on second beam, Fig. 240.

Figs. 239 to 241.

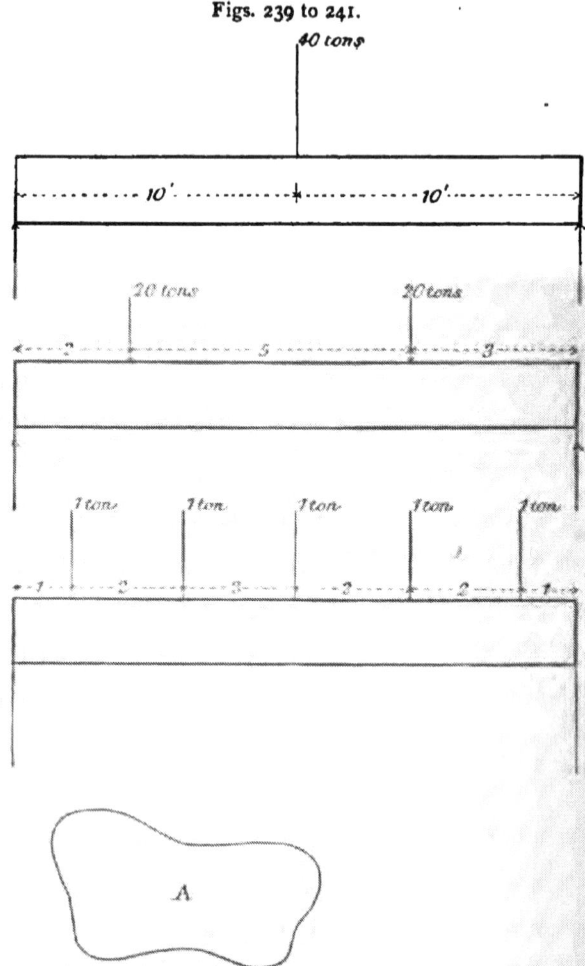

Ex. 271. Show the curve of bending moment, and also for shear strain in the third beam, Fig. 241.

Ex. 272. A beam 20 feet long has a uniform load of 1 ton to the foot of length. Show the curve of shear strain.

CHAPTER LX.

CENTRES OF GRAVITY.

229. ANY body on the earth is acted on by the force of gravity. This force acts towards the centre of the earth, and therefore the lines in which the forces act on the particles of which such a body as A is made up will converge towards the centre of the earth. But the bodies with which the practical engineer has to deal are so limited in size compared with the distance of the earth's centre, that we may treat the lines in which gravity acts on bodies as parallel lines.

In finding the centre of gravity of two such bodies as A and B, we suppose the resultant of all the forces acting on the particles to act at the geometrical centre of the body and in parallel lines.

Fig. 242.

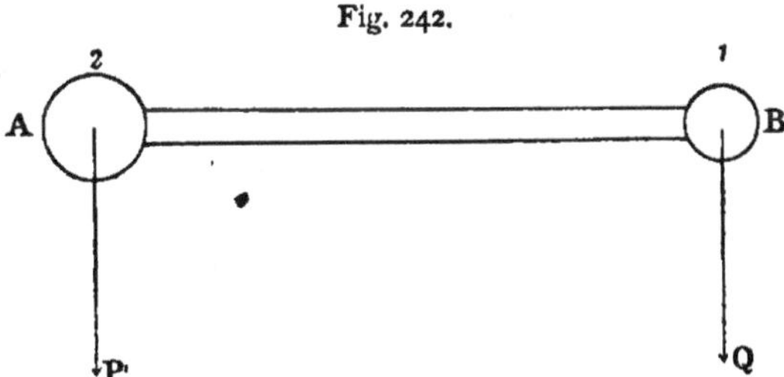

The centre of gravity will be in the line joining the centres. Its position will be a point in that line, found by dividing the line in inverse proportion to the masses.

Ex. 273. Find the centre of gravity of two balls; one 2 lb., the other 7 lb. The centres are horizontal, and 9 inches apart.

Ex. 274. Find the centre of gravity of three 4-lb. balls, one at each corner of an equilateral triangle, 3 inches side.

The centre of gravity of a triangle is in the line drawn from the middle of any side to the opposite corner, and at a point one-third the length of that line from the side.

The centre of gravity of a cone and of a pyramid is a

point one-fourth up the line drawn from the centre of gravity of the base to the apex.

Fig. 243.

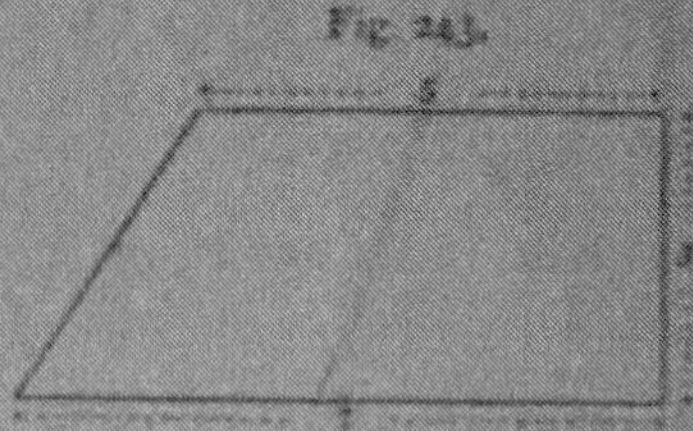

Ex. 275. Find the centre of gravity of two cones standing on H.P.; one with base 2 inches diameter and 4 inches high the other with base 2½ diameter and 4 inches high, distance between parallel axes 3 inches.

Ex. 276. Find the centre of gravity of two cones: one with base 2½ inches diameter and 3 inches high, the other with base 1½ inch diameter and 4 inches high, axes parallel and 3 inches apart.

Ex. 277. Find the centre of gravity of a pyramid with square base of 2 inches side, and axis 1¾ inch long; and a cone with 2 inches base, and axis 4 inches long, axes 4 inches apart, both standing on horizontal planes; one axis being 2 inches from V.P., the other 2¾ inches from the V.P.

230. The centre of gravity of a thin lamina, Fig. 244, is found by dividing it into a number of strips of equal breadth. The divisions are shown thick. The middle line of each part being very approximately the mean length of the part, may be taken to represent the weight of the part. In the figure A we may suppose the lengths of the thin middle lines to represent the weights of the parts. Representing these weights by a polygon, by taking a pole *o*, by drawing a link polygon on A, we get a point through which the resultant of the forces acts, as shown in Fig. 244.

Then dividing the figure into a number of equal parts by lines in another direction, and finding the resultant of the weights of these parts, we get two resultants crossing each other. The centre of gravity is contained by both resultant lines. It is, therefore, at the point where the lines cross.

Ex. 278. Find the centre of gravity of a semicircle of 2 inches radius.

Fig. 244.

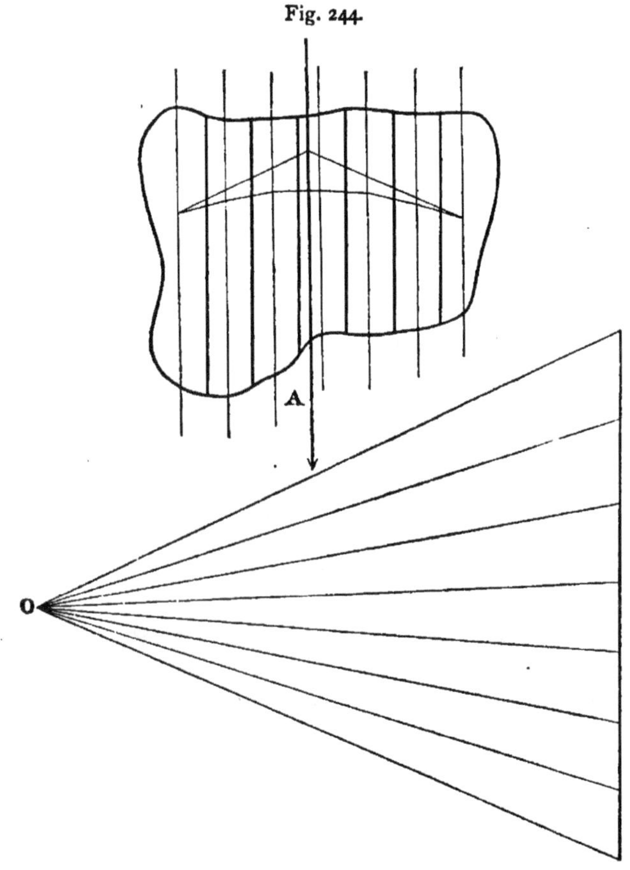

Ex. 279. Find the centre of gravity of any parabola of 3 inches axis.

Ex. 280. Find the centre of gravity of half of an ellipse, major axis $2\frac{1}{2}$ inches and minor axis $1\frac{1}{2}$ inches.

Ex. 281. Suppose the surface of England to be quite flat, find its centre of gravity. How far is the centre of gravity from London?

Ex. 282. Find the centre of gravity of Fig. A on page 218.

SECTION XII.

VALVE MOTIONS.

CHAPTER LXI.

THE ACTION OF THE SLIDE VALVE.

231. SUPPOSE, for the purpose of illustrating the motion given to a valve by the eccentric, that the crank and eccentric are worked on two different shafts, the eccentric being above the main shaft, as shown in Fig. 245. As the eccentric is fixed to the same shaft as the crank, it goes round with the crank, always moving through the same angle as the crank in the same time; so we will suppose like conditions for the crank and eccentric in their new places.

232. The simplest case which can present itself to anyone studying the motions of a valve, is the case in which the valve just covers the ports and no more when the piston is at the end of the stroke, and is full open to steam at one end when the piston is at mid-stroke and travelling from that end. Fig. 245 shows the valve just covering both ports against the admission of steam to either end of the cylinder while the piston is at the end of its stroke. It will also be observed that the centre of the eccentric is at right angles to the direction of the crank, and that the valve is at mid-stroke when the piston is at the end of its stroke. Fig. 246 shows the piston at mid-stroke and the valve at the end of its stroke admitting steam to the left end of the cylinder. Fig. 247 shows the piston at the other end while steam is shut off. When the crank has moved through another quarter of a revolution the valve will have moved to the end of its stroke, and will be admitting steam to the right side of cylinder, and

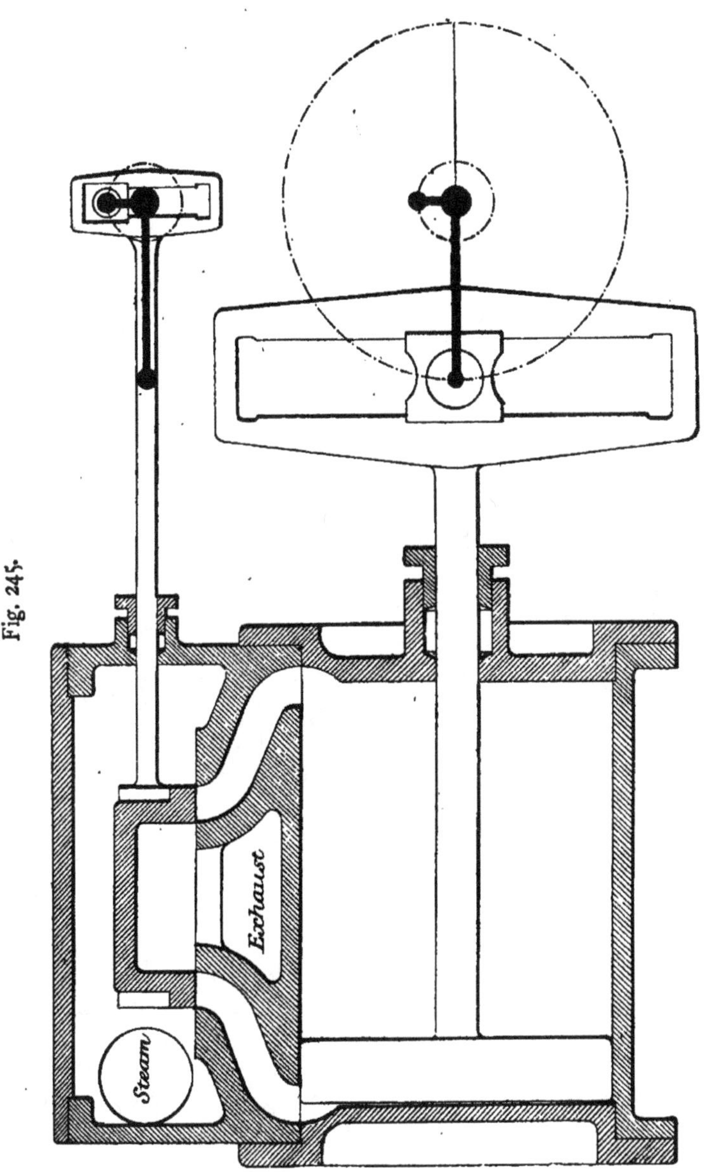

Fig. 245.

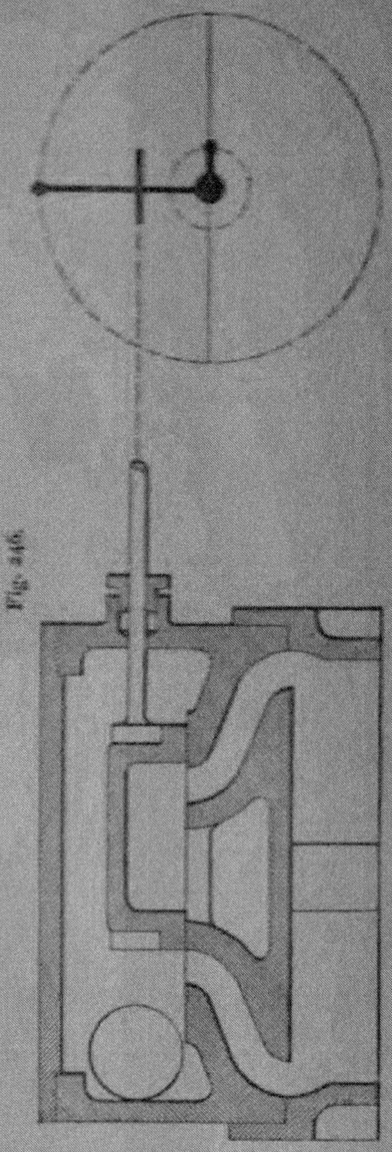

Fig. 246.

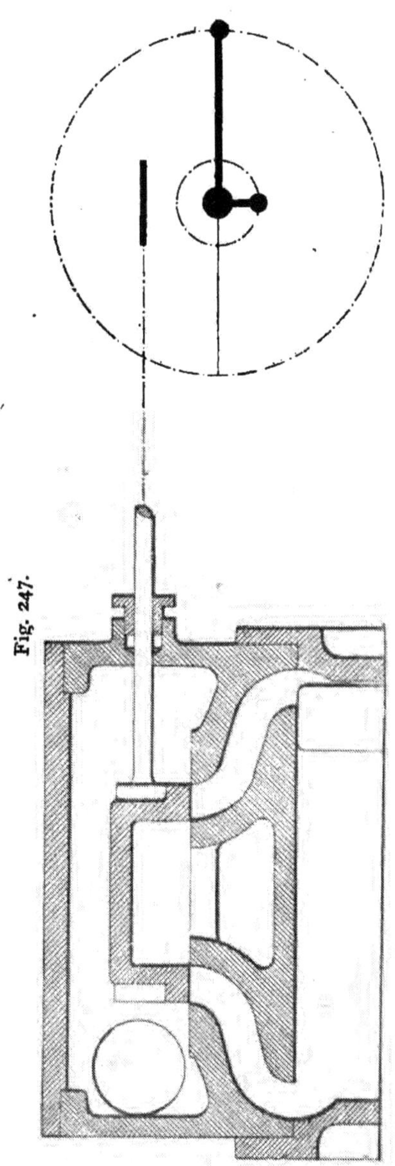

Fig. 247.

Fig. 245 shows the condition of things after a complete revolution has been made and another cycle of operations is just beginning. This kind of valve is called the normal valve. Such a valve does not allow any expansion of steam, for it does not cut off steam until the piston has travelled the whole length of the stroke.

CHAPTER LXII.

NORMAL VALVE DIAGRAM.

233. THE motions of the valve are mostly studied by the aid of a valve diagram. At the beginning of the study of those motions by such aid it is often imagined that the matter is very complicated; but it is not so after some perseverance. And the student is therefore advised not to be discouraged if he does not understand it quite clearly at first.

Fig. 248.

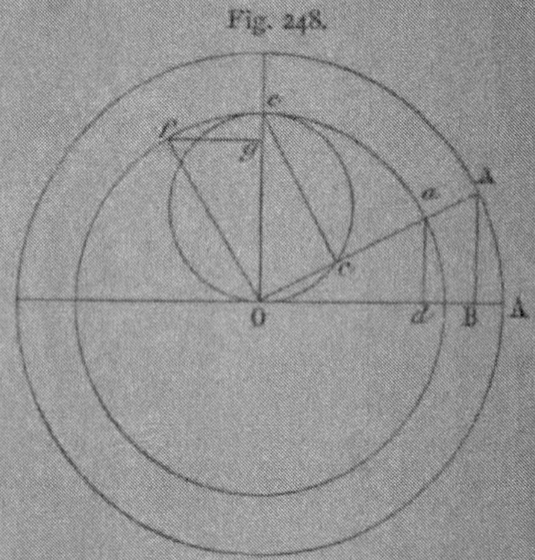

Suppose O A, Fig. 248, moving in the opposite direction to the hands of a clock shows the position of a crank at a certain instant. If the inner concentric circle represents the path of the centre of the eccentric, then the eccentric being

90° in advance of the crank, *o f* will be the position of the eccentric, and *f g* will represent the travel of the valve from its mid position. Now since *o f* is equal to *o a*, and the angle *f o e* equal to the angle *a o d*, the perpendicular *a d* will be equal to *f g*. And therefore *a d* may be taken to represent the travel of the valve from its middle position.

If *o e* be drawn at right angles to the position of the crank when it is at the end of the stroke, and a circle be described on *o e* as diameter, then *o c* being equal to *a d* the intercepted part *o c* of the crank will represent the travel of the valve from the middle position. For if we join *e* and *c*, we have *o e c* and *a o d* complements of the same angle *e o c*, and, therefore, equal to each other.

And $\angle\, eco = \angle\, oda$, being right angles,

and $eo = oa$;

$\therefore\ \Delta\, eoc = \Delta\, oad$,

and $oc = ad$.

And *o c* the part of the crank intercepted by the circle, described on *o e* as diameter, represents the travel of the valve from the middle position.

Thus, by drawing a line to represent the crank in any position, the travel of the valve from its middle position can at once be found; for it is the part of the crank line intercepted by the circle on *o e*.

CHAPTER LXIII.

EXPANSION OF STEAM.

234. JAMES WATT, when experimenting with the crude steam engines of his time, found that it was much more economical to stop the admission of steam before the piston reached the end of its stroke. For by thus cutting off the steam, that steam already in the cylinder was allowed to expand, exerting pressure through space as it did so; and thus the work done

by the steam on the piston from the point of cut off to the end of the stroke was got from the expansion of the steam and not, as formerly, from extra steam being admitted.

235. Let us compare the work done by a cylinder full of steam when no expansion takes place, with that done by the same amount of steam when expansion does take place. When no expansion takes place steam is admitted during all the time, and at the end of the stroke a cylinder full of steam has been used. With this amount of steam one stroke at full pressure has been performed. But when expansion takes place the action is modified. For example, if the cut off took place at half-stroke, the half cylinder full of steam expanded and did a certain amount of work by expansion. During the next stroke the same thing was done. So during the two strokes a cylinder full of steam was used, and in this time two half strokes at full pressure were made. But beside this amount of work there was an additional amount of work due to expansion, namely, two half-strokes at varying but considerable mean pressure. So by using expansion we get two extra half strokes at considerable mean pressure performed by the cylinder full of steam.

236. The advantage of the expansion is best shown by comparing two areas which represent the work done in each case by the same amount of steam.

Fig. 249.

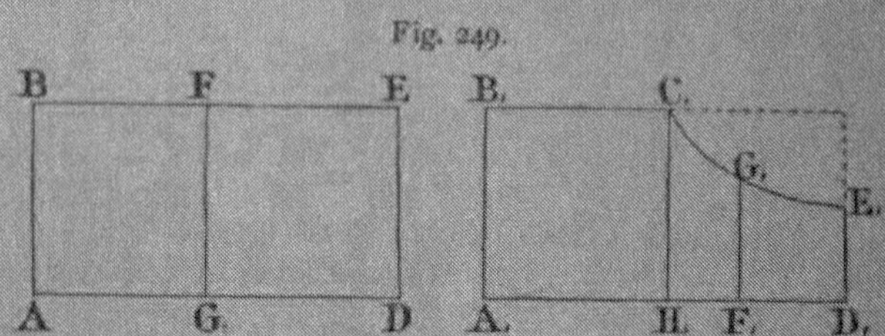

If A B represent the pressure of the steam in lbs., and A D represent the stroke of the engine. When the pressure is constant, the pressure at F when the piston is at any position F G will be just equal to A B. And this will be the same for any point along A D. But in the second case the pressure is reduced after the middle of the stroke, for at any point like F, it will be represented by the line F, G,, which is reduced in length. But the work done in the two cases by the same quantity of steam is very different. In the first case the full cylinder of steam does the work represented by the rectangle A B E D, and in the second case half a cylinder full of steam does the work represented by A, B, C, H,, and in the next stroke the next half cylinder full of steam does the work represented by the same area. Twice the area A, C, is equal to the area B D, so that the work done in the second case in the first halves of the two strokes is equal to the total work done in the first case. But in the second case the work done in second halves of the strokes are still to count. The work done in each will be represented by the area C, G, E, D, F, H, and this is considerably more than half A C. The extra work got out of the steam by expansion is represented by twice C, G, E, D, F, H, A,.

237. Or putting it in another way—

Work done by one cylinder full of steam when there is no expansion is represented by area

A B E D.

Work done by one cylinder full of steam with expansion is represented by the areas

2 A, B, C, H, + 2 C, G, E, D, F, H,,

but

2 A, B, C, H, = A B E D

is represented by

A B E D + 2 C, G, E, D, F, H,.

Advantage of expansion over no expansion is represented by

2 C, G, E, F, H,.

CHAPTER LXIV.

THE VALVE PROBLEM STATED.

238. THE problem which would come before the designer of the valve, and the fitter who sets the eccentric, would present itself somewhat in this fashion.

Fig. 250.

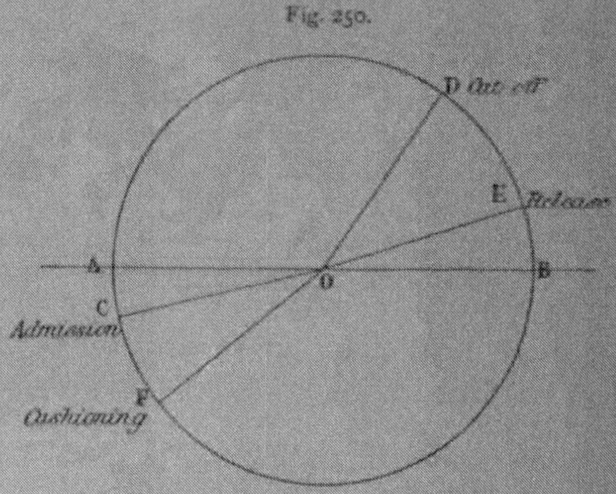

He would be given the stroke of the engine A B, Fig. 250; the position of the crank O C when steam is to be admitted; the position of the crank O D when expansion has to begin; the position of the crank O E when the steam is to be released; or in place of this last the position of the crank O F when cushioning has to begin. And he has to find the radius of the eccentric, or the eccentricity; the outside and inside laps, the lead, and the angle of advance of the valve.

239. Now in the normal valve we have the arm of the eccentric just 90° in advance of the crank arm; so that if O A, Fig. 251, is the position of the crank at the beginning of the stroke, then O *a*, which is 90° in advance of this position, is the place where the eccentric arm will be. When the engine

has to be constructed to allow expansion to take place, the relative positions of the two arms are different. For, suppose we have the problem set above and represented in Fig. 250

Fig. 251.

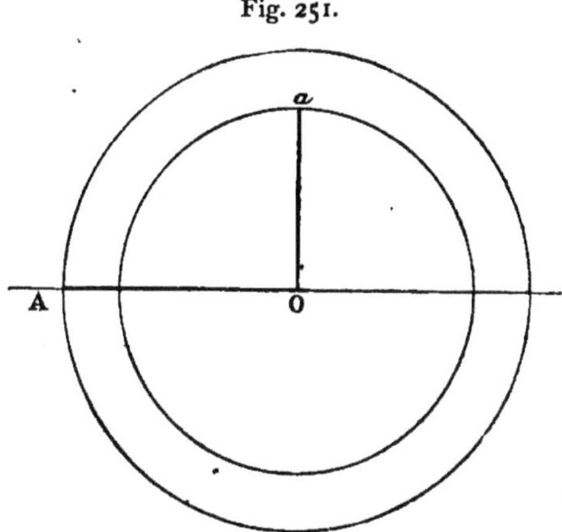

to solve. The angle moved through by the eccentric arm will just be the same as the angle moved through by the crank arm. That is, between the points of admission and cut off, the eccentric arm must move through an angle equal to the angle C O D, Fig. 250.

CHAPTER LXV.

THE RADIUS OF THE ECCENTRIC BY CALCULATION.

240. Now let us examine the action of the eccentric. Suppose O *a*, Fig. 252, shows the position of the eccentric arm when steam is just going to be admitted, and *e* represents the position of the valve V. When the eccentric arm comes to *c*, V will have reached *f*, its furthest position to the right, and *e f*, which is equal to *d c*, is the greatest amount of opening to steam. Now, before V can have come back to the point *e* the eccentric must come into the position *o b*, the point

[illegible]

[illegible]

Fig. [illegible]

[illegible]

[illegible] by construction.

Let

w = width of port.

n = fraction of greatest opening [illegible] steam.

nw = greatest opening to steam.

$$nw = dc = oc - od.$$

But

$$oc = \rho = \text{radius of eccentric}$$

Then

$$nw = \rho - od$$

but

$$\frac{o\,d}{o\,a} = \text{cos. } a\,o\,c$$

$$o\,d = o\,a.\ \text{cos. } a\,o\,c$$
$$= \rho \text{ cos. } \tfrac{1}{2} \text{ C O D}$$
$$\therefore \quad n\,w = \rho - \rho \text{ cos. } \tfrac{1}{2} \text{ C O D}$$
$$= \rho\,(1 - \text{cos. } \tfrac{1}{2} \text{ C O D}) \ .$$

$$\rho = \frac{n\,w}{1 - \text{cos. } \frac{1}{2} \text{ C O D}} = \frac{\text{greatest opening to steam}}{1 - \text{cos. } \frac{1}{2} \begin{Bmatrix} \text{angle moved through} \\ \text{during admission.} \end{Bmatrix}}.$$

This is the formula for finding the radius by calculation; but it may also be found by construction.

CHAPTER LXVI.

RADIUS OF ECCENTRIC BY CONSTRUCTION.

243. SUPPOSE that the angle C O D, Fig. 254, is the angle moved through by the crank while steam is being admitted. Half this angle is to be moved through by the eccentric arm

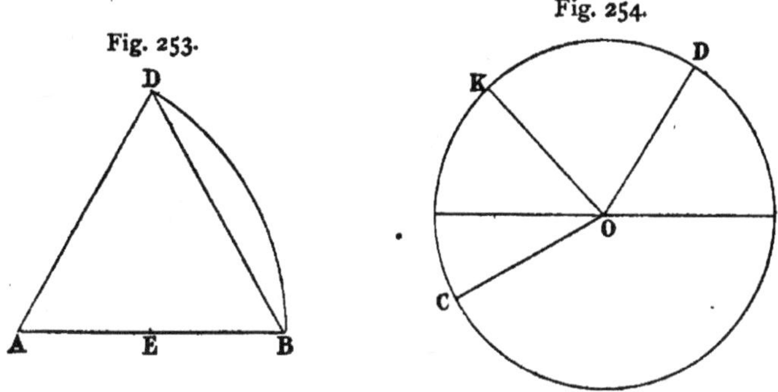

on each side of the line of centres. Take then a horizontal line A B, Fig. 253, and set off D A B equal to *c o a*, Fig. 252, half *b o a*, which is just half the angle C O D, Fig. 254. Drop a perpendicular from D on A B, Fig. 253. Suppose this perpendicular meets A B in E. Then if E B is just equal to the greatest opening to steam required, A D would be the length of the eccentric arm. And note that A D and A B are equal, being radii of the same circle.

244. Should E B be not equal to the opening to steam, then draw A D and A B inclined at an angle equal to half the angle C O D. From D drop a perpendicular on A B, and let this perpendicular meet in E. Produce D A, D E and

Fig. 255.

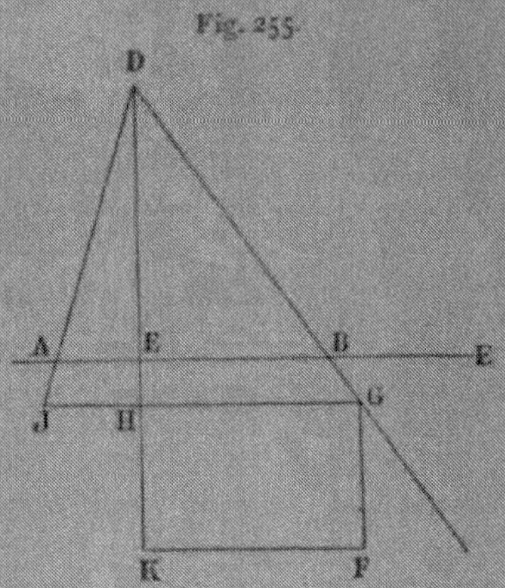

D B. From any point K in D K draw K F perpendicular to D K and equal to $n w$. Through F draw F G parallel to D K, and let it cut D B, or D B produced in G. Draw G H parallel to K F, and let G H meet D A, produced if necessary in the point J. J D is the radius of the crank.

$$\text{H G} = n w = \rho(1 - \cos. \text{D J G}).$$

But

$$\begin{aligned} \text{H G} &= \text{J G} - \text{J H} \\ &= \text{J G}(1 - \cos. \text{D J G}); \end{aligned}$$

but

$$\text{J D} = \text{J G},$$
$$\text{H G} = \text{J D}(1 - \cos. \text{D J G}),$$

$$\therefore \text{J D}(1 - \cos \text{D J G}) = \rho(1 - \cos. \text{D J G}),$$
$$\text{J D} = \rho.$$

CHAPTER LXVIII.

LAP.

245. Now to find the inside lap, outside lap, and the lead of the valve, describe any circle A E B′, to represent the path of the crank pin. For convenience the radius may be taken greater than the length of the eccentric arm, which has been found above. Lay off O C the position of the crank when admission takes place, and O D its position at cut off, O E the position at release, and O F at cushioning. Next with O as centre and the length of eccentric arm as radius, describe the circle

Fig. 256.

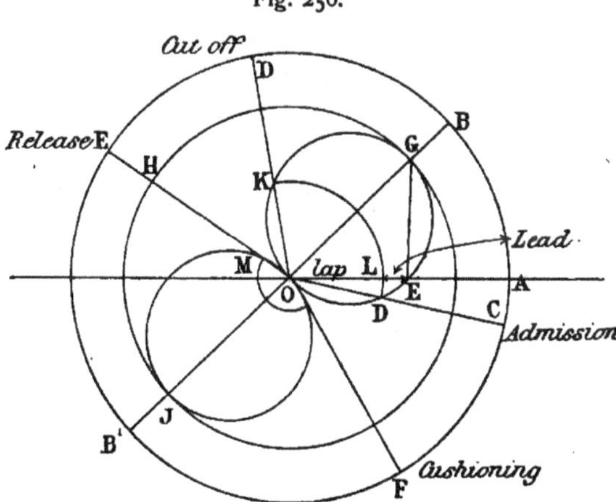

G H J to represent the path of the eccentric centre. Bisect D O C with the line O B, and on O G as diameter describe a circle. This circle will represent the motion of the valve. This circle will cut O C, the line of admission in the point D, and O D shows the amount of travel of the valve from its mid position before admission takes place. The length O D therefore represents the outside lap of the valve. Describe the lap circle D K. K of course is already found, for it is the point where the cut-off line O D cuts the valve circle.

246. At the end of the stroke the crank pin is at A, and the travel of the valve at the beginning of the stroke is O E, and therefore the amount of opening to steam will be O E, minus the lap, that is L E. This amount of opening at the beginning of the stroke is called the lead. Lastly, the inside lap is to be found. The line O H, which represents the position of the crank when release takes place, will cut the lower circle described on O J at the point M, and O M will show the travel of the valve from the mid position when the valve is just opening to exhaust. The length O M will therefore show how much inside lap must be put on to keep the steam shut to exhaust while the valve travels from its mid position by a distance O M.

247. All that is required for the construction of the valve is now found, having given the positions of the crank when admission, cut-off, and release takes place.

The radius of eccentric is ..	J D,	Fig.	255.
The outside lap	O D	„	256.
The inside lap	O M	„	„
The lead	L E	„	„

248. In the case of the normal valve we showed that the arm of the eccentric was 90° in advance of the crank arm; but when expansion takes place the angle is greater. The amount of advance of an eccentric arm which gives expansion is always measured by the difference between the angle that it is in front of the crank arm and the arm of the normal valve. If *o c*, Fig. 257, represents the position of crank, then *o d* represents the position of the normal eccentric arm; and if *o a* represents the position of the arm of any eccentric which gives expansion, then the angle *a o d* is the angle between the normal and expansion arm. It is called the angle of advance. It may be put in this other way. The eccentric arm is 90° + angle of advance in front of crank arm.

249. A change in the angle of advance makes a great change in the amount of expansion performed by the steam. This can be very clearly shown by drawing the probable valve

diagrams obtained by using different angles of advance, the other conditions remaining the same.

Fig. 257.

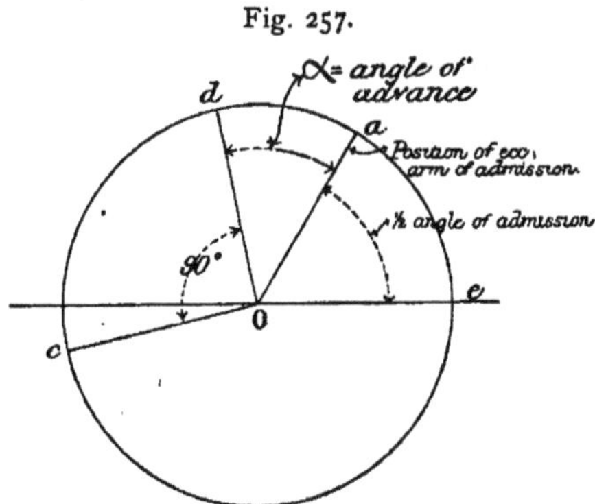

250. For example, take first the angle of advance to be $l\,o\,b'$, Fig. 258. Let $o\,m$ be the lap. Describe with $o\,m$ as radius the lap circle $m\,n$. Also describe the inside lap circle $p\,q$ with the inside lap as radius. On $o\,b'$ as diameter describe a valve circle, and where $m\,n$ cuts the outside lap circles draw the admission line $o\,a_1$, and the expansion line $o\,o_1$.

Now project the points A and B on to a horizontal line $g\,h$. Set up $h\,e$ to represent the pressure of steam in the boiler.

From a_1 draw a projector. Admission will take place at some such point as k_1 in this projector. Project down o_1 to the horizontal line through e. The cut off takes place at e, and the pressure begins to drop from that point, but not nearly so quickly as shown in figure. Now draw $o\,r$, through the intersection of the inside lap circle $p\,q$ and the lower valve circle whose diameter is $o\,d_{\prime}$ corresponding to $o\,b_{\prime}$. Drop a projector from $r_{\prime}$. The exhaust opens to steam at some such point as f_1 (though it is not quite so low as shown), and the condenser pressure will be $g\,h$. Draw $o\,c_1$ through the second point of intersection of the two circles $p\,q$ and the valve circle on $o\,d_1$. The projector from $o\,c$, which meets $g\,h$, shows that the cushioning of the steam or air left in the cylinder begins at the point h_1. This cushioning helps to pull up the speed of the piston before it comes to the end of the stroke, and so prevents injury to the parts.

Fig. 258.

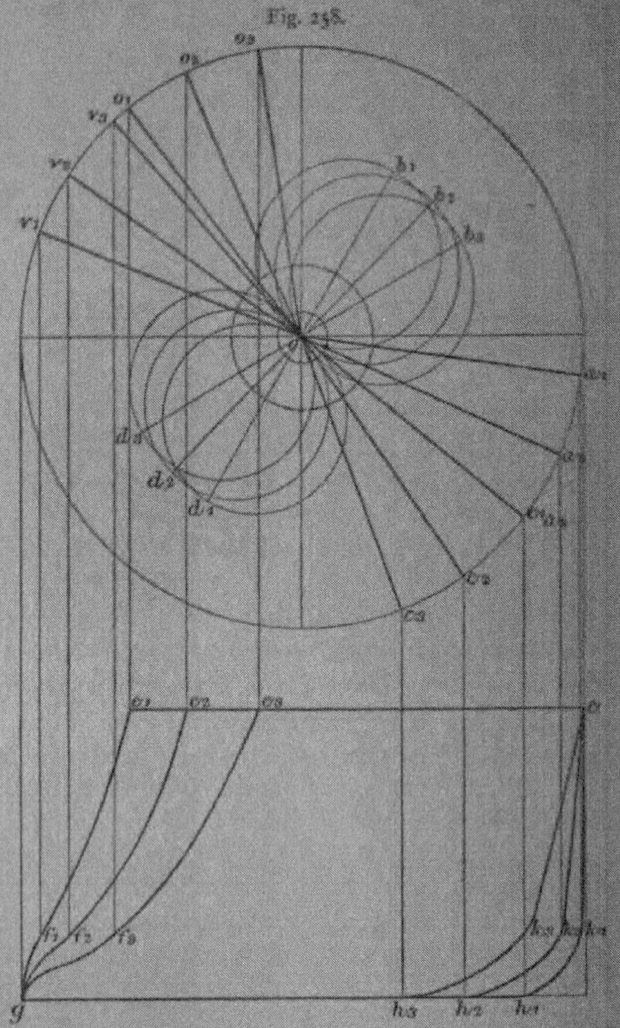

Take next $l\,o\,b^2$ as the angle of advance, and by the valve circle constructed on $o\,b_2$ find the points e_2 f_2 h_2 and k_2 to show where expansion, release, cushioning, and admission, respectively take place. So when $l\,o\,b_3$ is the angle of advance, find [illegible] and k_3.

Now it will be observed that the areas enclosed by the curves joining these sets of points vary a great deal, and that the variation of areas, and therefore the work done which is represented by the areas, is due to the variation of the angles of advance.

CHAPTER LXIX.

DOUBLE ECCENTRIC.

251. THE locomotive engines of our railways have to be so constructed that they can run backwards as well as forwards. This capability of going in both directions depends on the piston and connecting rod being capable of driving the axle round in either direction. The capability of the piston, which may be travelling from one end of the cylinder to the other in a particular direction and then before it reaches the end to suddenly receive steam on the opposite side and proceed in the opposite direction, depends on the possibility of sending steam into either end of cylinder at will. This admission of steam into either end of the cylinder at will depends on the capability of suddenly shifting the valve and causing it to cover the port which it has opened, and opening the port which it had closed.

252. The shifting of the valve is brought about by having two eccentrics instead of one. One of the eccentrics is fitted on the shaft relatively to the crank, to cause the valve to work the engine and shaft in one direction; while the other is fitted relatively to the crank, to enable the valve to work the engine and shaft in the other direction.

The power of the double eccentric to cause the engine shaft to revolve in either direction is best shown by sketches. We have already seen that the centre line of the eccentric is in the normal valve, always 90° in advance of the crank, and that when expansion is in request the eccentric centre line is (90° + the angle of advance) in advance of the crank. So if *o* A, Fig. 259, represents the position of the crank and *o a* the position of the eccentric, then the engine will be revolving in the direction of the arrow. But if, leaving the position of the

Fig. 259. Fig. 260.

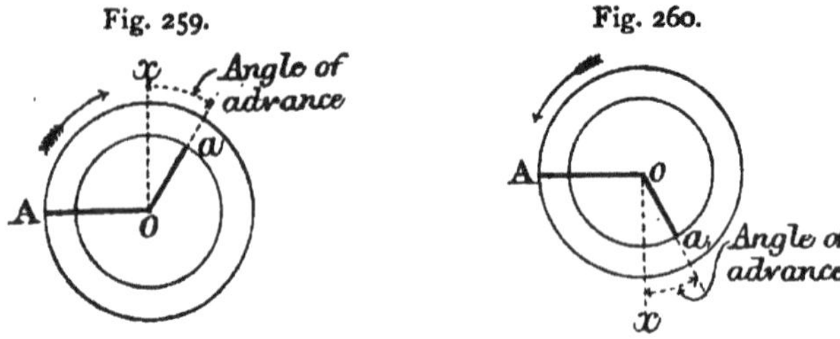

crank just as it is, we arrange that the eccentric centre line lies along $o\ a_{,}$, Fig. 260, then the engine will revolve in the opposite to direction as shown by the arrow.

253. Suppose next that we join the two eccentrics together and have some means of detaching suddenly the eccentric rod from a and attaching it to $a_{,}$ and *vice versâ*, then if we can do this we have power to reverse the motion of the engine.

Fig. 261.

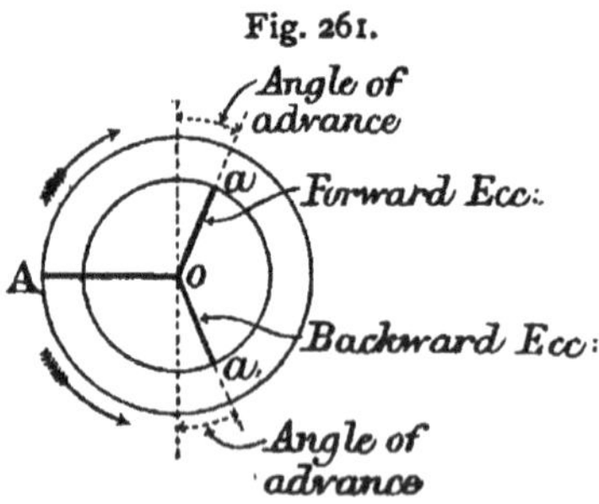

If when the eccentric rod is attached to a, the direction of the engine is forward; when it is attached to $a_{,}$ it will move backward. In consequence of this forward and backward motion produced by the eccentrics, the eccentric which produces the forward motion is called the forward eccentric, and that which produces the backward motion is called the backward eccentric. The eccentric $o\ a$ is called the forward, and $o\ a_{,}$ the backward. The eccentric rods are named in the same way: that attached to $o\ a$ is called the forward rod, while that attached to $o\ a_{,}$ the backward.

CHAPTER LXX.

LINK MOTIONS.

254. NOW the sudden shifting of *o a* out of action, and *o* $a_{,}$ into action, is not done at the eccentric end of the eccentric rods, but at the other end.

Fig. 262.

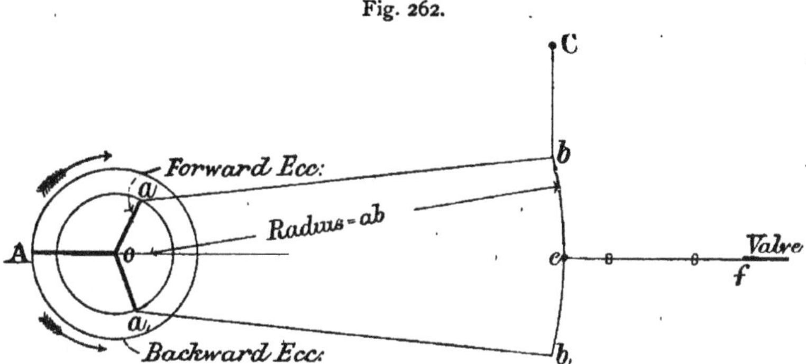

The two eccentric rods *a b* and $a_{,}$ $b_{,}$ are attached to another link *b* $b_{,,}$ which can be pulled quickly up and down by the rod *b* C. When it is required that the engine should go forward, the link *b* $b_{,}$ is suddenly pushed downwards by means of the rod *b* C until *b* coincides with *e*, as shown in Fig. 263. The effect of the motion of $b_{,,}$ the other end of the link moved by $a_{,,}$ is not felt by the valve, and the motion of *e f* and the valve are as if actuated solely by *o a*. The result is that the engine shaft revolves as shown by the arrow, Fig. 263. On the contrary, when it is required that the engine should go in the backward direction, the rod C *b* is suddenly pulled up until $b_{,}$ coincides with *e*. The position of the links when $b_{,}$ coincides with *e* is shown in Fig. 264. In this second case the effect of the motion of *b*, the upper end of the link moved by *a*, is not felt, and the rod *e f* and the valve move as if solely actuated by $a_{,}$. The result is that the engine shaft revolves in a backward direction.

255. It will be observed that the radius of the link *b b*, which is made to move round the centre *o* and slide on the block *e*, is equal to the length of the eccentric rod, and that it is concave towards the shaft. This system of link motion is called Stephenson's.

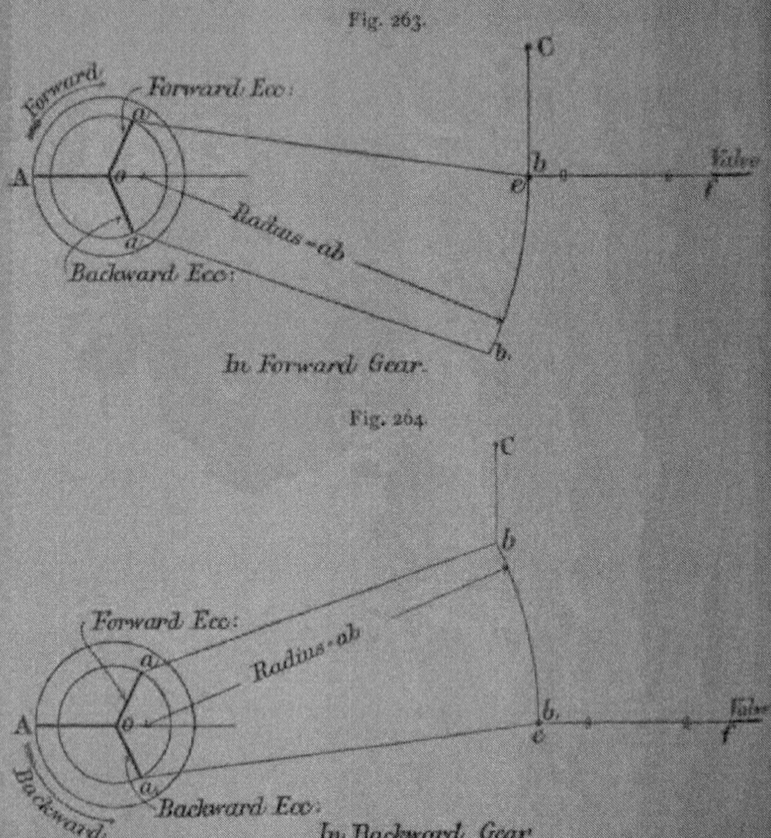

Fig. 263.

In Forward Gear.

Fig. 264.

In Backward Gear

Sometimes Stephenson's eccentric rods are crossed, as shown in Fig. 265. This only reverses the order of things at the link end. When *b*, the lower end of link which is drawn by *a*, is at *e* the motion of the shaft is forward, and when *b*, is at *e* backward. The eccentrics still fulfil the same function.

256. Another modification is to have the link stationary

suspended by a link K*l* and the valve rod *ef* free to move about the joint *f* and *e* to slide quickly up and down the link. As *e* moves round *f* it necessitates the link being curved the other way; that is convex towards the shaft. The radius of curvature of the link is the length *ef*. The dotted line $n_1 f$ shows the eccentric rod pulled up and the forward eccentric giving motion to the valve. This system of link motion is called Gooch's.

Fig. 265.

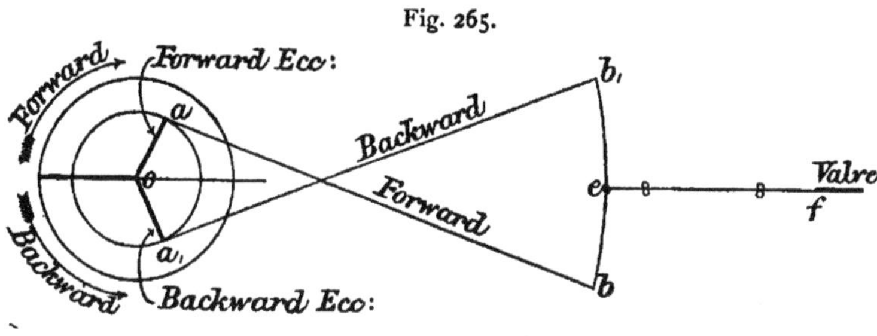

Fig. 266.

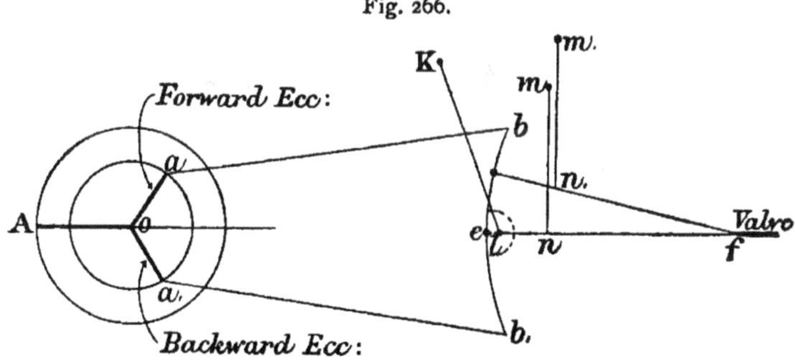

257. In Allen's link motion both the slide and the link in which it slides, move. If a forward motion is required the slide is pulled up as in the Gooch, and the suspension link is pushed down as in the Stephenson. The effect of the two motions is to make the suspension link straight. For as the lifting or lowering of the slide caused the link to be curved concave towards the valve, and the lifting or lowering of the suspension link caused the link to be curved concave towards the shaft, so when both take place together the effects are neutralised and the link made straight.

CHAPTER LXXI.

ANALYSIS OF THE MOTIONS OF ECCENTRICS.

258. WHEN describing the action of the link motions, it was pointed out that the reverse motion was obtained by suddenly shifting the position of the slide block from *b* to $b_{,,}$ Fig. 268 ; but nothing was said of what would happen should the slide remain at some intermediate position between the extreme positions *b* and $b_,$. What would be the effect on the valve should the slide remain at a point like *e*? This can be best answered by explaining first the kind of motion each of the end points *b* and $b_,$ have, and then showing what is their influence on other points of the suspension link $b\,b_,$. We are imagining that *b* stands still, for the purpose of examining only the effect on $b_,$. If $b_,$ is kept moving in a horizontal line it will only receive the reciprocating motion which is communicated to it by the eccentric $o\,a_,$.

Now the horizontal motion produced on $b_,$ will be just the horizontal motion of $a_,$ itself, and the motion of $a_{,,}$ the centre of the eccentric, is just the same as a point in the circumference of a circle which revolves about the centre with a radius $o\,a_,$. But what is the horizontal motion of a point in the circumference of a circle?

259. Suppose a point is moving with uniform velocity round the circumference of the circle *f l g*, Fig. 267. Then it will move over equal spaces in equal times. And if *f h*, *h k*, *k l*, &c., are equal spaces, the time taken by the point to move over these spaces will be the same. Now if we imagine that there is a point rigidly connected to the point in the circumference; but always remaining in the diameter, and always situated just under the point in the circumference; so that when the point in the circumference P is at *h*, then the point *n* is at *a*, and when at *k*, the point *n* is at *b*. It will be seen that when P travels over the distance *f h*, the point *n* will travel over the

small distance $f\,a$, and when P has travelled over $h\,k$ the point n will have passed through $a\,b$, which is greater than $f\,a$. It will be observed that when the point P is near the ends of the diameter, the point n travels slowly and moves over very little space; but when the point P is at the top of the circle the space passed through by n is almost equal to the space passed through by P. The motion then, of n is slow at the ends of the diameter and quick at the middle. It starts at the end from rest, increases its speed to a maximum at the middle, and then diminishes towards the end. Now this kind of motion is the horizontal motion of the point P. This kind of motion is called harmonic motion.

Fig. 267.

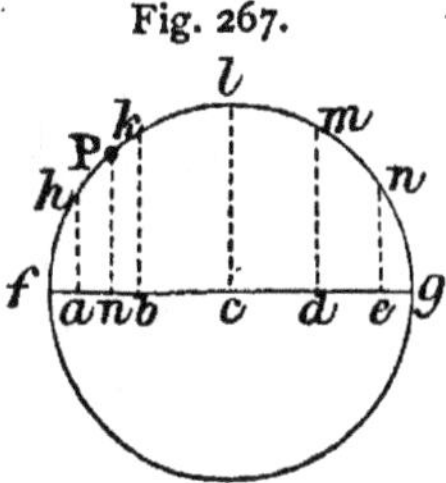

The horizontal motion of a, Fig. 268, is just like n, Fig. 267, for a moves in a circle at a uniform speed. The horizontal motion of b is the same as that of a, and $b_{,}$ the same as $a_{,}$; these four moving backwards and forwards with a motion like the motion of the point n, which we have just analysed.

260. Now suppose $b_{,}$ to become stationary and to act as a centre, about which the lever $b\,b_{,}$ swings. The point b is swinging backwards and forwards with a harmonic motion, the point g, half way down, will have exactly the same motion, only its extent will be just half that of b, and any point e will have a motion exactly of the same kind as those two, but of an extent something between the extent of b and g.

261. But this is not the whole motion of e, for $b_{,}$ does not stand still as we have supposed, but moves in exactly the same way as b, only when b is going to the right $b_{,}$ is going to the left. But to understand the effect of the motion of $b_{,}$ on e we must proceed as before, and suppose that b stands still and acts as the centre to the swinging lever $b\,b_{,}$. The point $b_{,}$ will have a harmonic motion like $a_{,}$, and its effect on g will be to give it a harmonic motion exactly similar to its own but just half the extent. The effect on the point e will be

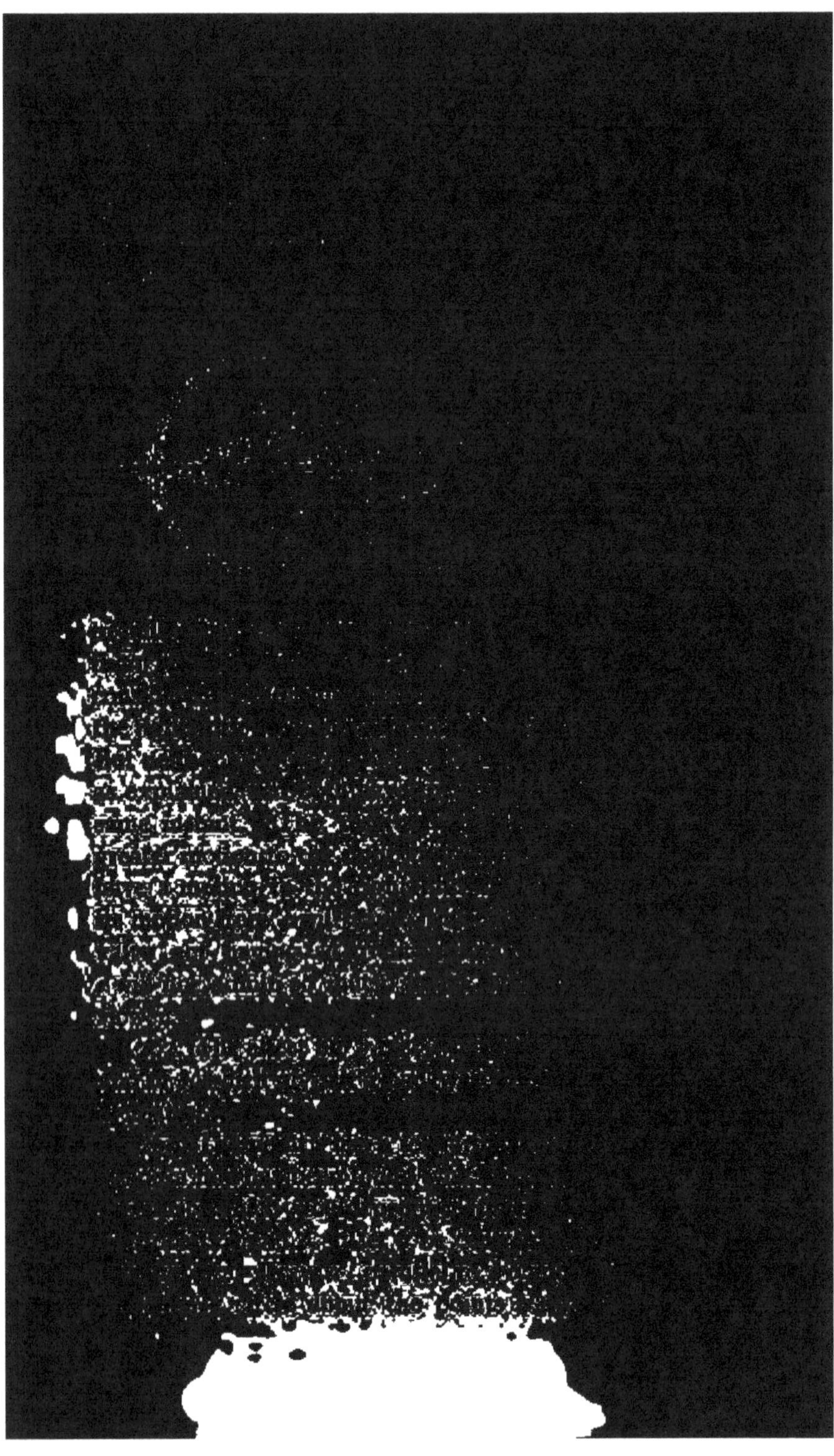

circle between $a\,a_{,}$ will contain the centres of the supposed eccentrics.

The eccentric arm which will produce the same effect on e as b and $b_{,}$ is m. The point m being a point of section of the curve $a\,a_{,}$ got by dividing $a\,a_{,}$ into $a\,m$ and $m\,a_{,}$ in the same proportion as $b\,e$ and $e\,b_{,}$.

264. When the links are crossed the parallel lines $a\,l_{,}$ and $a_{,}\,l_{,}$ come between the shaft and the suspension link, and the circle comes as shown $a\,a_{,}\,l_{,}$. The curvature of the arc which contains the centres of the supposed eccentrics being the other way.

CHAPTER LXXII.

NOTCHING-UP.

265. THE effect of the position of the slide in the suspension link is beautifully shown by drawing a number of probable indicator diagrams, from the valve diagrams, taken from the supposed eccentrics.

Suppose A B, Fig. 269, to represent the stroke of an engine, and $x\,o\,a$ the angle of advance at full forward stroke. Let $o\,a$ be the position and length of the forward eccentric centre line, and $o\,a_1$ the position of the backward eccentric, and let $o\,e$ and $o\,f$ be other eccentric arms for other corresponding positions of the slide in the suspension link.

Describe on $o\,a$ the valve circle, and draw through $h\,h$, the points where it cuts the outside lap circle, the lines $o\,A_1$ and $o\,C_1$. This will give us the points of admission and cut-off. Drop a projector from A_1 and so obtain a' the point of admission in the diagram. Drop a projector from E_1 and obtain the point of cut-off I in the diagram.

Through the two points where the lower valve circle cuts the small inside lap circle, draw the lines $o\,R_1$ and $o\,C_1$. From R_1 drop a projector and find the point of release r^1 in the indicator diagram. From C_1 drop a projector and find the point c_1 where cushioning begins. Then describe the valve circle on $o\,e$ and go through exactly the same process, and so find the point a_2, 2, r_2, c_2 of the probable indicator diagram. Lastly find a_2, 3, r_3, c_3 of the indicator diagram, corresponding to the position of the eccentric $o\,f$.

The difference of areas and of work done are apparent.

Fig. 269.

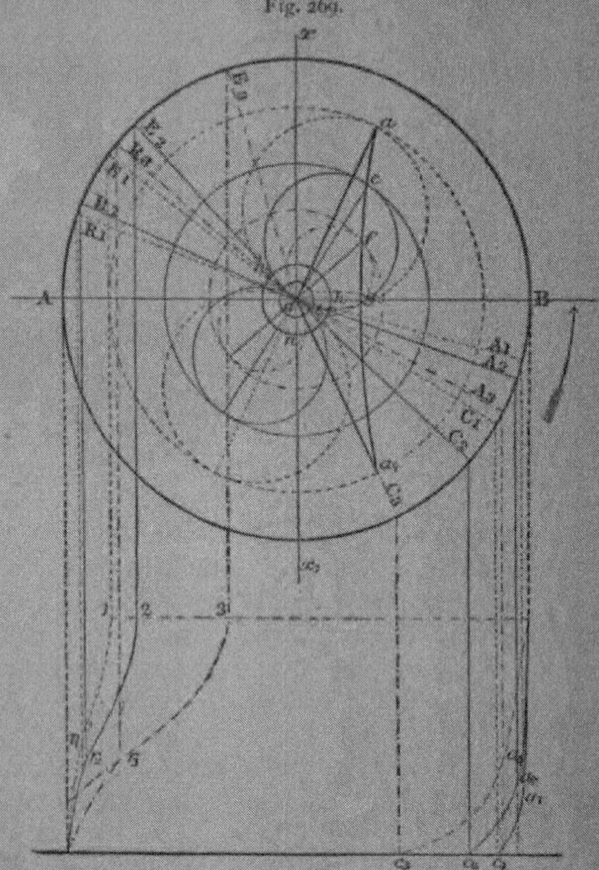

Fig. 270 shows another set of probable indicator diagrams got from the position of the resultant eccentric arms $o\,e$, $o\,f$, $o\,h$. The difference of areas in this case are even more apparent. It will be observed that the curve B C, which contains the centres of the eccentrics, is straight. This is due to the suspension link being straight.

Fig. 270.

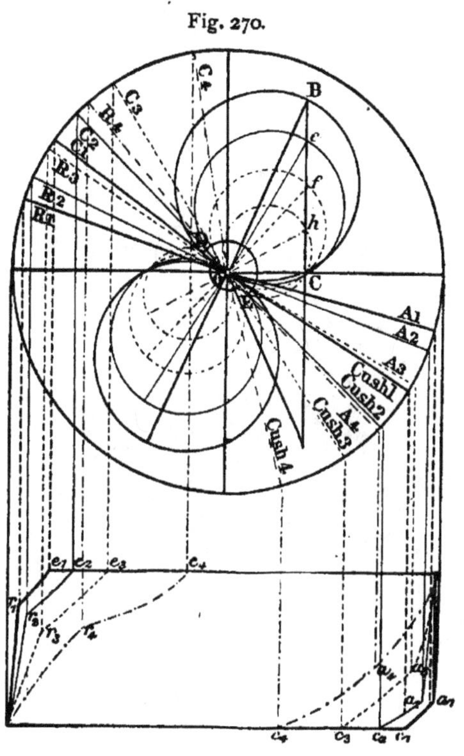

Ex. 283. Steam is admitted $\frac{1}{32}$ of the stroke before the piston reaches the end, is cut off at $\frac{3}{4}$ stroke, and exhausts at $\frac{7}{8}$ stroke; the port is $\frac{1}{2}$ inch wide, and the valve opens full to steam; find the radius of eccentric, the outside and inside lap, and the lead.

Ex. 284. The diameter of steam cylinder is 1 foot and the width of port is ·075 of the diameter of the cylinder, while

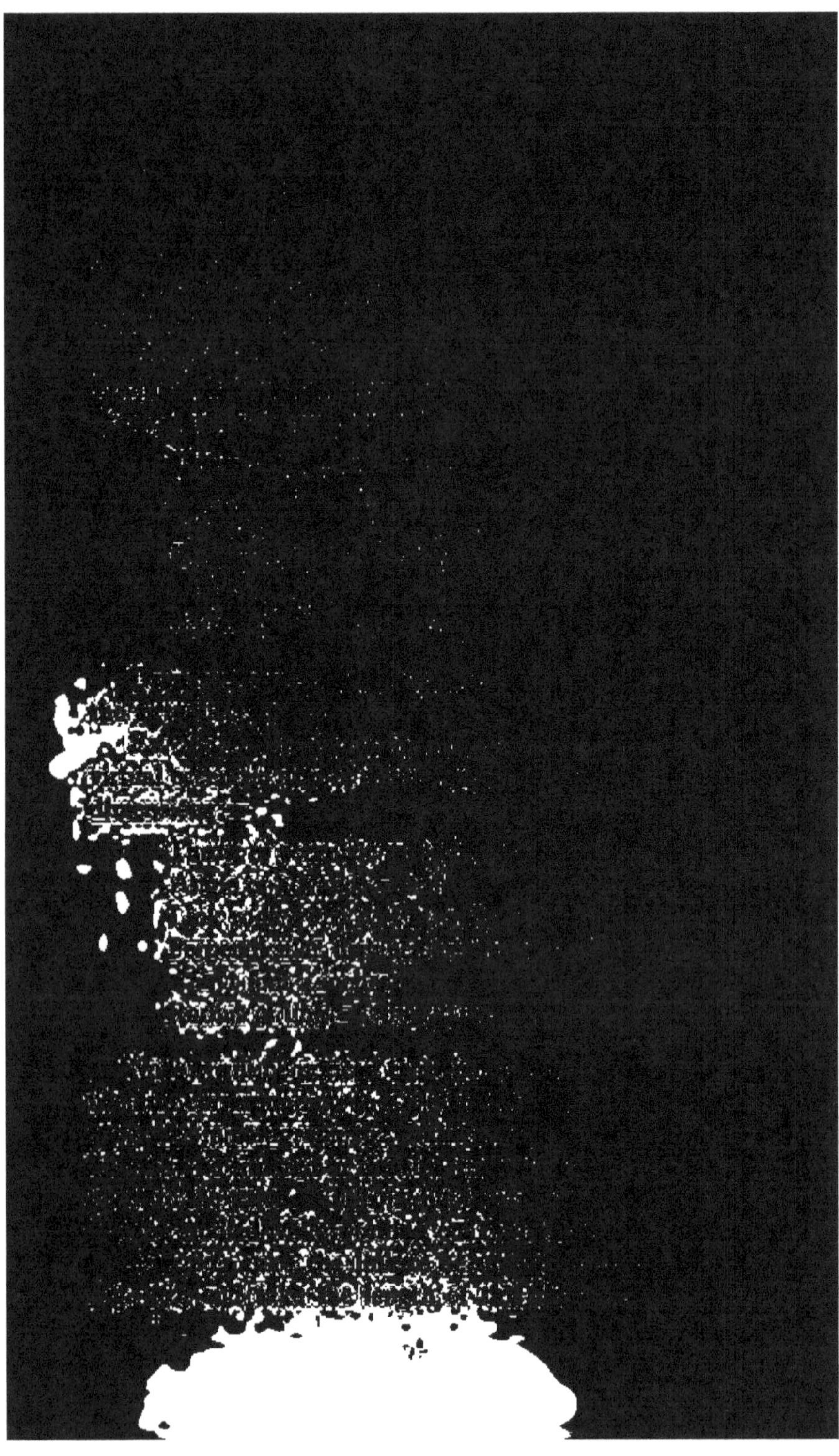

when everything is in mid position, 1 foot 5 inches. Trace out the curves in which the points *b* and *b'* move when the block is in mid position, (*a*) for the express engine, and (*b*) for the tank engine.

Ex. 290. Suppose next that the suspension link is so constructed that the expansion block does not rise so high as when it is in full forward gear; but that it can only rise to such a position in the slot of the expansion link $b\,b_{\shortparallel}$ as only to give a travel of 3¾ inches instead of 6 inches; find first the position of the point *m* showing the virtual eccentric arm under these conditions; then find the position of the block in the expansion link, (*a*) for the express engine, and (*b*) for the tank engine.

Ex. 291. Draw the valve face showing the ports, having given the following dimensions of express engine:—

Width of steam port = 1⅜ inches.
Width of exhaust port = 3 inches.
Thickness of bridge between exhaust and steam ports = 1⅛ inches.
Total width of face = 12 inches.
Length of ports = 14 inches.

Then draw a section of valve, making centre line of this section coincide with centre line of valve face.

Extreme width of flanges = 10 inches.
Width of flange = 2⅜ inches.
Inside of valve = 5¼ inches.

And show by dotted lines the valve covering the valve face in its normal position.

Ex. 292. Draw the valve face and valve for the tank engine under the same conditions as last case.

Width of steam port = 1⅜ inches.
" exhaust port = 3½ inches.
Thickness of bridge between exhaust and steam ports = 1 inch.

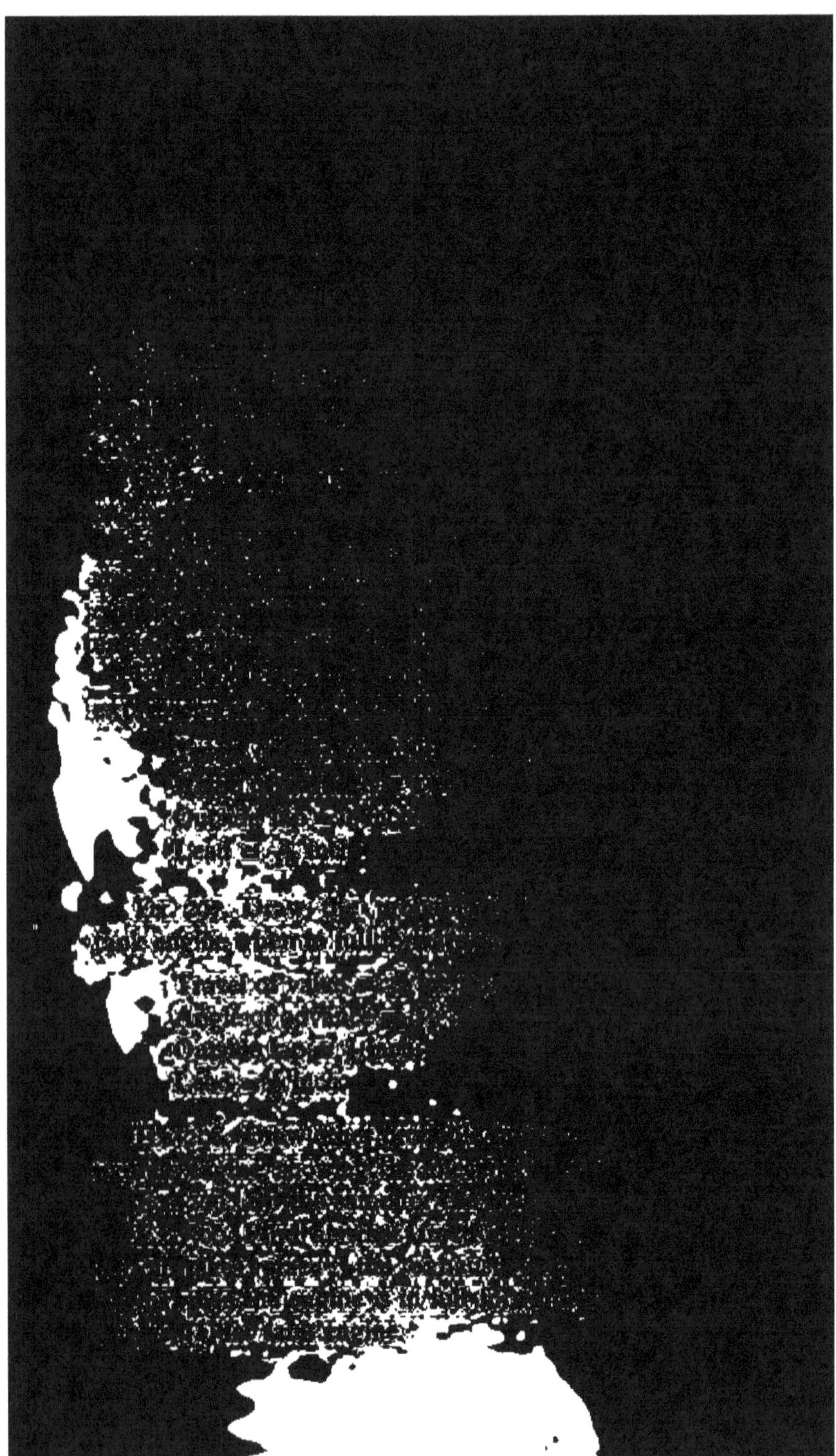

The following dimensions of the link motion of a Great Eastern locomotive engine have been kindly supplied by Mr. James Holden, locomotive superintendent of the Great Eastern Railway.

Ex. 301. Draw the curve *a m a'*, Fig. 268, for finding the lengths of the virtual eccentrics. The link is Sephenson's.

Throw of eccentric = $5\frac{3}{4}$ inches.
Angle of advance = 17°.
Link rods *a b* and $a_{,} b_{,,}$ Fig. 268, = 4 feet 2 inches.
Perpendicular distance between *b* and $b_{,,}$ Fig. 268, = 1 foot $4\frac{1}{2}$ inches.
Radius of link = 4 feet 2 inches.

Ex. 302. The link is suspended from its middle point *g*, Fig. 268, and take the distance between centres to which link rods are attached to be 1 foot 4 inches. Trace out the curves in which the points *b* and $b_{,}$ move when the block is in mid position.

Ex. 303. The expansion link at its lowest position, that is when the engine is in full forward gear, allows the centre of expansion block to come within $3\frac{1}{4}$ inches of *b*; find the position of the point *m* in the virtual eccentric curve corresponding to this position of the expansion block at full gear, and measure the travel of the valve.

Ex. 304. Draw the valve face showing the ports having given the following dimensions :—

Width of steam port = $1\frac{1}{2}$ inches.
Width of exhaust port = $3\frac{1}{4}$ inches.
Thickness of bridge between exhaust and steam ports = $1\frac{1}{8}$ inches.
Total width of face = $11\frac{1}{4}$ inches.

Then draw a section of valve, making centre line of this section coincide with centre line of valve face.

Extreme width of flanges = $10\frac{1}{2}$ inches.
Width of flange = $2\frac{1}{2}$ inches.
Inside of valve = $5\frac{1}{2}$ inches.

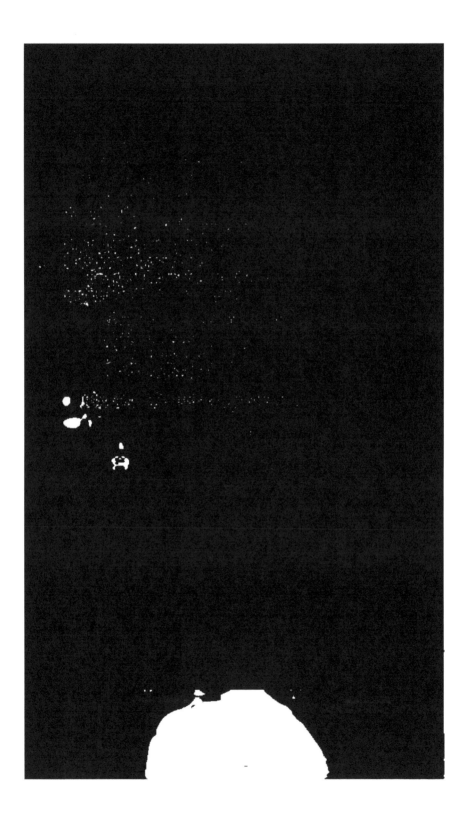

INDEX.

A.

B.

C.

D.

E.

F.

G.

H.

I.

L.

M.

N.

O.

P.

R.

S.

T.

V.

W.

LONDON: PRINTED BY WILLIAM CLOWES AND SONS, LIMITED, STAMFORD STREET
AND CHARING CROSS.

In Imperial 4to, sewed, with 12 Plates, Price 2s.

MECHANICAL DRAWING:

A FIRST COURSE

OF

MECHANICAL DRAWING

(TRACING),

ARRANGED FOR USE IN TECHNICAL AND SCIENCE AND ART INSTITUTES, SCHOOLS, AND COLLEGES.

By GEO. HALLIDAY

(WHITWORTH SCHOLAR),

INSTRUCTOR OF MECHANICAL DRAWING, AND LECTURER ON MECHANISM AT THE CITY AND GUILDS OF LONDON TECHNICAL COLLEGE, FINSBURY.

REVIEWS.

"Beginners begin with tracing in the drawing office, because it is a mechanical job (dirty work), which almost any one can do, and as it has to be done, cheap labour is employed. This is the philosophy of tracing in the drawing office. I have only used tracing as an extra voluntary work to help those who wanted to improve their chances of getting into the drawing office."—W. T. ROWDEN.

"Mr. Ruskin once horrified the drawing-masters by recommending the use of ruler and compass until the pupil has learnt to appreciate the niceties of straight lines and curves, when he may be safely trusted to draw them accurately without such aid. Instructors of mechanical drawing in many a college and institute may possibly be equally scandalised at the novel departure which Mr. Halliday, who occupies a similar position in the Finsbury Technical College, has struck out by the advocacy of a course of tracing exercises leading up to instead of following the art of mechanical drawing. Neither the Education Code nor South Kensington offers the slightest encouragement to Science Schools and Colleges teaching this the A B C of mechanical drawing, and the result is that pupils very generally begin their course of instruction, so far as scientific drawing is concerned, at the wrong end. Mr. Halliday insists that the same method should be adopted in the class-room as prevails in every practical drawing office; and the book before us contains a series of progressive examples as a first course, with instructions for the pupil's guidance, whether under a master or not. It is to be desired that Mr. Halliday's method and his vindication of it should be known to every science teacher in the kingdom."—*The Electrician.*

E. & F. N. SPON, 125, STRAND.

www.ingramcontent.com/pod-product-compliance
Lightning Source LLC
LaVergne TN
LVHW010152070326
832903LV00073B/111

* 9 7 8 1 3 5 8 3 1 3 9 1 2 *